October and the World

Also by Paul Dukes

A History of Russia: Medieval, Modern, Contemporary

The Emergence of the Super-Powers: A Short Comparative History of the USA and the USSR

Catherine the Great and the Russian Nobility

Russia under Catherine the Great (2 vols)

The illustration on the cover of Lenin is taken from *Links! Links! Links! Eine Chronik in Vers und Plakat 1917–1921* by Fritz Mieran (Berlin: Rutter und Loening, 1970) from a Russian source.

October and the World:

Perspectives on the Russian Revolution

PAUL DUKES

First published 1979 by
THE MACMILLAN PRESS LTD
London and Basingstoke

Associated companies in Delhi Dublin
Hong Kong Johannesburg Lagos Melbourne
New York Singapore and Tokyo

Photoset, printed and bound
in Great Britain by
REDWOOD BURN LIMITED
Trowbridge & Esher

British Library Cataloguing in Publication Data

Dukes, Paul, b. 1934
    October and the world.
    1. Russia – History – Revolution, 1917–1921
    2. Russia – Politics and government, 1917–1936
    I. Title
947.084'1   DK265

    ISBN 0–333–18391–6
    ISBN 0–333–18390–8 Pbk

Contents

To Daniel and Ruth
and their generation

Preface

The Russian Revolution, which occurred just over sixty years ago, was hundreds of years in the making. The purpose of this book is to throw some light on the origins and significance of the great event by making use of such chronological perspectives. It aims in particular to show how one of the Revolution's major aspirations, to universality, was developed from the seventeenth to the twentieth century by Russia's increasing involvement in world affairs, especially in the revolutions of those modern times. It then illustrates the manner in which that aspiration was radiated and echoed during the years of the Russian Revolution itself, culminating in October 1917 and the immediate aftermath. Finally, it directs attention to at least some of the ways in which objective appraisal of the Revolution has been hindered and helped during the decades since its occurrence.

Although not originally a specialist on the Russian Revolution, I developed a close acquaintance while conducting a Special Subject on it for ten years at the University of Aberdeen before passing the course over to the capable supervision of David Longley, a genuine specialist. The basic idea for the book came to me in 1970 during the course of a sabbatical, round-the-world study tour and was taken up again and enlarged during the course of another, spent largely at the University of Auckland, New Zealand, in 1974. While the research and writing were being completed, I received much help and encouragement from a large number of sources. Some of these are acknowledged in the notes. I should also like to express my gratitude to colleagues, students and friends at the University of Aberdeen, in particular to John Hiden, in co-operation with whom I wrote the article on Nazi-Soviet comparisons referred to below, from which has been taken the first half of chapter 3 and a few paragraphs of Chapter 7. Special thanks must also go to Tsuyoshi Hasegawa, of New York State University at Oswego, who very kindly sent me a full summary of his reading of the work in Japanese referred to in Chapter 5. note 62. I am also very grateful to Stephen White for the loan of the typescript for his book, *Britain and the Bolshevik Revolution: A Study in the Politics of Diplomacy 1920–1924*, also to be published by Macmillan. The book would never have been completed without all kinds of help from my wife Rosie, varying from proof-reading to restraint of our children, the dedicatees. Neither they nor anybody else but myself is to be blamed for the book's errors and other inadequacies.

Part of the book has already appeared in a rather different form; I am grateful for permission from those listed below to use this material, which includes:

'Russia and the Eighteenth Century Revolution', *History*, vol. 56 (1971): Professors R. H. C. Davis and Keith Robbins.
'Russia and Mid-Seventeenth Century Europe: Some Comments on the Work of B. F. Porshnev', *European Studies Review*, vol. 4 (1974): Professor J. H. Shennan and SAGE Publications, London and Beverley Hills.
'Russia and the General Crisis of the Seventeenth Century', *New Zealand Slavonic Journal*, no. 2 (1974): Professor Patrick Waddington.
With J. W. Hiden, 'Towards an Historical Comparison of Nazi Germany and Soviet Russia in the 1930s', *New Zealand Slavonic Journal*, no. 2 (1978): Professor Patrick Waddington.

Translations from Russian are my own unless otherwise stated or implied. Transliteration is a variation of that adopted by the *Slavic Review*. Final -ii is rendered thus in the notes, -y in the text. Hard and soft signs have been eliminated from the text but not the Notes. Russian dates in chapters 2 and 4 up to March 1918 are given Old Style, that is eleven days behind New Style in the eighteenth century, twelve in the nineteenth and thirteen in the twentieth. An author cited in the notes is not normally included in the Index.

King's College, Old Aberdeen   PAUL DUKES
June 1978

Part One
Russia and Modern Revolutions

Modern history began with the end of the Thirty Years War and the English Revolution; the execution of Charles I was the culminating moment in the 'general crisis' of the seventeenth century. Russia has usually been placed on the sidelines of this great movement, or even beyond them, both by those Western scholars who specialise in its history[1] and those who do not.[2] In chapter 1, the following view of the Czech historian J. V. Polišenský is taken as a point of departure:

> It is perhaps not too much to say that a perspective for the study of the Thirty Years War has been opened which may be compared with the possibilities created by the October Revolution after 1917 for the study of international relations in the age of imperialism.[3]

The case is examined for considering Russia as an indirect participant in that war and as a not too remote respondent to pressures such as those which produced the English Revolution. While absolutism was crushed in England, however, it came to be entrenched in Russia.

The French Revolution followed American independence at the end of the eighteenth century to constitute the centrepiece of a wider 'democratic revolution' which left few parts of the Western world untouched. Again, the customary interpretation of Western specialists and non-specialists has been to place Russia on the periphery or outside it.[4] In chapter 2, a more positive argument is once more put forward, that Russian absolutism found itself under severe threat, but grew in confidence because of its survival.

During the nineteenth century, that confidence became increasingly shaken as even the tsars and their establishments came to realise that Russia was falling behind in the process of modernisation. Could Russia catch up without making any radical alterations in its governmental system? This has been a subject for much Western discussion of Russia under the last tsars.[5] In chapter 3, the subject is considered in the form of an estimate of the chances of Russia following two alternative routes, the German and American. Tsarism's failure to complete the process of modernisation in a peaceful manner would produce a revolution wider in its implications than those of the seventeenth and eighteenth centuries and make Russia the focus of what appeared strongly for a few years to be a threat or promise for the whole world.

1 The General Crisis of the Seventeenth Century

In 1965 Christopher Hill wrote that some agreement had been reached on seventeenth-century history. There was an economic and political crisis all over Western and Central Europe at that time; again this suggested that the comparative method, if discreetly applied, might be 'a useful tool for the historian, the nearest he can get to a laboratory test'. English history, Hill added, would not then be considered as 'something unique and God-given'.[1]

After some remarks about Russia's involvement in the evolution of Europe in the early modern period, this first chapter will use Hill's argument as a basis for estimating the degree of her participation in the 'general crisis'. But first of all it will be necessary to establish Russia's credentials to make an appearance in each of these two contexts. Western specialists in Russian history can be as parochial as those in any other field, often viewing the object of their specialisation as a country apart, while Western historians in general still tend to exclude Muscovy from their vision of seventeenth-century Europe. Was this how contemporaries saw the continent?

John Milton tells us:

> The study of Geography is both profitable and delightful: but the Writers thereof, though some of them exact enough in setting down Longitudes and Latitudes, yet in those other relations of Manners, Religions, Government and such like, accounted Geographical, have missed their proportions. . . . [This fact] perhaps brought into the mind of some men, more learned and judicious, who had not the leisure or purpose to write an entire Geography, yet at least to assay something in the description of one or two Countreys, which might be as a Pattern or Example, to render others more cautions hereafter, who intended to make the whole work.[2]

And so Milton decided to follow a certain precedent[3] in concentrating upon Muscovy and England, explaining that he 'began with Muscovy, as being the most northern Region of Europe reputed civil'. He therefore clearly believed that Muscovy was an integral part of Europe and that it bore comparison with England from the point of view of 'Manners, Religions, Government and such like'.

On this occasion Milton was not using his power of imagination but, as he himself said, following precedent. Many contemporary writers saw Muscovy as the eastern extremity of the European continent rather than as lying beyond it. Admittedly, there was little agreement among them as to where exactly Europe came to an end – the river Don, the river Volga, the Ural mountains or even points further east were all put forward. Moreover, the geographical, racial, linguistic, religious and other reasons for including Russia were not often mentioned. And a number of writers, although it would seem a minority, did exclude her.

The majority appear to have put Muscovite Russia in Europe from about the end of the sixteenth century, that is from just after the time at which travellers had started to open her up to Western infiltration after a long period of relative – if by no means complete – separation. J. Q. Cook says that 'as the seventeenth century progressed Western writers increasingly came to think of Russia as being geographically a part of Europe'.[4] Perhaps the majority opinion was most graphically expressed by the writer talking of the European body politic who likened the continent to a woman whose 'head is Spain, . . . bosom is France, arms are Italy and Britain, stomach is Germany, navel is Bohemia, and the other parts of the body are Norway, Denmark, Sweden, Finland, Livonia, Lithuania, Prussia, Poland, Hungary, . . . Greece, . . . and Muscovy'.[5] This is the context in which an examination of some aspects of the evolutionary formation of modern Europe will now take place.[6]

In a passive manner, then, Muscovy was brought closer to the rest of Europe by the voyages of the late sixteenth century around the northern cape and through the Baltic. Actively, the Russian people were able to recover from the great disaster of the Time of Troubles at the turn of the century, to drive out the Polish, Swedish and Turkic invaders and to re-establish something like their national integrity. This resurgence undoubtedly had an effect on Eastern and Central Europe and contributed to the agonies of the Thirty Years War. At the same time, the Russians were moving eastwards, consolidating their hold on Siberia.[7] Thus Russia was contributing to the political definition of the states of modern Europe and participating in the infiltration into Asia.[8]

Economically, too, Muscovy was becoming more integrated with Europe. A contemporary observed at the middle of the seventeenth century that:

All the peoples of Europe are co-operating among themselves, Spain gives iron, soft wool and fruits, England – leather, wool, tin and lead, France – grain, salt, wine and oil, Germany – horses, weapons, iron and silver, the Low Countries – money, Italy and Greece – silk, the northern countries – furs, copper and fats, timber for ships, Poland and Russia – luxury furs, honey and wax.[9]

Deficient in some of its details, this observation was correct in its general conception. Such a point was clearly made by Sir Thomas Roe, the itinerant ambassador extraordinary, who wrote to the Prince of Orange at the end of the 1620s:

The loss of the free trade of the Balticque sea is more dangerous to the kingdome of England and to the United Provinces than any other prosperity of the house of Austria, being the Indyes of the materialls of shipping, and consequently, both of their strength, riches, and subsistence.[10]

Russia's own part in the Baltic trade at this time is difficult to establish because it was carried out exclusively by middlemen; but its importance is reflected in the seriousness of the rivalry for Russian trade between the English and the Dutch and also the Swedes, both in the Baltic itself and by the alternative route around the northern cape.[11]

Muscovy could not become involved with the rest of Europe politically and economically and preserve her Slavic Orthodox culture complete and unaffected. Admittedly, it was not the spirit of scientific enquiry that infiltrated so obviously as that of ecclesiastical reform. In Moscow in the 1640s a group called the Zealots of Piety was formed, aiming at the purification of the church from impurities and deviations. The leader of the group was the tsar's confessor and its members included the two future protagonists of the Russian Schism, Nikon and Avvakum. Nikon was to become Patriach and to reform the church, while alienating the tsar in the overbearing manner in which he did it. After Nikon's disgrace, the church was on the road to the submission to the state which was completed in the reign of Peter the Great. Meanwhile Avvakum led the schismatic Old Believer movement in protest at the changes in sacrosanct tradition and at the impending nationalisation of the church. On first hearing of the Nikonian reforms, some of

Avvakum's followers at a monastery near the White Sea are reported to have lamented: 'Brothers, brothers! Alas, alas! Woe, woe! The faith of Christ has fallen in Russia, just as in other lands. . . .'[12] These monks were, of course, referring to the decline of Orthodoxy, but one may be permitted to speculate whether they did not also have in mind the great religious upheavals of the non-Orthodox Europe. Certainly, later historians have put forward the hypothesis that the Old Believer movement could well have been part of a wider phenomenon, the Jansenists in France and the Covenanters in Scotland both being suggested as parallels.[13] Throughout the continent established churches made a compromise with the self-assertive state, while schismatic or sectarian groups sacrificed themselves in the vain attempt to adhere to what they believed to be former standards of pure devotion. In a far less perceptible and more restricted manner, the newer European spirit of scientific enquiry was also being carried into the court of the tsar and other Muscovite centres.[14]

One further task remains to be carried out before we proceed to examine the violent events in Russia in the middle of the seventeenth century and assess their comparability with the contemporaneous revolutions of Western Europe. This is to describe the national development and international relations of Muscovy in the first half of the century. The Time of Troubles was appropriately depicted in a work by Henry Brereton published in London in 1614 and entitled: *Newes of the Present Miseries of Russia occasioned by the late Warre in that Countrey . . . together with the Memorable Occurrences of our own Nationale Forces, English and Scottes, under the Pay of the now King of Swethland*. Of a campaign launched by the Swedes in 1610, Brereton tells us:

> Now must the miseries of Russia be augmented by the coming of this Armie compounded of so many Nations, English, French and Scots. For though they came as a friend, and for their aide, yet who can stay an Armie from spoile and rapine, which the unhappy Russian found true in the pursuit of this bloody warre. . . .[15]

It was experiences such as this that made Russians get together to rid their land of foreigners and moved one of their leaders, Prince Dmitry Pozharsky, to declare in 1612: 'We do not now need hired people from other states. . . . We ourselves, boyars and nobles . . . serve and fight for the holy godly churches, for our Orthodox Christian faith and for our fatherland. . . .' Pozharsky further asserted: 'We will defend ourselves from the Polish and Lithuanian peoples with the Russian state and without hired people.'[16] In such a spirit of patriotism, the *Zemsky Sobor* or Assembly of the Whole Land came together in 1613 to bring the Time of Troubles to an end with the election of a new tsar, Michael – the first Romanov.

But the new dynasty soon discovered that it could by no means dispense with the service of mercenaries, hard-pressed as it was by Polish and Swedish attacks from the west and incursions from the south by the Turks and their henchmen, the Crimean Tatars. There were nearly 450 foreign officers in the Russian army in 1624;[17] and in 1630 Michael's government decided to form regiments on the European model with foreigners in charge as commanders and instructors. As a decree put it, all foreigners of the old and new emigration, whether landed or not, were to come to Moscow for military service under two colonels, Frantz Petsner and Alexander Leslie. An insufficient number answered the summons, and so at the end of 1630 Leslie proposed to negotiate for further recruits with the Protestant governments of Sweden, Denmark, the Netherlands, England, and the free towns of Hamburg and Lübeck. Leslie's plan appears to have met with some success, but Muscovy's ensuing attempt to wrest Smolensk from Poland ended in failure.[18] However, the tsar's government continued to devote its main efforts to building up the army. Peter the Great, who has often been given credit for the regularisation of the army, himself gave credit to his father Alexis, pointing out that in 1647 Alexis began to use regular forces on the basis of a military manual published in that year after its translation from the German.[19] In fact, as is clear enough from Leslie's activities in 1630, the process was more general, and it was not completed until the eighteenth century. Up to that time, highly trained mercenaries and Russians found themselves fighting alongside a peasant militia, Cossacks and savage tribesmen.[20]

In the great conflict of the seventeenth century, the Thirty Years War, Muscovy was an important, albeit indirect participant; the nature and context of this participation have been analysed by B. F. Porshnev[21] who gives the following analysis of the political structure of Europe in the 1640s. Stretched from the 1620s to 1653 in order to allow discussion of two chronological focal points – the 'Swedish' period of the Thirty Years War (1629–35) and the English Revolution coupled with the end of that war and the end of the French Fronde – this slice of time clearly reveals the interconnection of the continent from one end to the other. For example, the 1632–4 Smolensk War engaged Poland–Lithuania against Muscovy and thus allowed France's ally Sweden to complete its move into the heart of the Habsburg Empire.[22] The interaction goes beyond Europe, because Muscovy could not have entered the Smolensk War if her Asian neighbours had been causing her anxiety at this time. But the nature of the Thirty Years War shows that Europe itself was a

meaningful entity at that time, with all the states of the continent supporting or opposing the Habsburgs with men or money. The English
Revolution was essentially to the disadvantage of the Habsburgs,
besides having an influence in Europe and beyond in its own right.

Mazarin was worried about the spread of the English Revolution
to France and for this reason pursued peace at Westphalia so that the
dangers inherent in the Fronde could be overcome. Porshnev's principal primary sources here are Mazarin's letters, diplomatic correspondence and pamphlets. For example, going to take up the
position of ambassador to England in 1646, Bellièvre received instructions describing the 'dangerous consequences' which would
follow the destruction or the severe limitation of the English
monarch's power. The establishment of an English republic would
be

> ... a bad example, which the subjects of other sovereigns will
> extract from the revolt of the English and the Scots against their
> King, which sovereigns consequently must not allow that the evil
> so easily capable of arousing imitation will reach the limit of its de-
> velopment and culminate in a happy end.

Moreover, Louis XIV wrote, or had written for him, that 'We also
for important reasons feel a threat of the abolition of our own monarchical power . . .'.[23] France would have intervened in the English
Civil War if she had not herself been deeply immersed in domestic
troubles in the shape of the Fronde and foreign entanglements concerned with the last phase of the Thirty Years War. Mazarin sought
peace to protect stability at home and restore it in England, perhaps
with the help of the Scots. When it was too late to help Charles,
Mazarin was quick to see that Cromwell was the Napoleon rather
than the Robespierre of the English Revolution, to use Engels's
phrase, and made a *rapprochement* with him, even if official recognition of the republic did not come until 1653.

Pushed towards peace by France, Sweden was divided between a
Christina worried about civil disturbance and fear of isolation on the
one hand, and an Oxenstierna keen to take the Swedish successes of
1646 to their logical conclusion. Pomerania was the principal bone of
contention, with Brandenburg supported by Holland and other
powers fearful of Swedish domination of the Baltic resisting the concession to Sweden of the whole of Pomerania. Porshnev argues that
pressure towards settlement came from a quarter not properly appreciated hitherto by Western historians, Poland–Lithuania.

Porshnev follows a long line of Polish historians in his examination of the attempt of Władysław IV to strengthen his authority over

the nobility (*szlachta*). Failing in his attempt to gain sufficient internal support, the principal possibility – the Cossacks – proving too dangerous, Władysław placed his hopes on a vigorous foreign policy, hoping to find a base abroad for consolidation at home. Porshnev believes that the most progressive Polish–Lithuanian move would have been towards the west, as part of the anti-Habsburg coalition. Instead, Wladysław alarmed Sweden and other potential allies by continuing the policies of his predecessors by leaning towards the pro-Habsburg side while seeking for an anti-Turkish crusade. At the same time, he unwittingly succeeded in encouraging the Cossacks to fight for their independence under Khmelnitsky, a struggle with ramifications from France to Transylvania.

Porshnev now takes a closer look at another important element in the European situation, the Muscovite state and European politics in the 1640s. He divides Moscow's foreign policy from the peace of Polianov in 1634 to its abrogation in 1654 into three phases: from 1635 to 1642; 1643 to 1645; 1645 to 1654. The first phase was taken up for the most part by the construction of the Belgorod line, separating the Muscovite state from the wild steppe. The line's purpose was not only to keep out the Tatars but also to stop peasants from running away to join the Cossacks. A minor theme was the abortive negotiation for an anti-Turkish alliance with either the Poles or the Swedes. The second phase began with the energetic attempt of Habsburg diplomacy to activate the pro-Polish, anti-Swedish tendency in Muscovite policy, with the assistance of a papal attempt at *rapprochement* with Orthodoxy. A. L. Ordin-Nashchokin, often thought of as a precursor of Peter the Great, made unworthy concessions in the Polish direction when he should have been thinking of the primary historic task of uniting the 'two Russias'. With the accession of Aleksei Mikhailovich in 1645, Morozov and Nikon were soon in the ascendancy and Ordin-Nashchokin's policy reversed until the latter's return at the time of the Russo-Swedish War of 1656–8.

Returning to the other end of Europe and the centre of the book's attention, Porshnev deals with the Franco–Spanish struggle and the Neapolitan Revolt. Here he explains why, after pressing for peace with the Habsburgs with some urgency, Mazarin decided to delay it. The reason was that in 1647 there opened up before him the great hope of crushing the Spanish Habsburgs, who threatened France from three sides, from the Pyrenees, from Italy and from the Netherlands. Harassed already by a breakaway Portugal and a revolt in Catalonia earlier in the decade, the Spanish Habsburgs were stricken at the end of it by a revolt in Naples, – one of the many revolts of that troublesome time throughout Europe. While the Spanish and Austrian Habsburgs were undoubtedly split after 1648, this was not solely the result of a machinating Mazarin; the Netherlands had played a big part which was recognised in the separate Dutch–Spanish treaty and reflected in the general acceptance throughout Europe of the republican form of government as well as the recognition of nascent nationalism, for example in Germany. Nevertheless the English republican nation did not survive as, in the calm atmosphere following the peace of the Pyrenees, monarchical Europe was able to achieve the restoration of the Stuarts.

Next Porshnev considers the vertical and horizontal (or diachronic and synchronic) approaches to the problem of Russia and the states system. Part of the understanding is to be found in the Viking and Byzantine worlds of the tenth and eleventh centuries, not to mention the Turkic peoples who in the shape of the Mongols made their greatest impact in the next period, pressing in on Russia during the thirteenth century from the east while the Germans did so from the west. From the end of the fifteenth century, another period commences as both these threats receded and Muscovy was able to consolidate its existence in a situation still dangerous with the Asian front quiet but the Turks, the Poles and the Swedes all causing anxiety from the European side. These three states of the eastern barrier, as the French called it, were the protagonists of the horizontal situation of the seventeenth century. The Poles as the main obstacle to the reunification of the two Russias and the chief impediment to closer relations between Russia and the rest of Europe should have been the primary target and those statesmen who continued the anti-Polish policy of Filaret (Michael Romanov's father and chief adviser) were therefore the most progressive. Of the other two neighbours, the Turks were inhibited from European expansion by such circumstances as tension with Persia, although the unfixed nature of Russia's southern boundary and the turbulence of the Crimean Tatars meant that relations between Russia and Turkey could never be completely happy, even setting aside the problem of the Orthodox Balkans.

As for the Swedes, their expansion is the theme of the following section of Porshnev's arguments, deservedly so in the light of their successes under Gustavus Adolphus. Porshnev explains these largely through the support given to him by France and Russia. Russia's engagement of Poland culminating in the Smolensk War was recognised by Richelieu as an important factor in the situation allowing Gustavus Adolphus to penetrate deep into the heart of the Habsburg Empire, and the Swedish king was further assisted by subsidies from Muscovy in the disguised form of low-price grain resold on the markets of Europe at a great profit. But after the death of Gustavus Adolphus at the end of 1632, the Swedes were already losing their grip when Russian embarrassments brought the Smolensk War to an end in 1634 and allowed the Poles to turn their attention to them. Porshnev declares:

> What a complicated chain of inter-relations. Turkey because of war with Persia could not interfere in the Thirty Years War in time. The peasants raised a revolt in Russia. The Kalmyks did not want to go on a campaign together with the Tatars because of a difference in religion. And the Swedes suffered a defeat in Germany because of the changed situation in Poland. France under the control of Richelieu putting aside the interests of confessional politics was forced to rush into a difficult struggle for the salvation of its national independence.[24]

In conclusion Porshnev widens his argument to the Eurasian scale. The fact that two-thirds of the world's population probably lived in Asia in the seventeenth century makes it necessary not to omit that continent from any examination of widespread historical movements at the time, Porshnev argues. This is still so even though Asia did not interfere with Europe as much as previously. If China and India had not been busy with domestic conflict and Persia and Turkey had not been at war with each other, Muscovy would probably have felt more pressure on its southern and eastern frontiers and would therefore have been unable to devote its energies to the infiltration of Siberia and to the struggle with European rivals, principally the Crimean Tatars and the Poles. Towards the end of the century, relations with China became direct as Russians and Chinese came into confrontation in the Amur Valley.

Porshnev makes out a trenchant, perhaps over-assertive case. We cannot enter here into further discussion of his view of the Thirty Years War and its setting; suffice it to add that the eastern perimeters of European warfare at this time were described quite accurately by the Scottish and other mercenaries who were often to be found in the Russian service as well as in the Polish and Swedish service. The cost of hiring them to fight Central European foes as well as to maintain the fortified lines such as Belgorod against the Crimean Tatars added to the continual financial worries of the tsarist government. And so the slender resources of the Russian people had to be squeezed beyond endurance, and centrifugal tendencies, whether exhibited by runaway peasants or independent boyars, had to be ruthlessly crushed. In such a manner, Russian absolutism began to take shape in fundamental conformity with the Europeanwide movement described by E. N. Williams in the following manner:

Absolute monarchy arose out of the need for internal and external security which made a standing army as a royal monopoly essential. This army required higher revenues; the revenues required economic growth; they all required the formation of a royal bureaucracy to eliminate, or push aside, the manifestations of the corporate state.[25]

Of course, Russian conformity was not rigid. The military revolution did not strike exactly as it did elsewhere, and it would be wrong to draw too close a parallel between, say, the rise of the middle service class and that of the English gentry, itself a controversial enough subject for debate.[26] Economic growth was held back by geographical circumstances and closely controlled by the tsarist state.[27] The social system lacked the legal complexity of most of its counterparts, although parallels have been suggested with Spain and even with France.[28] But the essential integration of Europe was perhaps most clearly revealed when in 1648, under the great strains brought about by the Thirty Years War and its ramifications, states from one end of the continent to the other experienced civil disturbances of great magnitude.

Tension had been building up in Muscovy for some time before revolt broke out in 1648, and the last years of the reign of the first Romanov were disturbed ones. When the sixteen-year-old Alexis succeeded his father in 1645, the economic and social problems were compounded by a grain shortage and cattle plague. In such difficult times, the young tsar leaned heavily for support on the boyar Boris Morozov, his tutor.

The new government soon set about the fundamental task of balancing the budget and working out a stable financial system. To carry out the first aim, it tried to reduce expenditure by dismissing some officials and cutting the pay of others. Such a move obviously alienated many of the government's servants. To achieve the second aim, an indirect group of taxes was introduced in place of the direct. Of particular importance was the salt tax introduced in 1646.[29] This was so unpopular generally that it had to be withdrawn in February 1648. But discontent was not stilled, and flared up in a more virulent form in the summer of that year.

According to a Swedish report from Moscow, Alexis was returning to the capital from a visit to a monastery on 1 June 1648, when 'the ordinary people started to complain as they had often done before about injustices and the violence which was being inflicted upon them'. But the tsar would not receive their petition and his entourage started to beat the people with their knouts. The people responded by throwing stones at the boyars. Fifteen or sixteen of the insurgents who persisted in trying to petition the tsar were thrown into prison. On 2 June, as the tsar was walking in a religious procession, he was again accosted by the people asking for the release of those who had been arrested and for the surrender of their chief tormentors. Neither the tsar nor the patriarch could pacify the crowd, and the *streltsy* (musketeers) grew restless enough to join in the sacking of Morozov's house and the killing of an unpopular official. On 3 June fires broke out throughout Moscow and another unpopular official was handed over to the crowd to be killed. Before he died, this official denounced Morozov, and more fires started by the favourite's servants could not deter the crowd from demanding his life, too. The tsar protested that it would be better to kill him rather than Morozov, and the patriarch also came to the favourite's defence. Finally the crowd agreed to spare Morozov's life as long as he was dismissed and sent into exile.

The disturbances continued, and on 5 June Morozov's brother-in-law had his head cut off. The tsar ordered the *streltsy* to be given their back pay and on 6 June the tsarina distributed presents among the crowd. But other military groups then started to demand their pay arrears, and the crowd remained restless. Finally on 12 June Morozov went into exile, after a petition of 10 June in favour of this move came from some of the nobles and merchants, along with a request for the *Zemsky Sobor* to be summoned. Although the Swedish report refers to further troubles in August and October, the June days were the most important period of the revolt in Moscow.[30]

But the capital was not alone; other towns throughout Muscovy experienced violence in 1648. Siberia and the north-east were affected, so were the centre and the south. The last of these regions was probably the most worrying to the government since it was adjacent to the Ukraine, which was itself in revolt against Polish domination under the leadership of Bogdan Khmelnitsky. It is by no means impossible that some of the Ukrainian rebelliousness percolated to Moscow; almost certainly it spread to such southern towns as Bolkhov and Bobriki. Moreover, the social composition of the revolts in these towns was wider than in Moscow, including not only *streltsy* but also Cossacks and other servicemen. The disturbances did not close with the year 1648 but broke out again in Moscow in early 1649, albeit on a minor scale. And then in 1650 there were further revolts, not so much in Moscow as in Pskov and Novgorod.[31]

Having given a brief outline of Muscovy's 'contemporaneous revolution', we must now go on to analyse it, first from the point of view of the tsar and his entourage and second from that of the 'revolutionaries', discussing their social composition and their ideology. After that, we should consider the *Zemsky Sobor* and the *Ulozhenie*,

or Code of Laws, that it produced. Only then can we be in a position
to estimate the extent of Muscovy's conformity to the pattern of the
'civil war' aspects of the 'general crisis'.

S. F. Platonov says that 'Tsar Alexis took a very active part in the
discussions with the crowd.'[32] While some of his other adherents
were executed, for example, he successfully pleaded for the life of
Morozov. The tsar swore that Morozov would be sent into exile and
perhaps promised an amnesty to the insurgents at the same time. If
the promise of amnesty was given, it was later broken. As far as the
exile of Morozov was concerned, it was put into effect, but soon rescinded. To arrange Morozov's return, the *streltsy* had to be bribed to
make a 'popular request' to this end, since the tsar's oath could only
officially be broken in such a manner. In other words, as
S. V. Bakhrushin puts it:

> In state conditions alien to all constitutional juridical forms, there
> was created a unique reciprocal relationship of the supreme power
> and the people, in which was possible a formal agreement between
> the tsar and his subjects reinforced by an oath. Thus peculiarly was
> composed the political life of Moscow.[33]

Of course, the tsar must not be looked at as a figure aloof from
Muscovite society. His place was largely defined by his entourage, to
which attention must now be drawn. At the centre stands Boris Ivan-
ovich Morozov, about whom Alexis wrote in 1650: 'He is our boyar,
who as our tutor left his home and his friends and has been with us
unceasingly and has served us and taken jealous care of our royal
health.'[34] Such a significant position, which Morozov had occupied
since the accession of Alexis and before, was strengthened in 1648 by
his marriage to the tsarina's sister. More generally, Morozov con-
structed around himself a network of patronage, most of the members of which were 'new men' who had not been prominent during
Michael's reign. Such an arrangement helped to make Morozov
appear 'democratic', at least to the newer nobility. Samuel Collins,
the tsar's English doctor, wrote of Morozov: 'He draws envious eyes
from the ancient nobility, whom he daily makes to decline, and
brings in creatures of his own.'[35] During the revolt, the opposition to
him could not attract support because of its exclusivist economic and
social policies, and Morozov was able to re-establish his position in
Moscow without difficulty after his return from exile, achieving the
reputation of the defender of the noble service class against the feudal aristocracy.

Not that the revolt of 1648 was the affair of the nobility alone, as
the above narrative has already shown and as will now become more

apparent as we turn to make some social analysis of the insurgents. For S. V. Bakhrushin the revolt was 'a movement of the middle strata of the town population, of the taxpaying burghers, joined by the *streltsy* and the town nobility'.[36] Although the Muscovite poor certainly participated in the revolt, and possibly even initiated it, its direction and development appear to have come from the craftsmen and traders of the capital, particularly the traders, who were seeking independence from the tight controls of the administration and the acquisition of a monopoly of trade. Nevertheless the bourgeoisie was by no means a solid class, for there was tension between its lower and upper strata, and between the groups living in Moscow and other towns.

The *streltsy* were essentially petty bourgeois in social origin, craftsmen and shopkeepers. Often joining up because of poverty, they were preoccupied with pay and showed resentment against the leaders who appeared to be responsible for pay arrears, such as Morozov who was head of the *Streltsy* Chancellery. As armed men, the *streltsy* obviously played a most important part in the events of June 1648. Once the government won them over with presents and promises, the real strength went out of the uprising. In towns other than Moscow, the *streltsy* were often joined by the Cossacks, who would be worried about encroachments on their liberty as well as pay arrears.

Just as the bourgeoisie was divided into different strata and groups, so was the nobility. While the leading nobles, old and new, struggled for power, the middle and lower ranking members of the service class took the opportunity presented by the revolt to voice their concerns about money and land payment. Many provincial nobles coming to the capital contributed to the petitions being presented to the tsar and added their voices to the town nobility's demand for the convocation of the *Zemsky Sobor*.

Soviet historians are not entirely happy with the social analysis of the insurgents carried out by Bakhrushin which has largely been followed here. M. N. Tikhomirov, for example, argues that the crowd played an important part throughout, although he agrees with Bakhrushin that the revolt was in the end taken over by the bourgeois and noble dissidents who, on 10 June, insisted on the exile of Morozov and the convocation of the *Zemsky Sobor*. The victorious nobles and merchants agreed at the *Zemsky Sobor* on the consolidation of their own power and privileges, at the comparative expense of their lesser brethren and to the ruin of the poor townsmen and rural inhabitants. The threat of Crimean Tatar incursions and the spread of trouble from the Ukraine were added incentives for the solidarity of the leading members of society.[37]

The principal features of the social composition of the revolt of 1648 might stand out more clearly after an examination of its ideology and of the Code of 1649. The ideology did not originate from theoretical or literary sources but from the experience of the participants. The first insurgents believed that their action was justified by its collective nature and that those who were killed were criminals since they had acted in a manner diametrically opposed to the common good. The further expression of their grievances took the form of petitions. Addressed to the tsar, these petitions did not blame him, adding to the traditional 'naïve monarchism' allowances for the youth and inexperience of Alexis. Morozov was the principal target of complaint. Not only had he been guilty of maladministration and misappropriation of money, he had also attempted to involve Muscovy in a war with Sweden 'in order to be in a secure position to be able to torture the insurgents', or to give up Pskov to the Swedes without a fight, or even worse 'to ally himself with foreigners to take Pskov' and then 'to move with the foreigners from Pskov against Novgorod, and from Novgorod against Moscow'.[38] When Morozov in particular was not the primary target of attack, the 'boyars' in general were. By 'boyars' the insurgents meant the upper nobility, whom they hoped the tsar would keep in order, both as landowners and as government agents. The petitions also complained about the bureaucracy as a whole, the bribes and the favouritism with which it seemed to be riddled. They requested that both civil servants and police should be made strictly accountable to the tsar. A fourth object of the complaints of the insurgents were the 'guests' and other top merchants. Like the leading nobles, these were unpopular in two capacities: as commercial entrepreneurs with special privileges, and as government agents used mainly for fiscal purposes, as collectors of the salt and vodka taxes. Often as well as these four complaints there were more local grievances, most marked perhaps in the Pskov and Novgorod disturbances of 1650, where the traditions of self-government were strong.[39]

The complaints of the first insurgents of 1648 did not take sufficient account of the tensions within the noble and merchant classes which became more apparent as members of these classes joined in. The nobles often argued about promotion in service and boundaries between their estates, and the lower members of the class were jealous of the privileges of the upper members. Similarly the less favoured merchants revealed their envy of the more favoured, and disputed possession of valuable government contracts and leases. These intra-class tensions were clearly apparent in, and resolved by, the decisions of the *Zemsky Sobor*, to which we must now turn.

The *Zemsky Sobor* was composed of representatives elected principally by the nobility and the bourgeoisie. From a number of sources, Byzantine, Lithuanian and Muscovite, the Assembly produced the *Ulozhenie* or Code of 1649, which consisted of 25 chapters and 967 clauses. Although the foreword of the Code stated that it aimed at justice for all, the interests of the mass of the people were if anything retarded rather than advanced. Serfdom was more entrenched, with the fiscal and judicial grasp of the state on the peasants being tightened. Stricter laws against runaway peasants satisfied the wishes of the nobility, who were also allowed to turn the estates won by service into their hereditary property. In fact, the way of the world being what it was, the leading nobles were assisted more than their junior colleagues. Much the same might be said about the smaller number of clauses that dealt with the bourgeoisie, even though a more equitable distribution of urban taxes was achieved. In the end, then, far from being weakened, the position of the senior members of the service nobility and bourgeoisie was strengthened.

And thus it was that a popular movement against the oppression of the upper classes ended in an assembly which not only reinforced their position but also solidified their connection with tsarism, thus entrenching absolutism. Although Morozov was soon back in power from exile, it would nevertheless be wrong to say that the crisis of 1648–50 made no significant impact on the evolution of Muscovy. The process of the formation of absolutism was undoubtedly accelerated in the positive manner just described and in the negative sense that the strength of the old independent aristocracy suffered a great blow. A firm foundation was being laid for the construction of the edifice of the Russian Empire to be completed by Peter the Great.[40]

We must now turn to the difficult question of the degree of connection between the Muscovite revolts on the one hand and the contemporaneous civil disturbances in other parts of Europe. Rather than attempting any broad comparative sweeps at the outset, we are perhaps on safer ground if we first look at the observations and activities of contemporaries. For their part, the Russians were reasonably well informed about developments in the rest of the continent. They acquired information from commercial, diplomatic and military visitors and sent missions of various kinds to the countries of Central and Western Europe. Several Muscovite ambassadors visited England, most notably G. S. Dokhturov, who arrived in London in August 1645 to bring the news of Michael's death and the accession of Alexis, and who left a year later taking with him some clear impressions of the troubles being experienced by the English and the Scots. Unfortunately for Dokhturov, he was not able to read later historiography on the subject and therefore acquired a rather simple

view of the English Revolution. To him, the clash between the king
and the parliament arose from the tendency of Charles towards arbitrary government and Popery, with commercial people supporting
the parliament while the nobility was for the king. However, from
Dokhturov and other Muscovite visitors, as well as from a number of
translations, at least a small number of Russians had a clear if not
completely accurate picture of the English Revolution.[41]

Dokhturov himself was involved in the Pskov revolt of 1650 and
might have had something to do with the reported remark of another
Muscovite official concerning this rebellion to the effect that God
was permitting even greater ones, in particular in England and
Turkey.[42] Before this, Alexis himself had not been won from his
Stuart affiliation by the parliamentarian offers that Dokhturov
brought back with him; on the contrary, he had received emissaries
from the imprisoned Charles I with kindness. At the same time, he
punished the English merchants in Moscow by withdrawing their
privileges, and when he heard of the execution of Charles he expelled
them altogether from Moscow to Archangel, declaring:

> At the request of your sovereign, King Charles, and because of our
> brotherly love and friendship towards him, you were allowed to
> trade with us by virtue of letters of commerce, but it has been made
> known to us that you English have done a great wickedness by kill-
> ing your sovereign, King Charles, for which evil deed you cannot
> be suffered to remain in the realm of Muscovy.[43]

And then in 1650 there was issued from the Low Countries 'A Declaration of His Imperiall Majestie, The most High and Mighty Potentate
Alexea, Emperor of Russia and Great-Duke of Muscovia, protesting
against the murder of Charles I'. In this pamphlet, Alexis calls upon
all Christian princes to come to a general diet in Antwerp on 10
April 1650 to make arrangements for a holy war against the regi-
cides. Scholars are agreed that the pamphlet was a forgery done by
Royalist sympathisers, one of them, Z. I. Roginsky, putting forward the interesting view that it was the work of Lord Culpepper,
who returned to France via Holland from Moscow in 1650 after a
mission there on behalf of Charles II.[44]

Throughout the 1650s the Stuarts attempted to retain the sympathy of the Romanovs that had first been established in the reigns
of James I and Charles I, when English merchants had lent money
to Michael and an English ambassador had interceded with Gustavus Adolphus to press the claims of Muscovy to Novgorod and
other parts of the north-west. For his part, Cromwell was interested
in the dénouement of the revolt of the Ukraine against Poland, in

the development of a vigorous Baltic policy and the acquisition of the sympathy of the Muscovites. Much relevant evidence is to be found in the papers of John Thurloe. To take just one example which included both Royalists and Roundheads, we have the following letter of intelligence from the Hague at the beginning of 1655:

> The resident for the king of Poland here is to go for England on the behalf of the said king, to compliment and congratulate the lord protector; but in effect to instigate the lord protector against the Muscovites, to the end that by a fleet he cause him to visit Archangel, and revenge the English nation, whom the great duke of Muscovy has banished, upon the request and desire of Lord Culpepper, agent on the behalf of the king of Scotland.

If Cromwell swallowed this suggestion, the letter of intelligence said, the real gainers would be the Dutch and the French, and the king of the Scots whom the Polish king was anxious to help. In the circumstances it was hardly surprising that Cromwell did not send an English fleet of intervention to Archangel.[45]

Many more examples could be given of the interconnection between Muscovy and the rest of Europe in the first half of the seventeenth century and its critical middle, but perhaps enough has been given to support our argument, which will now briefly be recapitulated. To return to the thesis outlined at the beginning (and to some of Christopher Hill's terminology), the study of the 'general crisis' becomes more of a 'laboratory test' if Eastern Europe is brought into the field of consideration as well as the west and centre of the continent. From the European point of view, the English was by far the most widely significant of the 'contemporaneous revolutions', even if it, like the others, was partly, even largely, brought about by circumstances peculiar to one country. But might not the English Revolution be more profoundly appreciated if its origins, course and consequences, as well as its early aspirations for the 'world's happiness',[46] are looked at in the broader perspective? Certainly such an approach contributes to a surer comprehension of the process by which Muscovy became transformed into the Russian Empire, a process brought forward by the events of 1648–50 and therefore placing Muscovy with France and Sweden in a 'half-way house'. Of course, this is not to deny that the large size and frontier situation of Muscovy gave it a peculiar position in Europe and in relation to other continents, particularly Asia. Of course, there are differences in a society where serfdom was being established at the same time as it was being dismantled elsewhere. But serfdom is more completely understood if viewed at least partly as a response to the comparative remoteness of Central and Eastern Europe from the major commercial routes and entrepôts of the period, at least partly as a counterpart to the exploitation of negro slaves and wage slaves in the overseas colonial regions and the Western European metropolis respectively.[47]

If not fatal, crisis[48] is followed by resolution.[49] Relatively speaking, seventeenth-century Europe conformed to this norm, although it might be more accurate to say that life and death gave way to touch and go. After all, England might no longer be rent by civil war or regicide but the fear of the renewal of domestic hostilities was constant and successive monarchs could by no means always sleep completely peacefully in their beds. The Restoration of 1660 was accompanied by the public disembowelling of Vane and Harrison and the persecution of sectaries. In the last years of the reign of Charles II, Whigs and dissenters were subject to legal terror, with the Rye House Plot of 1683 leading to some executions and much imprisonment. At the accession of James II in 1685, the invasion of Scotland by the Earl of Argyll and of south-west England by Monmouth led to more alarm and still more repression. There was peace but little calm until the removal of James and the arrival of William in 1688, and the matter of the throne had to be settled again in Ireland at the Battle of the Boyne in 1690. Even then, the exiled Stuarts were not finished. And more local state violence was endemic throughout the period down to the level of frequent hangings of members of the lower orders for the stealing of sheep and other offences deemed capital. 'A great revolution' in political practice, in economic enterprise and intellectual activity had taken place – 'Absolute monarchy on the French model was never again possible.'[50] This cannot be forgotten or denied, but it would be a further hundred years or more before the dust had finally settled and the new order revealed in sufficient clarity, before, to revert to our former metaphor, the effects of the crisis were transmitted to the full.

If we turn to look at one of Christopher Hill's 'half-way houses' – France – we may observe an absolutist state for the time being stabilised, but certainly not a society where insurgence was a stranger. Suffice it to mention the revocation of the Edict of Nantes in 1685 and the ensuing revolt of the Camisards, the great famines of 1693–4 and 1709–10 and the attendant unrest. Such is even more the case with the 'half-way house' that is the focus of our special attention – the nascent Russian Empire. Here perhaps we may not even speak of the stabilisation of an absolutist state, attributing at least the completion of the process to Peter the Great and his collaborators. For, while there was no repetition of the fissiparous Time of Troubles or fear of it quite as great as with the Moscow Revolt of

1648 and the accompaniments to it – with the revolts in other towns and most especially the widespread disturbance in the Ukraine – opposition to absolutism continued to make itself keenly felt as social groups in both town and countryside demonstrated their reluctance to be screwed down into subjection by the tsars and their upper-class allies. Moscow ignited again in 1662, when worn down by disease and taxation, and especially by a debasement of the coinage from silver to copper, the people ran riot and laid hands on the tsar himself. Alexis was able to extricate himself by an oath which he soon broke, and thousands were made to pay for their temerity with their lives, although those who survived were given the satisfaction of seeing the purity of the coinage restored. The principal adherents of tsarism in 1662, the *streltsy* turned against their royal masters again in 1682 and 1698, incensed by pay arrears and inspired by Old Belief. They were finally suppressed in a blood bath in which Peter the Great appointed himself superintendent. Away from the towns by far the most formidable threat to the stability of the government was posed by the 'peasant war' under the leadership of Stepan or Stenka Razin. This huge upheaval was brought about by circumstances similar to those which caused the revolts in the towns. Basically, as before, the root of the trouble was to be found in the necessity for the government to defend itself against internal and external enemies. Calls on the peasantry for taxes as well as for military and labour services were answered with increasing reluctance and growing frustration. The further entrenchment of serfdom after the Code of 1649, and the spread of the institution into the Volga and other regions, met with resentment, or at best smouldering acquiescence. Even when the exactions of the government and the landlords were just about tolerable, famine, epidemic or cattle plague could take the patience of the people up to or beyond breaking point. The 'safety valve' of flight was not as open as before as the absolutist power of tsarism grew stronger and spread. This last circumstance was particularly irritating to the Cossacks, who provided the leadership of the 'peasant war' of 1670–1 as they did for its successors. Razin himself first made a name as a bold freebooter along the Caspian Sea. Then in the summer of 1670, he led a band of Cossacks and an ever-increasing number of peasants against Rus, that is Moscow, and not so much against the tsar as evil advisers. Initial success was followed by failure and retreat after an unhappy experience at the hands of a formidable detachment of the regular army. Razin's attempt to revive the enthusiasm of his surviving followers and to gain new support from among the Cossacks did not succeed, and he was taken by the Cossacks loyal to the government and handed over to it, then executed in Moscow in the summer of 1671. Razin was dead, but his name lived on in the legends and songs of the Cossacks and peasants.

At the beginning of 1672 the victory over Razin was celebrated and those who had fallen to help bring it about were commemorated in services in Moscow. Charles II, ever mindful of the execution of his father and of the condemnation of the deed by Tsar Alexis, sent congratulations to his Russian brother on the suppression of the revolt, and unalloyed relief was felt throughout Europe, except perhaps in Poland, Sweden and Turkey where the continuance of the Muscovite difficulties could have been used as an excuse for intervention, although there was some sympathy from this quarter too. Further east, the Shah of Persia, whose own subjects had suffered from the depredations of Razin in the Caspian, also sent his congratulations. Consolidating their position along fortified lines to the south and east of Moscow, the Russians were now able to probe more deeply into central Asia, giving the Shah of Persia cause no doubt to consider eating at least some of his words, into Siberia, making more explorations and gathering more furs, and as far as China, where commercial possibilities seemed to be great. For the Manchu dynasty, which itself had recently been experiencing huge internal troubles, a Russian presence in the Amur Valley was not welcome, and local muscle was used to persuade the Russians to accept the not particularly favourable conditions of the Treaty of Nerchinsk in 1689.[51]

Thus, towards the end of the seventeenth century, the Romanov dynasty and its adherents were succeeding in maintaining and extending their grasp over the nascent empire after the conquest of a series of internal enemies and at least an adequate performance against foes from without. The administration was expanding to new demands and adjusting to them, and society was taking on a new and firmer shape, with the nobility coalescing at the top and the serfs becoming more subject to its control at the bottom. Economic, diplomatic and cultural contacts from Western Europe to China were integrating Russia completely with the rest of Eurasia, if not yet, except indirectly, with the whole world. Peter the Great was thus enabled to carry out his famous reforms and further expansion with the way well prepared.

2 The Democratic Revolution of the Eighteenth Century

Western historians still tend to exclude Russia from their view of the great movement of the time that has come to be known as the eighteenth-century revolution. Two of them, Godechot and Palmer, expounded in 1955 their concept of an Atlantic revolution, including the American and French upheavals and their impact throughout the Western world, but giving very little attention to Europe's eastern extremity.[1] While Godechot does not appear to have modified his interpretation since 1955,[2] Palmer has moved considerably from the position set out then at the Tenth International Congress of Historians. In the second volume of his political history of Europe and America, 1760–1800, generally entitled *The Age of the Democratic Revolution*, Palmer poses the question whether discords during the reigns of Catherine II and Paul I 'in any way resembled those of Central and Western Europe, and whether a knowledge of the European Enlightenment and the French Revolution acted as a new cause of dissatisfaction, and contributed to a clearer formulation of goals. The best answer seems to be a cautious and indefinite affirmative.'[3] Not intended to be less cautious, this chapter seeks to make that affirmative more definite, and to argue for the positive extension of the idea of an Atlantic revolution to include the Baltic and the hinterland. To do this, it will range thematically somewhat more widely than Godechot and Palmer, placing considerable emphasis on economic and social development as well as on political, diplomatic and cultural history.

Although Godechot and Palmer do not give much attention to the economic aspect of European development in the second half of the eighteenth century, their argument is that Russia was basically too backward for it to be considered along with those participating in the Atlantic market. Certainly Russia was in some respects backward; this was recognised by Catherine II and her advisers at the beginning of her reign. Sweden, Denmark, Prussia, most German states, Switzerland, England and France all demonstrated economic development to such an extent that the eighteenth might be called the economic century. So said the foreword to the first number of the 'Works of the Free Economic Society for the Encouragement of Agriculture and Good Husbandry,' published under the imperial patronage in St Petersburg in 1765. In various ways the *Works* were to help Russia catch up, declared their editor.[4] But the gap between Russia and the others needs to be measured. How far ahead of Catherine's Russia was, to take the most relevant example, the France of Louis XVI?

In answer to this question, E. V.Tarle put forward in 1910 the contention that France was not even clearly ahead.[5] Even though Tarle's patriotism sometimes ran away with him, the impressive evidence that he made use of compels us to give at least some serious attention to an assertion that might at first glance seem ludicrous. Tarle argued that the general acceptance in the Western world of Russia's historic backwardness was the result of the growth of Russophobia in the nineteenth century and of the circumstance that Russia did indeed fall far behind the industrialising nations after the French Revolution. However, he continued, by no means all contemporary foreigners writing about Russian trade and industry at the end of the eighteenth century considered Russia an economically backward country.[6] Of course, such sources have to be treated with great care. As one of them himself says:

> It is rare that men maintain a *juste milieu* in the praise or blame of their fellow creatures. This can certainly be seen in the judgements that one hears held on the Russians. Some, filled with the prejudices of their fathers, regard the Russians as barbarians, and pity the misfortune of those who are obliged to go to a country that they believe to be inhabited by savages. Others, falling into the opposite excess, can only see in Russia a land of Cockaigne, an Eldorado, the abode of felicity, the home of the most perfect wisdom and justice, the theatre of marvels. Both let themselves be led astray by vulgar rumours which continually contradict each other, and by their own imagination.[7]

Although Catherine's desire for favourable publicity became notorious, and although some of the excesses complained of by Burja, the German writer of the above remarks, were undoubtedly the result of her patronage, he himself pointed out that the imperial economy benefited from freedom of internal trade and the absence of guilds. Tarle, after noting this observation and commenting that Burja published his impressions four years before the French

Revolution, which aimed at, among other things, emancipation from guilds and internal customs, went on to declare:

> Let us note by the way that even the revolution by no means immediately abolished the guilds; as far as internal customs are concerned, even their partial reduction in the course of the actual revolution aroused the most stormy enthusiasm. For example, it is enough to recall the exultation of the people of Paris, when in the spring of 1791, the authorities abolished the duty paid for the import of comestibles through the walls of the capital. Guilds also were abolished on 2 March 1791, i.e. two years after the beginning of the revolution. When Burja wrote his book, all educated people following politics, particularly Frenchmen, had a vivid memory of the attempt of Turgot to abolish the tyranny of the guilds and to free the grain trade from the obstructions in its path; they also remembered the resolute opposition of the French court to the plans of Turgot, his fall and the downfall of all his undertakings. No wonder that Burja paid close attention to the circumstances that the ideals of Turgot (at least in some respects) were a living reality.[8]

Tarle failed to make the essential point that guilds had never taken strong root in Russia and that restrictions on internal trade had never been as strict there as in France. Nevertheless, it is remarkable that a government associated with close bureaucratic control had abolished internal customs in the 1750s, and that this abolition should be in response to pressure exerted by the growth of an all-Russian market in grains and other items of production.[9] Catherine's economic policy was very liberal in comparison with that of Louis XVI, including as it did the removal of the remnants of guild restraints on industry, and again must be seen at least partly as a concession to strains put on the feudal economy.[10] Of course there still existed in Russia large pockets of a closed natural economy, but a backward and more advanced economic system existing side by side could be found in almost every country in Europe towards the end of the eighteenth century. F. Crouzet has written of France at this time that 'the sector of quasi-autarchic subsistence remained considerable and was dominant in vast regions, acting as a brake on the progress of the economy as a whole'.[11]

Continuing his argument, Tarle goes on to make a comparison between the external trade of France and Russia in the revolutionary age. Again he quotes a contemporary, LeClerc, who wrote that 'the balance of commerce is always advantageous to the Empire. The reason for this is palpable: the merchandise which is exported from Russia is of prime necessity for all the nations of Europe; most of that which is imported into Russia . . . can only be consumed by a very small portion of the nation.'[12] In other words, Russia imported luxury goods and exported items of more basic value. Making use of documents from the French national archives and eighteenth-century statisticians, Tarle elaborates this point with respect to France, adding that since France was still mercantilist in outlook, the fact that her balance of trade with Russia was unfavourable indicated the empire's indispensability to her as a trading partner. According to the figures provided by Tarle, Russia was exporting more to France in the 1780s than Prussia or Sweden, and importing less from France than she exported to her.[13] The Franco–Russian Treaty of 1786, France vainly hoped, would reverse the balance and provide France with, among other materials, a greater supply of timber and other naval stores, the growing shortage of which had been of great concern to the French government throughout the eighteenth century.[14]

Of course France's chief rival, Great Britain, had a corner in this market for most of the century, and made great efforts to retain it. As Albion says of British Baltic policy in general, 'it was chiefly a matter of keeping the sea open at all costs, in order to ensure a supply of naval materials. This policy was taken so seriously that on several occasions English fleets forced their way into the Baltic to protect the supply.'[15] In this and other ways, Russia's trade in particular was of great importance to Britain, as Mr Foster, the agent for the Russia Company, was able to argue plausibly at the bar of the House of Commons on 5 May 1774. Foster declared:

> The articles we bring from Russia, our hemp, our iron, our flax, are so indispensably necessary to us for every purpose of agriculture and of commerce, that had we no export trade, it would be very expedient we should attentively cultivate the friendship of Russia on account of our important trade only . . . without them our navy, our commerce, our agriculture, are at end; without them, where would be our wealth, where our naval honours? . . . You will never, Sir, think that trade a prejudicial one, which brings home the materials, without which commerce could neither be undertaken nor protected.[16]

According to the figures provided by Marshall, which Palmer and Godechot used to support their concept of an Atlantic revolution, during most years from 1763 to 1794 Great Britain imported from Russia goods of a greater value than from anywhere else on the continent, in fact from everywhere except the West Indies or the East Indies.[17] While the future workshop of the world already had to export or die, and markets were already absolutely necessary, the workshop could not function without imported raw materials or sell its products without protection from the navy.

Not that all imports from Russia were raw materials or naval stores. The greatest iron producer in the world in the late eighteenth century, Russia exported more of this metal to Great Britain than to any other country.[18] Her linen exports to Britain, albeit of poor quality, were, according to Mr Foster at least, chiefly used by the poor, and 'The want of them could not be supplied by our home manufactures.'[19] In these two sectors, metals and textiles, Russia was experiencing in the reign of Catherine something like the early stages of industrial revolution. Soviet historians, who have given the subject much attention, argue among themselves about the beginnings of this revolution, but most appear to place them about the middle of the eighteenth century.[20]

Tarle argued that Russia's industry, like her trade, was not backward in comparison with that of France during the reign of Catherine II. Again he quoted contemporaries in support of his contention. Von Storch, for example, wrote in the 1790s that in Russia, 'A great number of new factories and manufactures have arisen, of which many are flourishing excellently, the spirit of industry has spread everywhere in the most remote parts of the huge state.'[21] Tarle also supported his view that Russian industry was on a par with the French or even in advance of it by a detailed comparison of numbers of factories and workmen. He pointed out, too, that while French industry was subsidised and protected at least down to the days of the Directory, Russian industry was booming relatively unaided. If Russian workmen still retained a close link with the land, said Tarle, so did the French and others throughout Europe, except perhaps in some parts of Britain, the most advanced industrial power of the time.[22]

Economically speaking, then, Russian backwardness does not appear very great when placed in a general European context, and compared in particular with that of France. Not only this; as indicated above, Russia was dependent on her trading partners in Europe mostly for luxury goods. If need be, she could be self-reliant to an extent probably greater than any other country on the continent. Moreover, if the eighteenth-century revolution was intimately connected with the early stages of industrial revolution, as many would agree, Russia was at an economic stage of development sufficiently advanced for her to be included in any comprehensive consideration of such a connection. To quote a more recent writer than

Tarle, Roger Portal:

> The Russia of Catherine II, by virtue of the number of its factories
> and workshops, the volume of its production and the part it played
> in European trade, took its place among the great economic
> powers of the eighteenth century.[23]

But, it will no doubt be asked, if Russia was not so backward in the
reign of Catherine II, where was her bourgeoisie? Why was serfdom
still so deeply entrenched in the empire? In answer to these questions,
the development there of a considerable degree of social mobility
must be noted. Along with the decline of the subsistence economy
went an increase in the stratification of the peasantry, and the top
stratum played the part of an unofficial, if rudimentary, bourgeoisie.
Several contributors to the 'Works of the Free Economic Society'
complained of the threat to agriculture posed by the movement of the
peasants from the rural areas to the towns and factories. One of them
declared that the number of people in agriculture was half what it
had previously been.[24] Moreover, even Russia's official social system
bears comparison with that of other European states. Before the outbreak of the French Revolution, town population was small and
town government in chains throughout the continent.[25] The peasantry was by far the largest class in France and other Western states,
and if it was not often shackled by serfdom, feudal restrictions and
impositions were still strong enough for the Western situation at
least to bear comparison with that obtaining in the East.[26] Of course
such an evaluation would probably reveal that Russia did possess
peculiar socio-economic features, such as, for example, the important part played in industry by the nobility, although even here West
and East might be seen to be more similar to each other than has
often been supposed.[27]
Certainly Russia cannot be dismissed from the society of eighteenth-century Europe by a bare reference to serfdom, or to the predominance of *Gutsherrschaft* in the East and *Grundherrschaft* in the
West. If the attempt is to be made to look at the age in which the
French Revolution occurred as an economic and social entity, there
is at least as much case for excluding the United States as for keeping
out Russia. Where is American feudalism, an American aristocracy?
Rather than excluding either Russia or the United States from the
revolutionary era, it is surely better to include them both as frontier
variations of the central theme, and to make any exceptions on a
firmer basis than that of an Atlantic civilisation.
It is the same with politics, diplomacy and the Enlightenment.
Russia has probably as often been excluded from Europe on account

of her autocracy as for her serfdom. Again such an assertion is based on form rather than content. Constitutionally more of an absolute monarchy than France and many other European states, Russian government was in fact like them subject to social checks. Although professional bureaucrats from the lower classes were increasingly to be found in the administration, most of the important decisions there and in the armed forces were taken by hereditary nobles. It was by no means a rare occurrence for Russian nobles to serve in both the military and civil branches of service. It would be quite possible for a noble who had led a regiment to head a college or lead a diplomatic mission, while drawing an additional income from both agriculture and industry. Hence, there was a very real aristocratic dominance of the empire, even if the close identity of the aristocracy with the state made unnecessary the constitutional expression of this basic fact, even if the defenders of Europe's steppe frontier had little time for many of the refinements of their Western peers.[28]

What sense can be made of the period from the Seven Years War, when Russian troops entered Berlin, to the conclusion of the Napoleonic Wars when Tsar Alexander I led his men into Paris, if Russian diplomatic and military activity is not given close attention? Can the American Revolution be fully understood if Russia's leadership of the Armed Neutrality is ignored?[29] Can the French Revolution be seen in its proper context if Russia's part in the wars against it be forgotten?[30] The answer to all these questions is sufficiently obvious for it not to require elaboration here.

With regard to the Enlightenment, Western historians have given Russia short shrift. Sometimes, it is true, in their attempt to redress the balance and to make up for such Western neglect, Soviet historians go too far the other way. For example, discussing a group of intellectuals who were active in the 1720s and 1730s, one of these historians writes, 'already in the first decades of the eighteenth century Russia was one of the world centres for the formation of enlightenment'.[31] This is an exaggeration, but by no means complete nonsense. The rest of Europe was far from being entirely ignorant of Russian cultural attainments at this time. To give a small example, D. Francisco de Menezes, an intellectual Portuguese nobleman, was a corresponding member of the St Petersburg Academy of Sciences, which had been founded in 1725, and published in Lisbon in 1738 the contents of that Academy's transactions. Menezes living by the Atlantic belonged to a group not much bigger, possibly no bigger, than its counterpart at the other end of Europe, and similarly alienated from indigenous society at large. Enlightened cosmopolitans in Portugal were known as the *estrangeirados*, as opposed to others unsullied by new ideas who proudly called themselves 'the chaste

ones'.[32] Here is an obvious parallel with the bearers of the new culture as fostered by Peter the Great and his successors on the one
hand, and those adhering to the old ways on the other, a parallel that
could be made in most of the countries separating Portugal from
Russia.

By the second half of the eighteenth century the ideas of the Enlightenment had penetrated as far as the extremities and lowest social
classes of the Russian Empire. The extent of such penetration is difficult to measure, and probably not many were affected in Siberia or in
the humbler ranks of the peasantry. Nevertheless there were over
60,000 students in educational institutions by the end of the century,
and probably at least as many more receiving some less formal
schooling. Over 8500 books were published in Russia between 1750
and 1800.[33] Such figures are low compared with those for Western
European states,[34] but were sufficient for the foundation of a native
intelligentsia, both noble and non-noble.[35] Russians showed great interest in such people as Voltaire, Montesquieu, Diderot and
d'Alembert, and the interest was mutual.[36] Russian savants were in
contact with foreign counterparts from Sweden to America.[37] Catherine herself must be given credit for her patronage of the arts and sciences and for her encouragement of a free discussion of the great
questions of the day, at least during the first years of her reign.[38] If the
empress became an extreme reactionary and an obscurantist secret
police became more active with the advent of the French Revolution,
do not such developments as these also reveal Russian conformity to
a European pattern?

What about the revolution? Even conceding that at least a prima
facie case has been made out for the extension of the Atlantic
economy and society, its political, diplomatic and cultural entity to
Russia, a critic could still argue that the empire withstood the shock
wave of the eighteenth-century revolution in its more violent aspect
without a tremor, exerting its strength only to help suppress the
revolution at its climactic point in the French Revolutionary and
Napoleonic Wars. Such an argument would be false.

Like other nations in the second half of the eighteenth century,
Russia had its own 'shooting revolution', or rather, two such revolutions, both of them abortive, in the 1770s and 1790s. The second of
them, which will be discussed below, had connections both with the
French Revolution and with its domestic predecessor, the Pugachev
Revolt of 1773–5, to which attention must now first be given. This
enjoyed wide support, and shook Catherine, her establishment and
the nobility at large; sympathy for it was evident both in the army
and in the capitals. Consider the following excerpts from the dispatches of the most sober and judicious of the foreign diplomats in

Russia at the time of the revolt, Sir Robert Gunning. On 25 February/8 March 1774, he reported that 'though it is kept very secret, I am assured, that part of the regiment detached by General Bibikov to attack the rebels, has gone over to them'. Just after the death of General A. I. Bibikov, which he thought might increase disaffection among the soldiers, Gunning wrote on 26 April/6 May: 'It is positively said, that the regiment commanded by young Prince Dolgoruky was prevented from desertion, merely by his liberality.' Concerning the situation in the old capital, Moscow, Gunning communicated on 26 August/6 September the information that: 'Several people continue still to be taken up at that place for treasonable practices. Eighteen of them have been hanged. . . . Some of them have been taken up here', continued Gunning, referring to St Petersburg, 'for drinking Pugachev's health.' Three days later, Gunning wrote that 'a general dissatisfaction continues to prevail. The Governor of Moscow was under the necessity about ten days ago of firing upon a number of the common people who were tumultuously assembled, and could not be prevailed upon by any other means to disperse.'[39]

The memoirist Andrei Bolotov perhaps had such circumstances in mind when he wrote later:

> . . . my hearing was struck by a general rumour which suddenly spread through the people of all Moscow and which shook me to the core and made me regret a thousand times that I had sent my horses away. . . . everybody began to speak openly about the great and incredible successes of the miscreant Pugachev. Particularly that he with his evil band had not only smashed all the military detachments sent out to suppress him, but had collected together almost an army of thoughtless and blind adherents and not only sacked and destroyed everything and hanged in evil executions all the nobles and lords, but also taken, sacked and destroyed Kazan itself and was already appearing to make directly for Moscow, and this was confirmed by the danger posed every minute by his accomplices. . . . we were all convinced that all the lower orders and the mob, and particularly all the slaves and our servants, were all secretly in their hearts, when not openly given over to this miscreant, . . . and were ready at the least spark to make fire and flame.[40]

Moscow was at the time of the revolt a province consisting of eleven counties as well as the former capital town, and a closer examination of developments there should lead to an appraisal of the general accuracy of the observations of Gunning and Bolotov, and thus to an

evaluation of the extent to which the Pugachev Revolt deserves to be
called a 'peasant war' as opposed to a 'frontier jacquerie', to use two
of the labels applied in recent analysis.[41] We cannot go here into the
whole question of the origins of the Revolt – the dissatisfaction of the
Cossacks and Pugachev's first claim to be Peter III – nor follow its
course through the earlier stages, from the siege of Orenburg through
the Urals to the defeat at Kazan. We begin after that defeat when, as
Pushkin put it in a well-known phrase, 'Pugachev was fleeing, but his
flight seemed to be an invasion.' As the pretender moved down the
Volga, violence broke out along that mighty river and to the west of
it. From 25 July to 4 August, there arose a great fear during ten days
that shook the Moscow province.

About the middle of July 1774 the commander-in-chief of Moscow
town, Prince M. N. Volkonsky, began to receive news about
Pugachev's movement west from Kazan and his potential threat to
Moscow itself. On 25 July, soon after learning that the rebels were at
Kurmysh, something over 500 kilometres away, Volkonsky called
together the Moscow departments of the Senate to discuss in extraordinary session arrangements for the defence of the old capital. Volkonsky himself would make a sortie against him with three regiments. Each senator was to assume responsibility for a section of the
konsky himself would make a sortie against him with three regiments. Each senator was to assume responsibility for a section of the
town. Government offices, documents and money were to be sealed
away, and members of suspicious gatherings arrested. As for the rest
of the province, instructions were to be sent out to the marshals of the
nobility to gather together the landlords and their retainers for the
defence of their districts and if necessary of the capital itself. The
Moscow senators accepted most of Volkonsky's proposals, often
modestly elaborating, slightly emending or simply repeating them.
They immediately communicated to the county chiefs, the *voevody*,
orders to send back to the Senate any news of Pugachev; to transport
their treasuries to Moscow or some other convenient place should
danger approach; and to co-operate with the marshals of the nobility
in preparations for defence against the miscreant, including the raising of levies composed of household servants and in some cases of
townspeople too.[42]

The very next day, 26 July, Volkonsky issued a new directive not to
carry out most of the measures just prescribed for the town of
Moscow. The reason given was fresh news, which altered the situation and made it unnecessary to spread alarm throughout the town.
A Soviet historian argues that the fresh news could not have come
from the revolt, but rather concerned the peace of Kuchuk-
Kainardzhi and the appointment of General P. I. Panin as com-

mander-in-chief of the anti-Pugachev forces. Volkonsky was not so much less worried about the threat to Moscow of the insurgents as apprehensive lest Panin should reprimand him for having forestalled any measures which the superior officer was contemplating.[43]

Let us leave the town for the moment and consider how the rural areas reacted to the threat of Pugachev's approach. The Gorokhovets *voevoda*'s chancellery reported on 22 July to the governor of Moscow province, Count F. A. Osterman, that travellers had brought news of 'the great danger' in which the inhabitants of Nizhny Novgorod believed themselves to be after the fall of Kurmysh. Kurmysh was little more than 120 kilometres east of Nizhny, Gorokhovets a mere 100 or so further to the west. The report concluded with a request for help, since the town was defenceless – without fortifications, soldiers or arms. The neighbouring Vladimir county chancellery was informed as well as the Moscow governor. On 23 July the local nobles were called together by the Gorokhovets *voevoda*, but there were only five of them, so they had to confess themselves unable to do much unaided. Vladimir itself was not in a much better position. Its chancellery informed Volkonsky and Osterman on 24 July that there were scarcely enough troops locally to look after 152 local convicts, including 78 Turkish prisoners. There was nobody left to defend the city itself, some of the local military detachment having been sent to the aid of Nizhny and others to look for brigands in the nearby districts.[44]

In Suzdal, near Vladimir, after some initial reluctance to believe the news of the approaching threat, the county chancellery set about planning its defence on 27 July in co-operation with the local nobility, while the local treasury was sent off to Moscow. The alarm spread by 25 July to Iurev-Polsky, a little further to the west, when Sergeant Timofei Chuprov reported to the county chancellery that the day before he had met a band of eleven men coming along the road from Suzdal. They were dressed in grey and were armed with swords, so he had assumed that they were soldiers. But when he asked them who they were, they replied: 'Detachments of the Sovereign Emperor Peter Fedorovich. Do you think he's dead then? No he's not dead but alive!' Supplied with tobacco and food, they were on their way towards Moscow. The report of Sergeant Chuprov, along with the news of the seizure of Kurmysh, convinced the Iurev county chancellery of the need for extraordinary measures. Neighbouring and other cities were to be alerted to the danger that suspicious people 'without proper passports' might try to lure simple folk away from their loyalty. The suspects must be caught and sent to Iurev. All noble landlords or their stewards were to commit themselves to setting up guard in the villages, and arming the inhabitants as much as possible, if only with sharpened stakes. Everybody was to be in complete readiness in case the insurgents should attack. Retired soldiers were to be ready to report to Iurev immediately, and all the local nobility and important merchants were to gather together with the *voevoda* to discuss further preparations for the defence of the town itself. Blockades were to be set up on all the roads and all travellers investigated. Only those peasants, who had written testimonials signed by the appropriate priest or steward could enter the towns on market days. Small lanes were to be sealed tightly or to have holes dug in them. The merchants were to make sure that food supplies would be sufficient if a large number of folk were to gather in the town. Murom, a hundred kilometres or so to the south-east of Vladimir, was also very much affected by the alarms and excursions of late July. The necessity for precautions there was confirmed by intelligence received on 26 July from Arzamas, less than a hundred kilometres to the east, that a band of about forty unarmed men was proceeding towards Murom, possibly as the vanguard of a large detachment of Pugachev's men.[45]

Thus disturbing news had spread quickly throughout the most exposed part of the huge Moscow province, and the great fear was not confined to that area; almost every county and district chancellery has left us some evidence of its disquiet. For example, at Meshchovsk near Kaluga, to the south-west of the old capital, the *voevoda* instructed the local marshal of the nobility on 28 July to assemble the nobles for a conference. In his turn, the marshal appointed ten supervisors to make sure that their fellow nobles turned up on 5 August, the day appointed. The conference duly took place, and 29 nobles signed a series of resolutions (as opposed to 16 signing the local instruction to the Legislative Commission of 1767–8). These resolutions included the recruitment of a levy, composed of the nobles themselves and 1 per 200 of their serfs, not younger than twenty and not older than forty, mounted, armed and provided for. As well as wondering if they should not perhaps purchase powder and shot at their own expense since there was none available locally, they also agreed to be ready for action at a moment's notice. The Meshchovsk townspeople followed the lead of the *dvoriane*, adding a further 3 to the estimated levy of 191. If court peasants and economic (formerly monastic) peasants had added their due quota, the grand total would have been about 225, making this extraordinary levy about half the size of the regular quinquennial recruitment (laid down in 1766 as 1 per 100 souls). But considering the expense and the importance of the point reached in the farming year, as the peasants were concentrating their minds on the all-important harvest, this was an impressive enough figure. Both the *voevoda* and other local leaders were perturbed enough by the news they received to carry on preparing for action until they received the 'all clear' decree of 4 August on 7 August.[46]

The frightening news had come not only from remote Vladimir, but also from other districts of Kaluga county. The peasants everywhere appeared to know about Pugachev, his aims and movements. One Rodion Efimov from the village of Senkov in the Kozelsk district was reported to have declared: 'We've heard that the sovereign will free us from the landlords.' A clothworker in the Maloiaroslavets district at the other end of the county, a certain Sutiagin, allegedly announced on 3 August: 'Pugachev has come to Arzamas and the Arzamas *voevoda* Siniavin has brought him out bread and salt, welcomed him with honour and ordered the bells to ring three days for his arrival.' Another worker, Naidenov, when informed that he was going with others to guard against the incursions of the miscreant Pugachev, not only refused to go but also protested: 'How can you call him a brigand? How will you answer for this?' The apprentice Ivan Ratastikov, when told that his wife would be held to account for inadequate work, threatened his masters thus: 'If God brings us the sovereign Peter Fedorovich, they will have to cope with him and will not be able to restrain him.'[47] Not far away, Andrei Bolotov, recently appointed steward of an estate by Prince Gagarin, addressed the detachment of serfs arrayed for joining a levy. As he later put it, he exhorted them:

> ...in case the affair should come to a battle, they should remember whose they were and not shame themselves before the whole world with cowardice, and should fight well, and turning to one of them, the strongest and smartest of the lot, I said: 'They won't want to fight with him, one of him could clean up ten of them.' 'Yes,' he said to me smiling wickedly, 'if I started to fight with my brother! And if it be you, the boyars, I shall be ready to fix ten on this spear.' Hearing this, I stiffened, and swallowing this bitter pill, could only say: 'Idiot! Son of a bitch! How this demeans you!' I thought to myself: 'That's how these protectors and defenders are in their hearts, and there you are expecting good from them.' Later, having asked for his name and written it in a notebook to remember it, I said to him further: 'All right, all right brother! Be off with you! Perhaps things won't turn out for you in this way, and then we'll see.' My muzhik lost his nerve when he heard this and saw that his name was written down; but since nothing could be done about it and he babbled on so stupidly and carelessly, he went off with the others hanging his head. Later he was rapped on the knuckles for this in a clever fashion; because when he happened to commit an offence and it was necessary to

punish him, I remembered these words and trebled his punishment for them.[48]

Regrets and retribution may have come later, but at the time there were many like Bolotov's muzhik ready to be insolent and threatening. And not only were there such statements in favour of the pretender, his agents were at work in and around Kaluga too. One such, Sergeant Tikhon Popov, was caught in Peremyshl on 12 August and examined in Kaluga county chancellery a week later. Popov said that there were many others like him. He himself had watched troop movements and converted peasants to the cause, including Rodion Efimov mentioned above. The *voevody* of Mosalsk and Serpeisk, along with the Serpeisk marshal of the nobility, reported on 2 August that Polish prisoners making their way back from Siberia were attacking villages and towns 'in the name of Pugachev'. (The Soviet historian M. D. Kurmacheva has argued that these 'Poles' were in fact peasant insurgents, and that the officials blamed their actions on the Poles in order to reduce the chance of mass outbreaks in support.) Poles or peasants, the disturbers of the peace were sufficiently active for the *voevody* and the marshal to say:

> Everybody knows that the name of the miscreant Pugachev has become known to all, even to rural inhabitants since the time that he has begun his evil deeds. His exploits inimical to the laws of society and God, have evidently infiltrated the hearts of simple people, as if to win them over to his band as he has done those in Kazan province, giving them hope that their dues will be reduced and that they will be freed from their duties to their landlord. Here nobody speaks directly about it; but many undoubtedly feel it, or pick it up easily from strangers, or take it in from their own menials who treat them without respect, abandoning their simplicity. There is no proof of this, indeed none is necessary, because the noble managing his own villages best of all recognises it for himself; however it cannot be ignored. The illusion of being free from the landlord and the advantages of paying the lightest taxes powerfully incline the peasant and the servant everywhere to base causes and desperate undertakings. And although it is in no way possible to hide completely for long from them the direct signs of permissible precautions, at least it is necessary to try for a time to hide from them the desperate strivings of the accursed Pugachev.[49]

With such ideas in mind, the *voevody*, the nobles and their allies among the townspeople set about their 'permissible precautions'.

Their work was certainly cut out because Kaluga was without defence, arms or munitions, or significant military detachments. Immediately all townspeople were told to be on the alert for vagrants without passports, and tavern keepers were told to look out for doubtful characters and to close their doors and not to sell drinks at night on pain of death. Such military personnel as there were in the neighbourhood (retired disabled soldiers keeping watch or carrying out escort duties, a recruiting detachment and a detachment of the second Moscow regiment) were to hold themselves in strict readiness with daily drill.

Soon these measures were supplemented. Boats on the river Oka were to be gathered together and kept under close guard. Inspectors from the nobility were to go around the areas under their jurisdiction three times a week, keeping a lookout for malefactors and attempting to catch them. A levy was to be recruited in Kaluga and elsewhere at a rate of 1 soul per 100 fully equipped. The clergy were asked to do their bit by suppressing the name of the accursed Pugachev as much as possible, and local officials in both towns and rural areas were to co-ordinate the mobilisation. The *voevoda* of Mosalsk was the most zealous of the higher local officials, apparently, being perturbed even about the lack of a drummer. In Mosalsk there was a drum, but no drummer. And what good were military detachments without a drummer? Just in time he recalled that there was in nearby Meshchovsk a drummer on leave, and so he wrote to the *voevoda*'s chancellery in that town requesting that just for the present critical time this drummer should be sent to Mosalsk.[50]

Neither the drummer nor the 300 flints brought back from Tula to Serpeisk and Mosalsk at a cost of 2 roubles 40 kopecks would have contributed much to the defence of the county of Kaluga had Pugachev's forces attacked it in strength. And yet the 'Home Guard' elements in the preparations of the *voevody* and their noble and commoner associates should not blind us to the deadly seriousness of the situation as they saw it. And only two examples have been taken here: the regions around Vladimir and Kaluga. Similar stories could be told of nearly all parts of the Moscow province. In most places there was a positive response to the Senate decree of 25 July 1774. Arrangements were made for the recruitment of levies, the blockade of rivers and roads, the protection of official buildings and treasuries, the suppression of subversive propaganda, and the arrest of suspects. It is true that little is known about the actual implementation of such arrangements, and that many were dependent on aid from Moscow. Levies are known to have been raised for certain only in Gorokhovets, Kolomna, Rostov and Mikhailov. And solidarity was not always complete among the anti-Pugachev forces; even among the most highly threatened nobility (*dvorianstvo*) friction sometimes occurred about status. Nevertheless fear of the common people in the towns and especially in the rural areas was sufficient to keep such tension within reasonable bounds. Nobles and their stewards, merchants and local officials, were all agreed as to where their principal enemy was to be found.[51]

Back in Moscow town the interference of Catherine from St Petersburg, the tension between her and Panin as well as between Panin and Volkonsky, in addition to the spasmodic and sometimes contradictory nature of the news about the whereabouts and mode of action of Pugachev himself, all contributed to a somewhat erratic policy of preparations for defence. Near the end of July Volkonsky came to believe that the danger had passed, and was in favour of giving a negative response to the demands of the counties for arms and aid. On 1 August the Senate agreed that county levies were no longer necessary. The provincial governor Osterman replied to a request from Kolomna on the same day in a similar manner, arguing that the rebel forces had been scattered and that the recruitment of armed men would create feelings of alarm rather than security. On 4 August the Senate sent out a decree to the counties rescinding its decree of 25 July. The peasants should now be encouraged to work on essential farming tasks, while the town officials would be sufficient to watch out for suspicious people. On the same day, Osterman again wrote in negative terms, this time to Iaroslavl, pointing out that the assembly of large numbers of people in the town could hinder the collection of state taxes.

Yet the day before, 3 August, the Moscow commander-in-chief, Prince Volkonsky, summoned the nobility to his house, before which the whole square was set with cannon. He announced that there were insurgent detachments in the neighbourhood of Nizhny Novgorod and that the nobles should therefore set up a levy of their own people. The proposal was accepted unanimously and Count P. B. Sheremetev was elected commander. And on 4 August the Senate received news that some court peasants had refused to contribute their quota of 2 men per 100 to a levy. Perhaps these two developments were connected, in which case the formation of a levy in the capital rendered superfluous the formation of levies in the counties, which could promote as well as inhibit social disturbance, a consideration in a sense dovetailing with that of Osterman.

Meanwhile, P. I. Panin, commander-in-chief of the anti-Pugachev forces and himself a Muscovite, was beginning to assert his own control. Although he had been assigned as his area of command only the provinces of Nizhny Novgorod, Kazan and Orenburg, he expanded it to include Moscow with the approval of most of the local nobility, many of whom would have been known to him personally. Panin delayed his departure for the main theatre of operations, aiming at consolidating his position in Moscow before advancing on the insurgents. Towards the end of July Volkonsky had sent out Major-General Chorba to Vladimir with a detachment of no fewer than three regular regiments and instructions to pay attention to requests for help from all districts of Moscow province. And so the policy of decentralisation inaugurated by Volkonsky himself and the Senate on 25 July was rescinded, while the county and district chancelleries lost their powers of initiative and resumed their subordinate position in the chain of command.

The threat of Pugachev and his adherents to the heart of the empire died away in the late summer of 1774, but as late as 15 September the Kadyi district chancellery from Kostroma county was reporting precautions taken against 'a band of the well-known state criminal'. More distant echoes of the revolt were heard even later, in 1775 and even in 1776.[52]

The reverberations were felt at the end of the eighteenth century as we shall soon see, throughout the nineteenth century and during the years of the Russian Revolutions, as we shall see in later chapters. The discussion concerning the significance of the revolt and its typification still continues today. Is it best described as a 'peasant war' or a 'frontier jacquerie'? Was it confined to Russia, just a part of it, or did its implications transcend the imperial boundaries?

The concept of 'peasant war' was first developed by Engels in his study of a series of hostilities in sixteenth-century Germany. It was taken up by Soviet historians, and has in recent years been at the centre of their analysis of the revolts of Bolotnikov, Razin, Bulavin and Pugachev. In their view a peasant war is one without concession or compromise, directed against the entire system of serfdom and the 'feudal' nobility in general, even though its radical nature is often disguised by the 'naïve monarchism' of the participants. Peasant war presupposes to a greater or lesser degree the existence of a unified centre of insurgent operations and of general slogans expressing the social hopes of the insurgents. Other groups, notably Cossacks, may participate, even provide leadership and driving force, but they do not change the peasant war's basic class alignment.[53] 'Jacquerie', on the other hand, is a concept originating in fourteenth-century France, developed by the American political scientist Chalmers Johnson, and taken up with a 'frontier' additive by the American historian who has written most in the English language on the Pugachev Revolt, John T. Alexander. The emphasis here is on 'a mass rebellion of lost rights or the removal of specific grievances. . . . a jacquerie aims at the restoration of legitimate government within a regime rather than at making unprecedented structural changes in the social system.' The prefix 'frontier' strongly implies the domination of the Pugachev Revolt by the Cossacks.[54]

The evidence presented above could provide some support for both definitions; perhaps most for the first. The verdict must to some extent depend upon the extent of one's agreement with the assertion of the Soviet historian M. D. Kurmacheva that representatives of the ruling class had no interest in exaggerating the success of the peasant movement. She and most of her colleagues would therefore accept at face value the estimation of the popular mood in Moscow made by Bolotov and already cited, and in the following remarks of Commander-in-Chief Volkonsky on 18 August 1774:

> This town is made up of all kinds of [ordinary] people, among whom, as is known to me through the affairs of the Secret Chancellery, baseness has almost completely spread from the propaganda of the accomplices of the miscreant Pugachev, and in the district[s], one may conclude, the rabble is imitating [them], as already in the Vladimir district a whole settlement of court peasants has become disobedient to its commanders.[55]

On the other hand, as R. R. Palmer has suggested, 'quotation, in which Russians dwell upon the reality or danger of revolutionary discontent in their own country, may in fact be more counterrevolutionary excitement or propaganda than actual evidence of a real social unrest'.[56] While this indeed may be so, the well-known observation of Carlyle needs to be borne in mind (and applied to the Pugachev Revolt) to the effect that most historians omit from their accounts of the French Revolution 'the haggard element of fear'.

A second, even more controversial point concerns the degree of the political consciousness of the Russian peasantry in the late eighteenth century. Can there be any justified talk of a 'serf intelligentsia'? This concept is completely acceptable to most Soviet historians, and might be more widely acceptable if M. D. Kurmacheva's definition of it is to be employed. She takes 'serf intelligentsia' to mean no more than those peasants who could read and write. Undoubtedly, there were plenty who had the basic *gramota*, if few such as those observed by a French visitor at the beginning of the nineteenth century surreptitiously borrowing from their masters' libraries the works of Voltaire and Rousseau.[57] How typical were the individual examples referred to by Kurmacheva and her colleagues, the Rodion Efimovs and Tikhon Popovs? This is a question that can probably never be definitively answered.

A third consideration must be of a man who failed even the basic test of literacy, that is Pugachev himself, his aims and intentions. In the testimony which he gave after his arrest in September 1774, he said that he had originally intended to march on Moscow, and would probably have done so after the winter of 1774–5. (Soviet historians sometimes argue that he changed his mind temporarily after the storming of Kazan because the harvest of 1774 was not very successful and supplies were easier to come by along the Volga than near Moscow.) In Pugachev's own further words: 'A further intention, to possess the whole Russian kingdom, I did not have because, considering myself, I did not think I was capable of government, because of my illiteracy.'[58] Illiteracy does not mean stupidity any more than literacy means political awareness, and both Pugachev and several of his associates were astute enough in their own way. Their 'War College' and organisation in general gave at least fitful direction to the revolt. And if they had no clearly formulated scheme to take over the whole of the empire, some of their purposes were straightforward and comprehensive, particularly in the decree of 31 July 1774:

And since . . . our name now flourishes in Russia, therefore We order by this Our personal decree: those who were formerly nobles in their estates, these opponents of our authority and disturbers of the empire and destroyers of the peasants catch, execute and hang and treat in the same way as they, not having Christianity, have dealt with you, the peasants. With the eradication of these opponents and villainous nobles, everybody may feel peace and a quiet life, which will continue for ever.[59]

These are hardly 'limited aims', in either scope or severity. Moreover, Pugachev's ideology did not point exclusively towards 'the restoration of legitimate government . . . and of lost rights'. Of course, there were pronounced elements of both restorations, in the 'naïve monarchism' of the insurgents which could find no wrong in the 'true tsar', and in the desire to grow hair and beards in the Old Russian fashion without tax or penalty. But there were backward-looking aspects to the views of fully fledged revolutionaries in seventeenth-century England, eighteenth-century America and France, and twentieth-century Russia. The 'freedom and liberty' promised by Pugachev to his supporters would mean the establishment of a fraternal commonwealth, with strong Cossack ingredients but also with the admixture of communal landholding and abolition of taxes and services more appropriate to the status of Great Russian peasants, and something more intangible but also more idealistic – 'the quiet life, which will continue for ever'.

A fourth question to be investigated revolves around the impact of international affairs on the Pugachev Revolt. This has been incompletely explored, in both Soviet and Western historiography. There is some substance in John T. Alexander's charge against his Soviet colleagues in this direction, but nor is Alexander's own article on this subject in any way comprehensive. However it is generally agreed that the conclusion of the peace of Kuchuk-Kainardzhi in July 1774 made an enormous difference to the outcome of the internal war. And European powers certainly watched Pugachev's progress as closely as possible, conscious that Russia's embarrassment could be to their advantage.[60]

A fifth and final question must be directed at the reasons for the revolt's failure. The Soviet answer, given also by some Western historians, is that Russia's social development had not progressed far enough by 1773–5 for the Cossacks and peasants to receive support or rather leadership from the bourgeoisie. We have earlier on in this chapter suggested that the Third Estate in Russia differed somewhat in its nature from its counterpart in some countries of Western Europe, but that, considered on a scale comprising the whole continent or even wider frame of reference, this class would not appear undeveloped. Nevertheless, there was obviously not present in Russia the kind of social alliance against the regime that France could provide fifteen or so years later.

Although the Pugachev Revolt failed, its impact was profound and lasting. The memory of the 'miscreant' was still fresh in the minds of most educated, upper-class Russians when the early stages of the French Revolution arrived. Many of them, no doubt, drew back from the brink of sympathy for this reason alone. It is just possible, too, that there was an agreement with the ideas of Prince M. M. Shcherbatov as expressed at Catherine's Legislative Commission in 1767–8. Strongly rejecting a fellow-noble's recommendation of England as a successful free society to be emulated, Shcherbatov had declared that England's freedom had cost the blood of thousands and the misfortunes of many virtuous and just monarchs. He also referred to the chaos caused by Russia's early seventeenth-century crisis, the Time of Troubles.[61] Neither this nor the Pugachev Revolt, however, deterred some noblemen, particularly the younger ones, from surrendering to the intoxication of the moment in both Paris and St Petersburg. Two Princes Golitsyn helped storm the Bastille. Count Paul Stroganov went nearly every day with his tutor Romme to the National Assembly at Versailles, and joined the Jacobins and other revolutionary clubs. He dreamed of becoming the Russian Mirabeau, writing as he left France at the order of his father: 'The cry of freedom rings in my ears and the best day of my life will be that when I see Russia regenerated by such a revolution.'[62] And the news soon broke through to Russia itself.[63] Back in St Petersburg the first slogans of the Revolution were welcomed and the Declaration of the Rights of Man quickly became a catechism, wrote a Swiss visitor, Dumont.[64] Segur, Louis XVI's ambassador, wrote about the reception in St Petersburg of the news of the fall of the Bastille:

> I cannot communicate the enthusiasm which was excited among the merchants, the tradesmen, the citizens, and some young men of a more elevated rank by the destruction of that state prison, and the first triumph of a stormy liberty. Frenchmen, Russians, Danes, Germans, Englishmen, Dutchmen all congratulated and embraced one another in the streets, as if they had been relieved from the weight of heavy chains.[65]

Catherine herself moved from a moderate suspicion to a complete abhorrence of the French Revolution. She wrote to Grimm in February 1790:

> As a person ignorant of the facts, I simply ask questions, foreseeing the destruction of everything that has been linked with the system of ideas of the beginning and middle of this century, which brought forth rules and principles without which, however, it is impossible to live one day.

In April 1792 she confessed to the same correspondent that 'I am frightened of going out of my mind because of the events which so strongly shake the nerves.' And then, in February 1794, she revealed that she had moved into a completely reactionary position, writing to Baron Melchior von Grimm:

> And so, you were right, never expressing the wish to be included among the luminaries, the *illuminés* and the *philosophes*, since experience proves, that all this leads to destruction; but whatever they have said and done, the world will never cease to need an authority . . . it is better to prefer the foolishness of one, than the madness of many, infecting with fury twenty million people in the name of 'freedom', of which they do not possess even the shadow after which these madmen rush forward to ensure that it will never be achieved.[66]

Until her death in November 1796 Catherine did all that she could to stop the French infection from spreading to Russia.

Nevertheless Count Rostopchin wrote in March 1794 that a discontent threatening the governing classes was general.[67] Three months later Catherine's secretary, Count Zavadovsky, wrote to A. R. Vorontsov that the situation was so threatening that 'God alone knows how and when this poisonous flame will die away'.[68] In the provinces[69] the Baltic governor-general, N. V. Repnin, sent instructions on 30 April/11 May 1796 to the commander of one of the units of Russian troops in the area, telling him that all suspicious people must be watched, particularly Jews. Repnin wrote:

> Unknown people . . . must not be allowed, on the contrary, particulars must be taken through the police of everybody without exception; where he came from, with what passport, on what business and to whom, with whom exactly he is lodging and what he is doing. Have your own people in all taverns and public places, to find out who is frequenting them and what is being said there, and do not allow anybody to stay there later than eleven o'clock, and arrest the disobedient. . . . On the main roads, in taverns and inns in both large and small towns . . . all this must be watched and reported to you immediately. In a word, all troops, all sentries and patrols must be in the highest military preparedness. Tell me about everything noticed by you. I am relying on you.[70]

The Baltic region, argues the Soviet historian Dzhedzhula, was no exception. Tsarism was terrified of the peasantry everywhere, and bourgeois historians have been mistaken in looking on the peasantry as an inert mass. The Russian peasant was by no means as stupid as was often alleged. Pugachev had played his part well, and his lieutenants theirs. His forces had stood up against regular soldiers and the best officers in Europe; they had even been a threat to them. And now the peasant in Russia understood in his own way what was going on in France. In his eyes the French Revolution 'was no different from the Pugachevshchina' and in this sense it was close to him and comprehensible. The French Revolution without any doubt served as a contagious example for the peasants too. How did the Russian peasants receive the contagion? Affirms Dzhedzhula:

> News about the French Revolution infiltrated the Russian villages through peasants working in the manor houses and hearing much

about it there; through peasant workers [othodniki] returning from the towns; through soldiers and officers quartered in the villages and small towns; through the serf intelligentsia, who read Russian and French periodical literature, and through many other channels. Among the people living in the villages there were not a few who intensively spread news about this revolution and summoned the peasants to follow its example.[71]

All this is by no means ingenious but empty rhetoric. Perhaps Dzhedzhula exaggerates the state of consciousness of the Russian peasant and the serf intelligentsia, the power and influence of Pugachev. But he also adduces an impressive amount of evidence from contemporary memoirs and from the archives. This and other information will now be used to show the nature and extent of social movements during the years of the French Revolution. S. N. Glinka later recalled that, in the years leading up to 1789, 'a general spirit of revolt went round the farms and villages' of Russia.[72] Citizen Genet reported to his government on 8 November 1791 that the Russian peasants were 'more ready than is thought to break the yoke of their masters' tyranny'.[73] S. R. Vorontsov wrote in 1792 that the French Revolution, 'a war between the haves and have-nots',[74] was too great a lure for the Russian peasants.

The peasants themselves soon gave positive testimony to the correctness of the views of Genet and Vorontsov. Except for that of Pugachev, no revolt was as widespread and penetrating in the later eighteenth century as that of the years 1796–8; according to an estimate made in 1904, 278 incidents occurred in 32 provinces. Few of these, it is true, led to much violence, but there were thousands of insurgents, battles with government troops, and some threat of separate groups coalescing into one peasant army.[75] Some of this disturbance was no doubt caused by local circumstances and some by the governmental changeover with the death of Catherine and the accession of Paul towards the end of 1796. And yet the connection with the French Revolution was made by contemporaries. The landlord Pozdeev commented about the character of peasant insurrection in 1797; 'All the peasants have . . . the thought that there should be no nobles. . . . This is the self-same illuminist spirit of insubordination and independence, which has spread through all Europe.'[76] The landlord Senator Bibikov declared that the people everywhere all this time had been led astray by false rumour of liberty and equality into dissension with other classes.[77]

Urban areas were affected as well as rural. According to Dzhedzhula, although here his argument cannot be corroborated by evidence from other published sources, disturbances occurred at factories in Kazan in 1796; in Moscow in 1797; in Iaroslavl in 1798; and so on. Moreover, the armed forces were not immune from the contagion. There were more military men than any other type in tsarist jails during the 1790s; more than a hundred soldiers and officers in two St Petersburg prisons, and about the same number in others elsewhere.[78] A group of officers from various garrisons throughout Russia and centred on Smolensk, wanted to kill the Emperor Paul and set up a quasi-democratic order, thus foreshadowing the growth of the Decembrist movement.[79] A guards colonel, Evgraf Gruzinov, was knouted to death in 1800 after having been accused and convicted on three charges, which were: boasting that he would take Constantinople, settle it with people of various faiths, and set up his own administration there; declaring that he would surpass Pugachev and his predecessor Stepan Razin; insulting the sovereign by sending away some peasants which had been granted to him, claiming that he did not need them. Gruzinov's younger brother and some Cossacks were executed soon after him, having shared his wild dreams.[80]

As well as military men, townspeople and peasants, intellectuals from the middle class and nobility were convicted of anti-tsarist activity during the 1790s. After Radishchev's *Journey from St. Petersburg to Moscow* had come out in 1790, Catherine called him 'a rebel worse than Pugachev', condemned him first to death and then to exile. His friend P. I. Chelishchev was called the second propagandist of the French Revolution in Russia after Radishchev by Catherine, who put him in jail. Released when proof could not be found that he had collaborated in the composition of Radishchev's *Journey*, Chelishchev went on to write his own. N. I. Novikov, the journalist and philanthropist, was jailed for fifteen years in 1792, Catherine deeming him 'worse than Radishchev'. In 1793 the freethinker F. Krechetov was given a rigorous cross-examination, the secret police writing that his works were filled with discussions of freedom and that 'with his propaganda and actions he could push people to an enterprise inimical to the state'. Krechetov was sentenced to life imprisonment and prohibited from reading and writing, and from communicating with friends.[81] The poet Derzhavin and other writers had to appear before the secret police, too, although without such serious consequences.[82]

There was much book-burning in Russia during the early years of the French Revolution, a sad end to the reign of that erstwhile liberal and patroness of the arts, the Empress Catherine. In 1792 in Moscow, according to one account, nearly 20,000 books were burned in connection with Novikov's arrest.[83] Tsardom censored talk as well as literature, completely forbidding the word for society, *obshchestvo*, and replacing *grazhdanin*, or citizen, with the more innocuous *zhitel*, or inhabitant.[84] One of the many anecdotes about Paul I tells of the emperor on a journey by coach to Kazan with his retinue, one of whom had the temerity to observe as they were passing through some wooded country: 'There are the first representatives [*predstaviteli*] of the forests which stretch far beyond the Urals.' Paul replied: 'Very poetically said, but completely out of place. Be so good as to get out of the coach immediately.'[85] Not only dangerous words, but fashions, too, were prohibited. A decree of 1798 ordered manufacturers to stop making tri-colour ribbons, for example.[86] And, of course, police spies were everywhere. Wrote Masson: 'A man who knows how to read and write, from whatever nation he be, is violently suspected. If he is French, there is no doubt – Jacobin. Whoever reads the newspapers is dangerous: whoever discusses them – Jacobin.'[87] For all this, French books, papers and pamphlets were still disseminated in Russia. The commander-in-chief of Moscow, Prince Prozorovskii, reported to Catherine in May 1792 that 'it can unmistakenly be said that as soon as books are published in France, they can secretly be bought here'.[88] Radishchev read *Père Duchesne* and other such works in exile in Siberia.[89] Moreover much manuscript work escaping the censor was disseminated. Emblems and badges were imported as well as books.[90]

The ideas and symbols of the French Revolution, then, certainly penetrated Russia to a degree comparable with that to be found in some other European nations, and sufficiently high to suggest the extension of the idea of an Atlantic revolution. Certainly the sequel to the era of the eighteenth-century revolution demonstrated the importance of Russia's involvement in it. For the rest of its existence tsarism retained a vivid memory of the revolution, and regarded a repetition of Russia's own peculiar contribution to it as something to be avoided at all costs. Largely for this reason successive governments shrank from the encouragement of the break-up of rural Russia, and supported the view that their empire was completely separate from Western Europe. Abroad, too, the tsars and their officials worked in the Holy Alliance and the *Dreikaiserbund*, to avoid or crush the revival of revolutionism. The Russian revolutionaries, for their part, from the Decembrists to the Bolsheviks, drew on the French (and, to a lesser extent, the American) traditions of liberty and equality. They sang their own version of 'La Marseillaise' in 1917. In 1917 and after, the course of the history of the Bolshevik government and the Third International was affected by the shadow of Thermidor and Bonapartism, at least up to the end of the 1920s.

There can be little doubt that the American and French Revolutions are the great events of the revolutionary age, signal moments in modern world history as a whole.[91] But neither of them (as Gode-chot and Palmer pointed out) can be fully understood if not seen in its proper context. That proper context, as Palmer has since recog-nised, goes beyond the boundaries of an Atlantic or Western revol-ution, even though progressive forces met with no comparable success elsewhere. By the standards of the eighteenth century, neither the economy nor the society of Russia was hopelessly backward. Its policy was recognisably European, and its diplomatic and cultural activity enmeshed it deeply in the Western world. In the climactic wars of the French Revolution, Russia played such a vigorous role partly because of opportunities for expansion afforded in Eastern Europe but partly also because the desire for liberty and equality was felt there as well as elsewhere in Europe. To suppress or at least contain revolutionary France was also to reduce a not inconsiderable threat to domestic stability. This threat may not in retrospect appear great, but was real enough at the time to commentators living in the empire and to such foreign observers as Edmund Burke, who wrote at the end of 1791:

> The Russian government is of all others the most liable to be sub-verted by military seditions, by court conspiracies, and sometimes by headlong rebellions of the people, such as in the turbinating movement of Pugatchef. It is not quite so probable that in any of these changes the spirit of system may mingle in the manner it has done in France. The Muscovites are no great speculators – but I should not much rely on their uninquisitive disposition, if any of their ordinary motives to sedition should arise. The little cate-chism of the rights of men is soon learned; and the inferences are in the passions.[92]

Burke points out the peculiarities of the Russian situation as well as the basic involvement of the empire in the eighteenth-century revol-utionary movement. Such has been the aim of this chapter, not to equate the Pugachev or any other revolt with the American or French Revolutions, which would obviously be a stupid claim, but rather to assert that their own domestic upheavals in the 1770s and 1790s appeared to Russians to bear a certain resemblance to those elsewhere. Conservatives trembled and did all they could to stop the infection from spreading; sympathisers rejoiced that the influence of the foreign revolutions had penetrated as far as their homeland and attempted to adapt the newly proclaimed ideas for the consumption of their fellow-countrymen. When Condorcet wrote in 1795 that in the aftermath of the American Revolution: 'The rights of man were freely investigated, and strenuously supported from the banks of the Neva to those of the Guadalquivir,'[93] his frame of reference was too narrow and should have been stretched further, from the Atlantic to the Urals.

3 The Peaceful Modernisation of the Nineteenth Century

Could tsarism have modernised without violent revolution? That is, could its autocratic government have successfully managed and adapted to the transformation of Russia from an agrarian to an industrial society with a new secular culture (including universal education) grafted on to the old religious ideology? This is the question addressed by much of Western historical writing on Russia in the nineteenth century, and answered too much in the affirmative.[1] On the other side, even if invariably giving the negative answer, Soviet historiography has also given some consideration to the question, and here as elsewhere it has followed the lead of Lenin, who talked of the possibility of Russia taking the Prussian and American paths.[2] These will be the subject of discussion in the present chapter.

First a few words about peaceful modernisation. Even where this process was achieved, the violence was only relatively absent and many people and ways of life were ruthlessly trampled underfoot even if the régime was able to continue its existence without radical alteration. The iniquities and savageries of modernisation in Britain and elsewhere were fully catalogued by a number of observers, not least Marx and Engels. But another preliminary point that needs to be made is that Marx and Engels did not believe the process to be retrogressive. Indeed they may be numbered among the more lyrical celebrants of capitalism, affirming in the *Communist Manifesto* that the bourgeoisie:

> ... has been the first to show what man's activity can bring about. It has accomplished wonders far surpassing Egyptian pyramids, Roman aqueducts, and Gothic cathedrals; it has conducted expeditions that have put in the shade all former exoduses of nations and crusades.[3]

Germany, like Russia, may be said to have begun the long process of modernisation in the seventeenth century.[4] By this time the basic nucleus was being formed in Prussia under the Hohenzollern family as it was in Muscovy under the early Romanovs.[5] Frederick William, the Great Elector (1640–88), set out on the long ascent which would take his successors to the titular hegemony of the German Empire. Assisted as was his contemporary Alexis Romanov (1645–76) by the partial decline in strength of Sweden, Poland[6] and the Austrian Habsburg Empire, the Prussian monarch achieved a clearer and stronger demarcation of his frontiers in the aftermath of the Treaty of Westphalia (1648) bringing the Thirty Years War to an end.[7] If the geographical area of concern was smaller for Frederick William than for Alexis, the problem of traditional local loyalties was probably greater, and the task of establishing overall control therefore formidable enough. The reduction of the Diets in Brandenburg, Cleves and Prussia and of their centrifugal Estates together with the restoration of the Privy Council pointed the way towards the establishment of the centralised bureaucracy. The institution of the General War Directory was a culminating moment in the reform of the army. The *Junker* class was fighting for the state and ruling it in a manner comparable to that which the *dvorianstvo* would assume in Russia.[8] Similarly the imposition of serfdom was just one part of a *dirigiste* economic policy applied by Hohenzollern as well as Romanov. The basic Protestant ingredients of the Prussian ideology were receiving an admixture of secular arguments which would soon be exported to the East.[9]

These included the propositions on government by such individuals as Leibniz and the Cameralist school of political philosophers who were to exert a considerable influence on Peter the Great. While such cultural transfer clearly indicates that Prussia was in several respects in advance of Russia, an Eastern European type of absolutism with features common to both of them and to some of their neighbours was already clearly formed by 1700, and development continued throughout the eighteenth century. Personalised comparisons within such a context and also throwing light on it may be made between Peter the Great (1682–1725) and Frederick William I (1713–40) and then between Catherine the Great (1762–69) and Frederick the Great (1740–86). The first pair shared a taste for hard work and simplicity of life style involving frequency and closeness of contact with their more humble subjects. And if Frederick William's achievements could be called filling out the sketch of the Great Elector,[10] then Peter the Great could be said to have done something similar for Alexis. The Prussian General Supreme Finance, War and Domains Directory set up in 1723 approached the overall command for which Russia also was striving. The collegial principles of administration and a rigorous control from above which obstructed them were to be found in both states, and Peter attempted – albeit without success – to introduce the *Landrat* system into local government. Russia's Table of Ranks – the basis of military and civil service from 1722 right up to 1917 – was to a significant extent of Prussian origin, and the *dvoriane* would henceforth be more explicitly expected to function as did the *Junkers*. Economic policy, although differing in some important respects such as land administration, was directed principally in both cases towards the upkeep of the armed forces. Eighty per cent of the revenues were expended in such a manner at the beginning of the eighteenth century, with government contracts for uniforms, weapons and munitions making an important contribution to industrial advance.[11] The peasants were ruthlessly exploited for these purposes and for the provision of revenues in the framework of serfdom. Altogether, if the reign of Frederick William I witnessed that 'complete intermarriage of army and state' which constitutes the 'real meaning of militarism,'[12] the same could be said with scarcely less relevance to that of Peter the Great.

After the death of Peter, Eastern European absolutism continued to consolidate itself with Prussia remaining the senior partner in cultural refinement if not in sheer strength. For example, the Prussian Academy of Sciences founded in 1700 was one of the models for its Russian counterpart inaugurated in 1725 and provided many of its first members. With some exaggeration it is true, the reign of Anna (1730–40) has been looked upon as an exclusively German if not altogether Prussian period in Russian history,[13] while the reign of Elizabeth (1740–61) did not witness the complete departure of the German influence for all the ascendancy of French fashion. Then, Peter III's occupancy of the throne was prematurely brought to an end, owing, at least partly, to his fanatical admiration for Frederick the Great and all things Prussian. Catherine II had nothing like the same veneration even though sometimes reputed to be 'Old Fritz''s daughter. If the two sovereigns did not have a blood relationship they shared a taste for the arts and the philosophy of the Enlightenment, and their patronage contributed towards the spread of awareness among their respective peoples,[14] including in each case a national self-consciousness formed to some extent in reaction to the impact of French culture.[15] Among his other achievements Frederick was able to bring the Prussian Code near to completion, although it was not actually made law until 1794, and if not arriving at constitutional monarchy, he and his immediate successors could be said to have introduced that *Rechtsstaat* that would be the basis for further advances in the nineteenth century during and after the Napoleonic interlude. Meanwhile Catherine failed in her attempt to foster the composition of a new code of laws for Russia, not so much through her own lack of capability or persistence as because of her adopted country's relative socio-political backwardness.

The physical superiority of the empire of the Romanovs over that of the Hohenzollerns, most pronounced near the beginning of the eighteenth century, was still evident towards the end of it. To a considerable degree, this was the consequence of position and size, Russia's remoteness from progressive developments in Europe being compensated for by aloofness from some of its more bitter struggles, and her huge distances as well as her inhospitable climate making a major contribution towards the downfall of invaders including Napoleon. But both states expanded their power and territory to an enormous extent during this period, largely because the decline of their neighbours, already detectable in the seventeenth century, had now gone much further. The outstanding gains were Russia's acquisition of the Baltic territories from Sweden followed by a drive to the Crimea against the Turks, and Prussia's seizure from Austria of Silesia. Having tried to bolster up Poland, the two rising powers then cooperated on its dismemberment, causing David Hume to lament that 'the two most civilised nations, the English and the French, should be in decline; and the barbarians, the Goths and Vandals of Germany and Russia, should be rising in power and renown'.[16]

The Seven Years War, an important part of this process in Europe, was also accompanied by the struggle between France and Britain for India and North America. The former's losses contributed to problems which resulted in the French Revolution, while the latter's gains added to the economic growth culminating in the Industrial Revolution. While this dual transformation rightly shifts the historical focus of attention on Western Europe for much of the period 1789–1848, we must not forget that it formed an important watershed for the course of development in Central and Eastern Europe, too. For Germany there was short-term collapse before French might, but also a far-reaching set of reforms which laid the ground for greater resurgence. Stein and Hardenberg between them during the years 1806–16 replaced the Prussian General Directory by a more flexible and up-to-date system of military and civil administration and emancipated the peasants. Neither Frederick William II (1786–97) nor Frederick William III (1797–1840) stood much in the way of such changes and even welcomed some of them. Meanwhile Alexander I of Russia (1801–25) was encouraged by the victory over Napoleon in the campaign of 1812 to reject the advice of Speransky and other liberal advisers for reforms comparable to those which were taking place in Prussia, and his brother and successor, Nicholas I, as we shall see, was even more of a conservative. Short-term success against foreign invasion was to contribute considerably in the long run to tremendous problems, intensifying Russia's backwardness.

The backwardness was relative, and has sometimes been applied too strongly as a label to Central and Eastern European societies because of the persistence in them of the agrarian mode of life and the absolutist form of government.[17] In an international comparative setting, the backwardness does not always appear great and from some points of view was at times barely if at all existent. Let us consider one of the central features of the label, the institution of serfdom, which accompanied the predominance of agriculture. Certainly, it is true that serfdom was introduced into Central and Eastern Europe at a time when it had largely disappeared from the West. But the institution was not set up because of the absence of a middle class or of capitalism from the regions concerned, but rather because of the preponderant influence in them of the landed nobility, usually in alliance with the crown, as was the case in both Prussia and Russia.[18] Moreover the new serfdom was not the same as the old. E. D. Domar has argued that there is a 'positive statistical correlation' in any society between available land and available labour, and that a relative shortage of workers tends to produce some form of involuntary servitude.[19] And so it was because there were no more than 2 million and 15 million people respectively in Prussia and Russia in the late seventeenth century (as opposed to about 5 millions in England and 20 millions in France) that peasant mobility had to be curtailed as soon as the control of the central government was strong enough. Moreover this was also the period during which the maritime powers of Western Europe were beginning to take full advantage of serfdom's sister institution, slavery. Without it, neither the Netherlands nor Great Britain would have been able to establish their capitalist prosperity. Denied full outlets to the Atlantic centre of such prosperity, the states of Central and Eastern Europe could not look outwards for their wealth to anything like the same extent, but had rather to turn inwards and squeeze it out of their own people. Such recourse, it must be emphasised, did not mean lack of development. The economy in Prussia and Russia was not irretrievably far behind that in at least some of the more advanced countries of Europe towards the end of the eighteenth century. Indeed the acceptance of economic liberalism contributed to the emancipation of the Prussian peasantry; Russia was the greatest iron producer in the world before the end of the eighteenth century and exported large quantities of it to Britain.[20]

The other principal characteristic of Central and Eastern European states was their absolutism, military–bureaucratic and autocratic at a time when parliamentary democracy was being grafted on to constitutional monarchy in Britain and republican revolution was reasserting itself in France. Here again, the backwardness recedes if we look at it in a wider context. British parliamentary democracy was not complete before the concession of equal female suffrage in 1918–28, and the ideals of French republicanism were put aside during the Second Empire of Napoleon III. Some kind of absolutism was the norm in Europe at least rather than the exception throughout much of the nineteenth century. Already by 1848, according to Marx and Engels, the comparative situation was such that they could declare in the *Communist Manifesto*:

> The Communists turn their attention chiefly to Germany, because that country is on the eve of a bourgeois revolution that is bound to be carried out under more advanced conditions of European civilisation and with a much more developed proletariat than that of England was in the seventeenth, and of France in the eighteenth century, and because the bourgeois revolution in Germany will be but the prelude to an immediately following proletarian revolution.[21]

Helped by the reforms of 1806–16 to regain and develop its strength sufficiently to exploit the opportunities presented by the Congress of Vienna (in particular the gains on the Rhine), Prussia had made enough use of its alliance with Metternich's Austria and of the expanding Customs Union after 1834 to be in a position by the middle of the century to make a bid for the leadership of the movement towards German unification. Frederick William IV (1840–61) made a distinctive contribution towards the establishment of Prussian hegemony;[22] but of course, if we are to speak in personalised terms, we must say more of Bismarck later. And we must not forget that the movement towards unification was accompanied by social changes which were indeed of a large-enough scale to encourage Marx and Engels.

Bourgeois revolution did not come to Germany as the *Communist Manifesto* predicted; rather it appeared to be following a course of peaceful modernisation. For this reason, so far as they entertained the idea of change at all, Nicholas I of Russia (1825–55) and his entourage looked to Prussia as a state for emulation, notwithstanding the pressures making for growing hostility between the two states after 1848.[23] Fortified not only by its suppression of internal dissidence in the years of the French Revolution and victory over Napoleon in 1812 but also by its leading participation in the formation and activity of the Holy Alliance, tsarism had found little reason to feel that it was in need of improvement.[24] True, Nicholas was somewhat disconcerted by the conscience-stricken nobles who led the abortive Decembrist Revolt of 1825 at the commencement of his reign and downright perturbed at the prospect of the fever of 1848 spreading into Holy Russia towards the end of it. He sent troops to suppress the Hungarian Revolution in 1849 and was fully prepared to send them over to the Rhine. But there was no strong cause for tsarism to doubt the strength of its 'patriarchal–feudal absolutism' until the fiasco of the Crimean War.[25]

However much it might have appeared in immediate retrospect to have been folly and blunder on all sides, a longer perspective on the Crimean War makes its significance look more than accidental. For Europe as a whole, it marked a key point in the development of Russophobia and in the realignment of the 'balance of power'. Almost unnoticed, a non-belligerent Prussia was creeping outwards to dominate the centre of the continent, while the Russian threat was now most marked in Central Asia. For Russia itself, the national humiliation was to lead to a final loss of that over-confidence born of 1812 and to the realisation that reforms in the armed forces and in the supportive social and political systems would be necessary if tsarism was to continue to survive in an increasingly dangerous international setting.

By the time of the Crimean War, too, although in spite of tsarism rather than because of it, the process of modernisation had gone far enough for the institution of serfdom to appear increasingly irrelevant, while even the committees set up by the tsar were not completely impervious to both free trade and humanitarian arguments.[26] And so, with the emancipation of the peasants in 1861 and other reforms, Alexander II (1855–81) took the first small steps towards transforming his people into fully fledged citizens and his government into a constitutional monarchy.

The emancipation of the American slaves in 1863–5 was more than a chronological coincidence, and an even wider context taking in the Taiping Revolt in China could add to our understanding of the end of Russian serfdom. Several observers including Lenin have argued that it was at least conceivable for Russia at this point to have taken the American road to modernisation as well as the Prussian.[27] That is, society could have been composed of free farmers rather than being dominated by *Junker*-type landlords. We shall say more about this below, for the American model was adopted mostly by the opposition; tsarist ministers tended to believe that the Prussian model was more appropriate for Russia, in particular for political arrangements, but for economic policy too.

Such a choice was being made partly because of domestic circumstances, partly because of the closer proximity of Prussia and its great success as unifier of Germany, and partly because of the fame of its outstanding statesman. Certainly Bismarck made a distinctive personal contribution to German development, but few historians would now want to maintain the cult of personality surrounding him which every schoolboy seems reluctant to abandon. In the first place even Bismarck had to work within the framework of the polity that he himself helped to construct with the aid of the great military victories of 1866 and 1870; the constitution of 1871 produced a Reichstag which may have been less than a parliament but was more than a 'fig leaf covering the nakedness of absolutism'. While the Reichstag on more than one occasion restricted Bismarck's freedom of action from below, Kaisers William I (1861–88) and William II (1888–1918) and their largely military entourage often impeded it from above.[28] Secondly the greatest economic surge forward took place after the pilot had been dropped, in the 1890s. Thirdly, in the German case as in others, the industrial and other features of modernisation were the product of socio-economic circumstances evolving over the centuries as well as more immediate political stratagems. Growth with a sufficient measure of control was achieved by an alliance between the *Junker* landowners and the middle-class industrialists as well as by a government basically responsive to it. This combination, seen clearly at work in the switch to protectionist tariffs after 1879, remained the basis of the Wilhelminine Empire for all the subsequent strains that sometimes threatened to undermine it.[29]

The population stood at about 67 millions by 1914 (well under half that of Russia). Manpower potential was absorbed sufficiently for most of the time, although indebted peasants were forced off the land either to leave Germany altogether or to work in towns. By 1914 less than 40 per cent of the population were in communities of fewer than 2000 as opposed to probably over 80 per cent in Russia. Figures for railway expansion, coal and iron production and for the newer engineering and chemical industries were all impressive. Banking techniques had become appropriately sophisticated and included the financial management of companies and cartels through the agency of the investment bank, which has been called 'perhaps the greatest organisational innovation' of the nineteenth century.[30]

While vast fortunes were being made by the few, very modest rewards indeed were the lot of most Germans. On the other hand the possibility of at least a measure of economic advancement presented itself to a substantial number, and those who realised the possibility joined the swelling ranks of at least the partially satisfied middle class.[31] Moreover the social legislation belatedly put through by Bismarck after 1881 and enlarged by his successors afforded at least a minimum of relief for those whose share of the national cake was not more than a few crumbs. These two factors contributed to the compromising nature of the Social Democratic Party (SPD), which Eduard Bernstein reflected at least as much as he promoted in his revisionist *Presuppositions of Socialism and the Tasks of Social Democracy*, to give its English title, first published in 1898.[32] Bernstein could refer to British precedent as well as German experience in arguing that improvements in the lot of the proletariat were leading it in the direction of reformism rather than revolution, towards a trade union rather than an extremist political consciousness. Further safety-valves for social discontent were constituted by emigration and expansion beyond unification, the phenomenon that Wehler has called 'social imperialism'[33] the export, as it were, of domestic strife, as well as people and capital. The extent of proletarian enthusiasm in this outward direction if limited contributed to the abandonment of its internationalist commitments by the SPD in 1914.

In this summary account stability has perhaps been overplayed and stress given insufficient attention. It is true that such measures as the lower agrarian import duties (to gain lower tariffs for the export of industrial goods) put strains on the *Junker*–bourgeois alliance in the 1890s.[34] It is also true that 'social imperialism' even in full flood could not completely drown internal protest from the left or even cries of anguish and accusation (including already a pronounced element of anti-semitism) from the right. Moreover expansion of German interests in Turkey and elsewhere at the same time as increasing reference to a Central Europe dominated by Germany alarmed potential enemies while patriots (among whom were militaristic extremists in court circles) still feared that Germany was being denied her proper 'place in the sun'.[35] Such national and international stress contributed to the advent of the First World War.

But for several years before 1914 these tensions had not appeared sufficiently marked for Russian admirers to drop their recommendation of Germany as a model for tsarism to follow. The chief candidates for a Russian Bismarck, who would of course be subject to comparable restricting circumstances, were Witte and Stolypin, whose periods in office were roughly divided by the Revolution of 1905. Sergei Witte, minister of finance at the turn of the century, produced in 1899 a secret memorandum on the industrialisation of Imperial Russia. In this illuminating work Witte actually made more specific reference to the other model:

> We must give the country such industrial perfection as has been reached by the United States of America, which firmly bases its prosperity on two pillars – agriculture and industry.[36]

But the spirit of the memorandum is far less that of American *laissez-faire* than that of Germanic *dirigisme*, the work with which it is most closely comparable being Friedrich List's *The National System of Political Economy*. Witte wanted Russia to cease to be an agricultural client of the more advanced West and to become its own self-reliant 'metropolis'. For this aim to be achieved, a high tariff and heavy taxes would have to be accompanied by the import of large amounts of foreign capital, guaranteed by the gold standard. And, of course, an important directing part would be played by the state.

During the 1890s Russia like Germany had experienced an economic boom of impressive proportions, but was less advanced and therefore subject to greater social strain. Some of the desiderata propounded by Witte had already been met, including the injection into the economy of much foreign capital. Complex financial and industrial arrangements were being developed to a degree sufficiently high for some analysts to believe that peaceful modernisation was taking place.[37] With no other foreign influence but money and expertise, such a process may indeed have taken place in the fullness of time. But in an age of highly competitive world imperialism, time was in short supply. And forcing the pace meant trouble at home and abroad. Domestic unrest was building up among peasants and workers, the armed forces and the nationalities, while members of the nobility and bourgeoisie both believed that a policy of vigorous expansionism had to be pursued. A Russian version of 'social imperialism' was succinctly put in the famous remark of Pleve, the minister of the interior, that 'To hold back the revolution, we need a small victorious war.'[38] The disastrous conflict with Japan in 1904 produced what it was hoped it would help to avert, and the Revolution of 1905 ensued. Persuaded by Witte that the only alternatives were military dictatorship or a constitution, and that the former would be difficult to impose owing to troubles in the army and navy, Nicholas II (1894–1917) conceded the latter.[39]

This concession, in any case grudging and limited and soon partially rescinded, did not change the minds of many leading Russians about the course of development to be followed. Even though the Duma had been set up, the tsar could retain at least as much real power as the kaiser, and other aspects of the national life might be undisturbed. Geoffrey Hosking talks of the 'imitation, conscious or unconscious, of the Bismarckian mode, and of the rhetoric of the National Liberals in the Reichstag'. He asserts that 'Germany was the model to which the centre and the right in Russian politics tended to look as an example of the successful integration of the authoritarian monarchy, an imperial patriotism and parliamentary institutions.'[40] Witte's successor as a potential Russian Bismarck, Peter Stolypin, necessarily followed many of his predecessor's policies, but gave particular attention to the peasant question. He believed that the modernisation of Russia would be most efficiently and speedily achieved by the formation of a 'broadly based class of capitalist farmers on the American model',[41] although his programme was by no means completely detrimental to the interests of the Russian *Junker*-type landlords, for all their protestations to the contrary. Between 1906 and 1914 even more progress was achieved than in the 1890s, although the overall mode, even in the economic sphere, remained less American than German. Gerschenkron says that 'Russia on the eve of the war was well on the way towards a westernisation or, perhaps more precisely, a Germanisation of its industrial growth.'[42]

Before he was assassinated in 1911 Stolypin argued that, for his programme to succeed, twenty years of peace were necessary. In both the internal and external situation of Russia in the early twentieth century, peace was not to be found. In the first place, because of what Trotsky called 'combined development',[43] tsarism both gained advantages and suffered disadvantages from the timing of the culmination of its modernisation process. On the one hand it could borrow not only money but also the most advanced forms of technological expertise. On the other its proletariat was formed too rapidly for it to be able to develop a trade union consciousness, and its government was obliged, for a transitional period at least, to be the client of its more mature seniors elsewhere in Europe. Already in 1882 Marx and Engels looked upon Russia as ripe for revolution, if not of the fully fledged bourgeois type, still less the proletarian.[44] By 1902, in his *What Is To Be Done?*, Lenin had moved several stages forward in an analysis which was also a counter-attack against the Bernsteinian and other heresies. Lenin argued that a political party with appropriate organisation and correct theory could lead the proletariat and the peasantry away from compromise to confrontation.[44] Coming near to realisation in 1905 and after, Lenin's diagnosis – now refined in other writings – was to achieve it in full measure in 1917.

Before then the Russian and German empires had joined together in August 1914 in a combat that would be mortal for both of them. Such an eventuality had been foreseen in February 1914 by several observers, among them the tsarist minister P. N. Durnovo, who argued in the face of growing pressures for war in the two empires that their interests were not incompatible and that war could bring them only great unrest, even revolution.[45] After the outbreak of hostilities, assertion of racial superiority that was barely latent before in this correspondence became completely explicit in such remarks as those by the German Foreign Secretary Jagow in a memorandum of

2 September 1915:

> Hitherto the giant Russian Empire, with its inexhaustible human material, its possibilities of economic recovery, its expansive tendencies, has brooded over Western Europe like a nightmare. In spite of the veneer of Western civilisation given it by Peter the Great and the German dynasty which followed him, its basically Byzantine–Oriental culture separates it from the Latin culture of the West, and the Russian race, part Slav, part Mongol, is foreign to the Germanic–Latin peoples of the West.[46]

By the end of the war Durnovo's gloomiest forecasts had been shown to be all too correct. Tsarism collapsed at the beginning of 1917, and the Provisional Government was so weak that starker alternatives than those of 1905 were already posed, of military right-wing or proletarian left-wing dictatorship.[47] The October Revolution constituted a clear choice, but several years of bitter civil war and intervention were to ensue before Lenin's government was fully established. And having dropped the Social Democratic label as an expression of their hatred for Bernsteinian revisionism and the abandonment in 1914 by the German Social Democrats of international socialism, the Soviet Communists, like Marx and Engels in 1848, turned their attention chiefly to Germany, hoping for a revolution there which would spread to envelop the whole world. The failure of the 1918–19 revolution in Germany left the Weimar Republic to clear up the mess compounded by the inequities of Versailles, while in the Soviet Union the government was pushed away from hopes of immediate world revolution towards the concept of 'socialism in one country'.

These developments are more centrally the concern of the second and third parts of this work, and will be enlarged upon there. They have been summarily introduced at this juncture to show where the Prussian path of modernisation was leading and how time did not allow Russia completely to take it. The essential point to be drawn from this exposition is that in this or any other kind of modernisation the fourth dimension is paramount; that, while models of modernisation and its factor analysis contribute to our understanding, the concrete manifestation of the process in each society is governed mostly by its chronological setting. Thus, although Russia had gone through the early stages of modernisation sufficiently for it to be one of the great powers of the eighteenth century, it fell behind during the years of the dual (French and Industrial) Revolution. The giant brooding over Europe like a nightmare during the nineteenth century, to revert to the terminology of Jagow, could not bring its threat

to the point of waking reality, for all the efforts made at the turn of
the twentieth century to emulate its more successful neighbour. For
by then the full process of modernisation had been carried out in
Germany for some time, even if autarchy had not been achieved.
And so, although the impact of imperialist competition and the First
World War was too much for both variations of Eastern European
absolutism, the more mature level of German development meant
that its ruling classes could withstand the onslaught of revolution,
while Russia succumbed to it at a critical moment of 'combined development'. That was not the end of the story, for the challenge
issued by the Russian Revolution might be immediately resisted but
could not be ignored in the longer term. In a world where Leninist
communism faced Wilsonian democracy, the pressures on the successors to the Romanovs and the Hohenzollerns and the respective
social élites would be intense indeed, and would force them to use
newly available means to take the coercion of the imperialist states to
a new peak of intensity.

We must turn now to consider the roots of Wilsonian democracy,
which will also give us the opportunity to discuss the second of the
two paths that Lenin suggested tsarist society could have taken: the
American. We have already seen that there were American elements
in the thinking of both Witte and Stolypin, but our search must go far
beyond them, back at least to the eighteenth century. For it was then
that the great and comparable potential of the future superpowers
was first discerned. One of Catherine the Great's many corre-
spondents, Baron Melchior von Grimm, wrote to the empress soon
after the outbreak of the French Revolution:

> Two empires will then share all the advantages of civilisation, of
> the power of genius, of letters, of arms and industry: Russia on the
> eastern side and America . . . on the western side, and we other
> peoples of the nucleus will be too degraded, too debased, to know
> otherwise than by a vague and stupid tradition what we have
> been.[48]

And some years earlier, not long after the commencement of the
American Revolution, the American diplomat Silas Deane had fore-
cast that Great Britain would share world hegemony with the United
States and Russia, asserting that 'Russia like America is a new state
and rises with the most astonishing rapidity'.[49] Indeed the writing
was clear enough on the walls of Europe at the dawn of the nineteenth century for those who chose to look, but it was not until some
decades later that the message positively obtruded itself on the public
consciousness. Even in the mid-1830s Alexis de Tocqueville could

claim that these

> . . . two great nations [had grown up] unnoticed; and while the attention of mankind was directed elsewhere, they have suddenly assumed a most prominent place among the nations; and the world learned their existence and their greatness at almost the same time.

De Tocqueville's further remarks may be taken as the basis for a discussion of these outstanding developments. He wrote:

> All other nations seem to have nearly reached their natural limits, and only to be charged with the maintenance of their power; but these are still in the act of growth; all the others are stopped, or continue to advance with extreme difficulty; these are preceding with ease and with celerity along a path to which the human eye can assign no term. The American struggles against the natural obstacles which oppose him; the adversaries of the Russian are men; the former combats the wilderness and savage life; the latter, civilisation with all its weapons and arts; the conquests of the one are therefore gained by the ploughshare; those of the other by the sword. The Anglo-American relies upon personal interest to accomplish his ends, and gives free scope to the unguided exertions and common sense of the citizens; the Russian centres all the authority of society in a single arm; the principal arm of the former is freedom; and of the latter servitude. Their starting point is different, and their courses are not the same; yet each of them seems to be marked out by the will of Heaven to sway the destinies of half the globe.[50]

De Tocqueville is impressive in his broad sweep, but inaccurate in nearly every particular. Many other nations may have reached their natural limits (although Prussia is an obvious important exception), but few were 'charged with the maintenance of their power' only, for imperial expansion was far from the limits of its extent. Granted, the spectacle of the United States preparing for the bustle of the Roaring Forties could hardly have failed to impress a visitor accustomed to the slower pace and smaller scale of Restoration France, nor equally could a percipient European over in North America have been less conscious of the expansionist Russian realities behind the mystical maunderings of the Holy Alliance – indeed distance may have lent more terror to the view. But de Tocqueville was looking at Russia too much from the standpoint of the West of his native continent and at America too much from the East of the continent that he was visiting. Indians on the frontier could not have agreed that the Americans were carrying on a struggle against 'natural obstacles' or 'the wilderness and savage life' with the assistance of the plough-share. Russians crossing Siberian wastes in winter would not have gained much comfort from the information that their adversaries were men, and also would not readily have believed that they were engaged in combat against 'civilisation with all its weapons and arts'. Mexicans could have been forgiven for doubting that they were threatened by nothing more than the ploughshare, while Georgians and at least a few of the other peoples of Transcaucasia would have been unjustified in any assertion that they had succumbed to the sword. The Anglo-American did not rely exclusively on personal interest when the federal government's land policy could be manipulated for private or corporate gain, to give just one example. Russians were likely to feel the weight of more than one arm in the course of a lifetime, and some of them were very much involved in private enterprise. Black slaves on the plantations of the South and white wage slaves in New England factories did not believe that their masters were principally motivated by thoughts of freedom, and Cossacks in addition to an increasing number of peasants were not profoundly conscious of being sunk in servitude. The rest of de Tocqueville's argument is more nebulous and therefore less open to comment; it undoubtedly contains a measure of truth.

This somewhat facetious exercise in criticism has not been carried out solely with the intention of scoring points off an otherwise often incisive political analyst of 150 years ago. It is principally directed at the congratulatory justification of expansion at the time and even more at a double historiographical standard that persists today. On the one hand even such a searching writer as Emerson could be ecstatic about American expansion in the mid-1840s:

> We cannot look on the freedom of this country, in connection with its youth, without a presentiment that here shall laws and institutions exist on some scale to the majesty of nature. To men legislating for the area betwixt the two oceans, betwixt the snows and the tropics, somewhat of the grandeur of nature will infuse itself into the code. . . . It seems so easy for America to inspire and express the most expansive and humane spirit; new-born, free, healthful, strong, the land of the labourer, of the democrat, of the philanthropist, of the believer, of the saint, she should speak for the human race.[51]

Russians could be equally lyrical at this time about their own movement into Asia, although a more sober analysis came some twenty years later from the chancellor, Prince Alexander Gorchakov, who considered that the state in his charge resembled' all civilised States which are brought into contact with half-savage, nomad populations, possessing no fixed social organisation'. Gorchakov's explanation was set out in the following manner:

In such cases it always happens that the more civilised State is forced, in the interest of the security of its frontier and its commercial relations, to exercise a certain ascendancy over those whom their turbulent and unsettled character make more undesirable neighbours. First, there are raids and acts of pillage to be put down. To put a stop to them, the tribes on the frontier have to be reduced to a state of more or less perfect submission. This result once attained, these tribes take to more peaceful habits, but are in their turn exposed to the attacks of the more distant tribes.

The State is bound to defend them against these depredations and to punish those who commit them. Hence the necessity of distant, costly, and periodically recurring expeditions against an enemy whom his social organisation makes it impossible to seize. If, the robbers once punished, the expedition is withdrawn, the lesson is soon forgotten; its withdrawal put down to weakness. It is a peculiarity of Asiatics to respect nothing but visible and palpable force; the moral force of reason and of the interests of civilisation has as yet no hold upon them. The work has then always to be done over again from the beginning.

In order to put a stop to this stage of permanent disorder, fortified posts are established in the midst of these hostile tribes, and an influence is brought to bear upon them which reduces them by degrees to a state of more or less forced submission. But soon beyond this second line other still more distant tribes come in their turn to threaten the same dangers and necessitate the same measures of repression. The State thus finds itself forced to choose one of two alternatives, either to give up this endless labour and to abandon its frontier to perpetual disturbance, rendering all prosperity, all security, all civilisation an impossibility, or, on the other hand, to plunge deeper and deeper into barbarous countries, where the difficulties and expenses increase with every step in advance.

Such has been the fate of every country which has found itself in a similar position. The United States in America, France in Algeria, Holland in her Colonies, England in India – all have been irresistibly forced, less by ambition than by imperious necessity, into this onward march, where the greatest difficulty is to know when to stop. . . .[52]

In fact, while all these imperial powers did indeed have elements of their expansionist policy in common, the two under present consideration shared some of them to the exclusion of the others.

Empire-builders everywhere believed that they themselves possessed 'the moral force of reason and of the interests of civilisation', but only the Americans and the Russians were faced with the problem of land-based empire which gave particular force to Gorchakov's variation of the 'domino' theory. Neither Washington nor Moscow was under threat of direct attack from the Indians or their Asian cousins, but direct contiguity with frontier regions still lent colour to concepts of what Gorchakov called Russia's 'special mission' and Americans had become accustomed by this time to call their 'manifest destiny'. True, Russia's sense of security was much more fragile than America's owing to the presence on the western frontier of powerful 'civilised neighbours'. And although colonisation, which the great historian Kliuchevsky called the dominant theme of Russian history, was even more central to the American experience, the nature of the process was very different in the two cases, with the Russians starting at the centre (first Kiev, then Moscow) and the Americans originating across oceans (to begin with the Atlantic, later the Pacific).

But a further feature common to both societies, which bound them much more closely than the differences separating them, has become more apparent only since the Second World War. For while all other empires of the developed world were dismantled, those of Russia and America remained. That was the fact of the matter, but it was disguised for several reasons, all facilitated by the landlocked nature of the original formations. Perhaps most important, locked in the dangerous embrace of the cold war though they were, the emergent superpowers were tacitly co-operating in the break-up of the other empires, to their common advantage. In the accomplishment of this task, they used the rhetoric of their respective ideologies to the full, and this involved the denial by each of its own imperialism at the same time as the attribution of what had become a label of opprobrium to the other. American patriots accused the Russians of enslaving the peoples of the other republics in the Union, all easily identifiable around the periphery. Soviet apologists attacked the American treatment of Indians, Mexicans and Blacks, conspicuous enough through the colour of their skin where not in a specific geographical location. Historians joined in such attacks, but also did what they could to marshal a defence. For some time the spokesmen for the heirs of the tsarist empire put forward the 'lesser evil' argument, which was based on the assertion that it was better for the nationalities to be subject to what would become the fraternal and progressive association of the USSR rather than becoming attached to another empire or remaining in primitive backwardness. The 'lesser evil' concept was later replaced by that of the 'friendship of peoples' which suggested that, while tsarist officers and officials were implementing their master's colonial policy, friendly contacts were made at the lower social level ready for fuller development after the Revolution. Less concerned for ideological consistency in their pluralist society, American historians have put forward a number of different explanations. The sins of the fathers may be expiated by the full confession of the sons: the enslavement of Blacks, the conquest of Mexicans and the slaughter of Indians were all disgusting episodes, but the situation with regard to all three groups is now better and still improving. Alternatively, Blacks were enabled through slavery to adapt from African tribalism to what later became full participation in American citizenship; the Mexican government was unstable and was not really capable of administering the area from Texas to California; and Indians were few in number with an antiquated way of life, unable to make full use of the natural riches in the vast regions through which they wandered without purpose; and so on. In neither the American nor the Soviet case is there much suggestion that the past might be unravelled, so to speak, for this could only result in the complete disintegration of the USA and the USSR, and the loss of their respective influences beyond their borders, in, for example, Latin America or Eastern Europe.

Imperial expansion was one of the most notable activities of America and Russia in the nineteenth century, and the historiographical double standard is perhaps most evident in its application to this subject. But discussion of the American path to modernity is more directly concerned with the pattern of development accompanying expansion, and so we must now address ourselves to discussion of this allied topic, for which a good point of departure is emancipation. At the time, since the Russian Proclamation came first in 1861 and the USA was involved in the Civil War, Northern journals gave it a welcome all the warmer for the propaganda advantage that it bestowed.

The *Liberator* declared:

The Manifesto of the Tsar is throughout in most striking contrast with the recent manifestos of the leaders of the rebel slaveholders in this country.

The *Atlantic Monthly* asked:

Who could have ventured to predict that at the end of one hundred years, the American nations should be engaged in a civil contest, having for its object, on the part of those who began it, the perpetuation and extension of slavery, while Russia should not be threatened with such a contest because her government, an autocracy, had abolished serfdom?

And looking in the other chronological direction, *Harper's* asserted:

Russia, like the United States, is a nation of the future. Like the United States, Russia is in the agonies of a terrible transition; the Russian serfs, like the American Negroes, are receiving their liberty; and the Russian *boiars*, like the Southern slaveowners, are mutinous at the loss of their property. To two such peoples, firmly bound together by an alliance as well as by traditional sympathy and good feeling, what would be impossible? An alliance between Russia and the United States at the present time would relieve both of us from all apprehensions of foreign interference.[53]

As the smoke of the Civil War lifted and the gloom of their ignorance of the Russian situation cleared, American journalists became less enthusiastic about the policies of the tsar, partaking indeed of the Russophobia that gripped their colleagues in Western Europe.

In the years following 1865 both emancipations were revealed to be far less radical measures than at first appeared. The Blacks soon found that the award to them of the ideal of the liberal philosophers – freedom without definition – was of little use. The 'Day of Jubilo' had given very few of them as much as 'two acres and a mule', and put nearly all of them heavily in debt to either their former master or a new one – storekeeper or company. Similarly the muzhiks were usually awarded an insufficiency of land, in many regions often unable to attain complete independence from the landlord or the commune. There was economic progress, however, in both societies, and at least some of the former slaves and serfs shared in it as the societies became more stratified in the wake of capitalist development.

But even those who might be expected to have derived great benefit from it – the American White farmers – did not. It was not until the end of the nineteenth century that agriculture was providing a good return for investment in the USA with any consistency. Some of the reasons for this have been exaggerated: falling prices, railroad manipulations, usurious rates of loan. The world setting, although not fully appreciated by nearly all of those who suffered from its market fluctuations, was probably at least as significant. Certainly the myth of the covered wagon taking the enterprising family to carve prosperity out of the wilderness has been too much exposed for it to deserve its all too healthy longevity. The Homestead Act and other legislation did work to the advantage of the corporation rather than the individual, and the path of the 'free farmer' was by no means as smooth as it might have seemed to some of its advocates in Russia.[54]

There, too, global circumstances were of considerable influence and they combined with the powerful legacy of serfdom and the half-hearted nature of emancipation to give the Russian farmer a large number of problems which made for deep discontent. Radical remedies of both domestic and foreign origin were prescribed, often not by the peasants but by well-wishers from other classes. Many of these may be put under the all-embracing heading of Populism, a phenomenon common to a considerable number of societies undergoing the process of modernisation, and usually a mixture of nostalgic retrospection towards a golden age and a fervent looking forward to a Utopia. In the Russian case argument was based mostly on the way of life of the traditional peasant commune, which was believed to contain within it the necessary ingredients for a future fraternal commonwealth. There was much more talk than action, and most of it by repentant or conscience-stricken nobles and members of the middle class.

American Populism was a genuinely popular movement, the consequence of a more advanced level of education, flexible society and open form of politics. American protesters were also confronted by a higher degree of industrialisation and urbanisation, which together gave them both a formidable problem and a vehicle for their protest. For the myth of the frontier was already strong by the time of its official closure in 1890, and the values of sturdy, independent tillers of the soil were aggressively adopted by patriotic town dwellers. Many urban voters joined in the Populist crusades of William Jennings Bryan in 1896 and 1900 because they believed that they should unite with other 'small men' such as their 'country cousins' in the struggle against a big business which was now rampant in town and country alike, undermining old American virtues in a savage and ruthless manner. And not a few of them had some experience of rural life, for the hundreds of thousands swelling the population of the cities were by no means exclusively new immigrants, as another myth of American history has led people to believe. The factory and the tenement were safety-valves for the discontent of multitudes of former farmers, albeit imperfect ones, since new grievances merged with the old rather than supplanting them.

By the end of the nineteenth century industry had overtaken agriculture, and farming folk were now in a minority. The vast potential of the USA as both a source of natural resources and a market for manufactured goods had been exploited by the 'robber barons' – the Carnegies and the Rockefellers – with a degree of success which would have made the Marx and Engels of the *Communist Manifesto* gasp. If the builders of the ancient pyramids and aqueducts and the medieval cathedrals had already been surpassed in 1848, by what distance had they been overtaken in 1900? Not that America's rapid rise went unnoticed by the Communist founding fathers, as they clearly showed in their preface to the Russian edition of the *Manifesto* in 1882, considering the sequel to 1848:

> It was the time when Russia constituted the last great reserve of all European reaction, when the United States absorbed the surplus proletarian forces of Europe through immigration. Both countries provided Europe with raw materials and were at the same time markets for the sale of its industrial products. At that time both were, therefore, in one way or another, pillars of the existing European order.
>
> How very different today! Precisely European immigration fitted North America for a gigantic agricultural production, whose competition is shaking the very foundations of European landed property – large and small. In addition it enabled the United States to exploit its tremendous industrial resources with an energy and on a scale that must shortly break the industrial monopoly of Western Europe, and especially of England, existing up to now. Both circumstances react in revolutionary manner upon America itself. Step by step the small and middle land-ownership of the farmers, the basis of the whole political constitution, is succumbing to the competition of giant farms; simultaneously, a mass proletariat and a fabulous concentration of capital are developing for the first time in the industrial regions.
>
> And now Russia! During the Revolution of 1848–49 not only the European princes, but the European bourgeois as well, found their only salvation from the proletariat, just beginning to awaken, in Russian intervention. The tsar was proclaimed the chief of European reaction. Today he is a prisoner of war of the revolution, in Gatchina, and Russia forms the vanguard of revolutionary action in Europe.
>
> The *Communist Manifesto* had as its object the proclamation of the inevitably impending dissolution of modern bourgeois property. But in Russia we find, face to face with the rapidly developing capitalist swindle and bourgeois landed property, just beginning to develop, more than half the land owned in common by the peasants. Now the question is: Can the Russian commune, though greatly undermined, yet a form of primeval common ownership of

land, pass directly to the higher form of communist common ownership?

Or, on the contrary, must it first pass through the same process of dissolution as constitutes the historical evolution of the West?

The only answer to that possible today is this: If the Russian Revolution becomes the signal for a proletarian revolution in the West, so that both complement each other, the present Russian common ownership of land may serve as the starting-point for a communist development.[55]

While Marx and Engels could only hint at the scale of American growth (at the same time as exaggerating the chances for proletarian revolution in the USA), they were not in 1882 in a position to sense fully the leaps forward that Russia too would be making in the following decades. The Populist overtones of their preface to the Russian *Manifesto* were somewhat anachronistic in that the assassination of Alexander II in 1881 marked an abrupt end to the Populist period in the history of the Russian intelligentsia. The movement now split in two general directions, towards liberalism on the one hand and socialism on the other, this bifurcation reflecting the growth of bourgeoisie and proletariat as well as continued stirrings among the landlords and peasants. Already apparent in the years following 1861, the urban problem had grown by the beginning of the twentieth century to proportions comparable with those in the Western world. Such a circumstance was to be made crystal clear in the Revolution of 1905, begun in St Petersburg and developing with a nationwide general strike and a full-scale insurrection in Moscow.

Meanwhile the United States managed to ride the storms of industrial unrest without revolutionary disturbance. The most celebrated reform movement, the Progressive, was essentially middle class in membership and moderate in aim, seeking to clean American cities of their ills and injustices without any significant change in the governmental system. Up to the outbreak of the First World War the Progressives were at least moderately confident that they were on the right track, and some of them believed that their policies contained lessons for less favoured lands, including Russia, for which Robert La Follette, for example, believed his own state of Wisconsin could be a model of reform. More extreme solutions never got very far in the USA, although Eugene V. Debs, the Socialist candidate for the presidency, received nearly a million votes in 1912.

We must remember, too, as in the case of Germany, that the achievement of peaceful modernisation in the USA did not mean the absence of tension or violence. American labour history contains almost as much gunfire as the winning of the West. Great strikes and the bloody breaking of them were widespread. Unions made only slow headway against the determined opposition of the bosses which included the hiring of gangs of 'detectives' or 'guards' approaching the scale and power of private armies. The leaders of the workers were ruthlessly persecuted, and a determined policy of 'divide and rule' was used against groups of differing ethnic origins. Even Progressives could do little to bring about a satisfactory truce, let alone a peace, in this large-scale conflict, which threatened at times to consume whole cities, even if the federal government itself could never have been said to have faced the danger of overthrow.[56]

Again, as in the German case, a form of 'social imperialism' helped to hold back the USA from such a cataclysm (a right-wing version of which was sketched out in Jack London's *The Iron Heel*). Looking outward or remembering the *Maine*, American citizens could celebrate their country's victories at the same time as denigrating those 'non-Americans' who either were not qualified or did not choose to join in the waving of the flag or the brandishing of the big stick. As John Higham writes of the 1890s:

> Two anti-foreign movements – one international, the other internal – complemented each other, so that the jingoist atmosphere of the decade helps explain the depth and intensity of its nativism.[57]

One of the most important areas of activity before 1900 was China, where the policy pursued was that of the 'open door', establishing an informal empire in which the USA would have an important share and stoutly resisting opposition movements such as that of the Boxers. Two years before, in the 'splendid little war' against Spain, the USA had consolidated its foothold in the Pacific and the Caribbean and also acquired a safety-valve to let off some popular steam. (It is interesting although also idle to speculate what would have happened if 'a small victorious war' – to use again the phrase of the Russian minister of the interior, Pleve – had been denied the American people as it was the Russian in 1904–5, or indeed what would have been the result if the USA's forces had taken on the Japanese at that time rather than those of the tsar.) Teddy Roosevelt, the rough-riding hero of San Juan Hill, was soon tall in the saddle of the presidency, and involved in showdowns from Panama to Algeciras. And before 1917 Woodrow Wilson was by no means the man of peace that he has sometimes been taken for. Asserting in 1912 that 'what we have been witnessing for the past hundred years is the transformation of a Newtonian Constitution into a Darwinian Constitution',[58] Wilson acted on the assumption of such a change in an area broader than that of the technicalities of government, namely international politics, intervening for example in the revolution of the Mexicans, condoning the suppression of the Kuomintang in China.

National expansion had indeed produced global contraction, in both peace and war. As early as the 1860s a telegraph company official could declare that 'We hold the ball of the earth in our hand, and wind upon it a network of living and thinking wire, till the whole is held together and bound with the same wishes, projects, and interests.'[59] Many nations had the ships, men and money to exercise on a world-wide scale the self-centred tenets of jingoism, including comparatively new entrants into the struggle for empire such as the USA and Germany, which had both successfully accomplished the process of peaceful modernisation. It was perhaps ironic that in the huge imperial contest the greatest threat to stability was seen in one of the weakest of the dynamic powers which had not yet successfully modernised, the unwitting begetter of the first jingoism (at the time of the Crimean War) – tsarist Russia. The aggression of the Russian bear was deemed to have reached appalling dimensions, the threat extending as far as New Zealand, where preparations were made in the 1870s and 1880s for raids by ships of the Russian navy.[60] This kind of threat, intensified by Russophobia, was of course exaggerated out of all proportion. Far from conquering the world with the opportunities afforded it by the age of imperialism, the tsarist régime became its most complete victim.

Part Two

The Russian Revolutions and Their Impact

In Part 1, we have argued that Russian history does not constitute an exception to the general course of world history, even though it does possess certain distinctive features. Russia was by no means a complete stranger to the general crisis of the seventeenth century, was fairly closely related to the democratic revolution of the eighteenth century and intimately involved with the peaceful modernisation of the nineteenth century. At the beginning of the twentieth century, tsarism was inextricably connected with the world-wide ties of imperialism.

In other words, Russia's most celebrated historical feature – backwardness – was throughout the modern period of world history no more than relative. Moreover this apparent handicap can sometimes act to the advantage of those who have been held back by it. Trotsky could write in the 1920s that 'The fact that Germany and the United States have now economically outstripped England was made possible by the very backwardness of their capitalist development'.[1] Similarly, as Trotsky and others have argued, even Russia was in certain respects in advance of some of its rivals soon after the beginning of the twentieth century as well as remaining behind them in others. Trotsky declared:

> At the same time that peasant land-cultivation as a whole remained, right up to the revolution, at the level of the seventeenth century, Russian industry in its technique and capitalist structure stood at the level of the advanced countries, and in certain respects even outstripped them.[2]

This circumstance, and its social consequences, resulted not only in the three Russian Revolutions that will be the focus of our next chapter, but also in some of their special features to which we shall have to draw our attention. Not the least of these is the unprecedentedly close relationship of the Russian Revolutions, especially the third or October, with the rest of the world.

The division of the world into three parts is widely accepted today, but there is some disagreement about the components of each of them. Most Western analysts would probably accept Frantz Fanon's concept of a Third World made up of the developing countries, with the other two constituted by the more advanced capitalist and socialist worlds.[3] For the Chinese, however, the First World comprises the United States and the Soviet Union together – 'the biggest international exploiters, oppressors and aggressors, and the common enemies of the peoples of the world';[4] the Second World consists of Europe and Japan while the Third World is made up of China with the rest. And growing Western schools of thought divide the world into four rather than three parts: the advanced industrial democracies; the communist camp; the relatively rich developing countries, particularly the oil producers; and a Fourth World of the poor. At least some of those sharing this view would want to emphasise that while the vast majority of this Fourth World is to be found in Asia, Latin America and Africa, a not insignificant amount of its members is to be found in the cities and backward rural areas of the other three.[5] Here we adopt what appears to be still the majority Western world view, especially since it conforms broadly to that shared by Lenin and his opponents in 1917 and after: Soviet Russia; Western empires and nations; and the victims of imperialism. This tripartite division will determine the shape of Chapters 5 and 6. And, as we shall now see again in Chapter 4, the division of the Russian Revolution was also tripartite.

4   The Three Russian Revolutions

The Russian Revolutions were three in one – an unholy trinity. Lenin called 1905 a 'dress rehearsal' and was the first to argue that October must follow on from February. For Trotsky the three Revolutions were all part of one continuous 'permanent revolution'. Writing of 1905 in 1922, he declared:

> . . . both in its origins and in its development the prologue carried within it all the elements of the historical drama whose witnesses and participants we are today. But in the prologue these elements appeared in a compressed, not as yet fully developed form. All the forces engaged in the struggle of 1905 are today illuminated more clearly than before by the light cast back on them by the events of 1917. The Red October, as we used to call it even then, grew after twelve years into another, incomparably more powerful and truly victorious October.[1]

Here we will attempt to give a brief description of the three Revolutions and of the relation between them, with emphasis on their aspirations for wider relevance culminating in the formation and early activity of the Third International after October.

Right from its beginning in 1894, the reign of Nicholas II went far from smoothly, and the going became even rougher after 1900. At about this time opposition political parties from social democrats to liberals were becoming more organised and increasing their agitation for the overthrow or at least the reform of the autocracy. Terrorism was also on the move again, and in 1901 an unpopular minister of education was assassinated, a fate that befell a despised minister of the interior in the following year. The latter's successor, V. K. von Pleve, took up as many arms as possible against a swelling sea of troubles composed of student agitation and unrest among the nationalities, peasants and, last and least in numbers only, workers. To relieve the pressure from the first of these sources,

Pleve encouraged attacks on Jewish communities in Bessarabia, the Ukraine and White Russia. He sent troops out into the rural areas to suppress peasant insurgency and suspended an investigation of the agricultural problem by the provincial *zemstva*. He sent more troops to quell industrial strikes and turned a deaf ear to demands for the eight-hour day and other concessions. If beating up Yids did not bring pacification, perhaps shooting 'yellow monkeys' would, although when war actually threatened against Japan Pleve was not as keen as before on his previously expressed notorious opinion that, 'In order to hold back the revolution, we need a small victorious war.' After all, he was already keeping the army busy enough in his fight against internal enemies. By July 1904 more than enough news had come through of Russian reverses in the war against Japan which had broken out in January for him to revise his opinion even more before being blown up by a terrorist's bomb in St Petersburg.

His successor, Prince Dmitry Sviatopolk-Mirsky, was comparatively moderate, but could only achieve too little too late. Even liberals were outraged by the treatment that Pleve had meted out to the *zemstva* in which they were often themselves active, and were by no means completely mollified by the new minister of the interior's concessions to them. In September a group of opposition groups including Socialist Revolutionaries, liberals from the Union of Liberation and representatives of various nationalities, both left-wing and moderate, met in Paris to form a bloc jointly resolved to work peacefully for the replacement of autocracy by a form of representative government elected by universal suffrage and offering the right of self-determination to the various peoples. In October the Union of Liberation went ahead with plans for a series of banquets which would celebrate the law reform of 1864 – the year which had also seen the introduction of the *zemstvo* boards into provincial government, and recall the campaign by French liberals in 1848. Discussions without a banquet continued, too, throughout late 1904 in St Petersburg and other towns. There was some disagreement about the extent of the demands that should be made, the men from the *zemstva* being less assertive than those from the Union of Liberation. But all could agree to be outraged by the government's warning to the opposition in December not to go beyond its sphere of competence and to be appalled by the loss of Port Arthur in the same month. In January 1905 occurred the event which made protest and disturbance spill over into revolution.

This was of course Bloody Sunday.[2] At the beginning of the new year a new wave of strikes had begun among the industrial workers of the capital and elsewhere, and a peaceful procession of strikers, women and children set out for the Winter Palace on 9 January. The personality and intentions of the leader, Father Gapon, have been the subject of much controversy, but there has been little disagreement about the purpose of his followers. Similarly it is by no means certain who ultimately initiated the action of the Cossacks, nor how many were killed, but beyond any doubt the shots fired upon the demonstrators ignited the fury of the opponents of tsarism and alienated many of its former friends. Lenin was surely correct to note that 'The revolutionary education of the proletariat made more progress in one day than it could have made in months and years of drab, humdrum, wretched existence.'[3] Never again would the workers of the capital march with their wives and children in devout supplication to their tsar under the influence of the oratory of a fervent priest. The prelude to Bloody Sunday may have recalled medieval Russia; the aftermath soon displayed a Russia firmly placed in the modern world. Trotsky wrote in February 1905:

Trade after trade, factory after factory, town after town are stopping work. The railway personnel act as the detonators of the strike; the railway lines are the channels along which the strike epidemic spreads. Economic claims are advanced and are satisfied, wholly or in part, almost at once. But neither the beginning of the strike nor its end is fully determined by the nature of the claims made or by the form in which they are met. The strike does not occur because the economic struggle has found expression in certain well-defined demands; on the contrary, the demands are chosen and formulated because there has to be a strike. The workers have to reveal to themselves, to the proletariat in other parts of the country, finally to the nation at large, their accumulated strength, their class responsiveness, their fighting readiness. Everything has to be submitted to the universal revolutionary appraisal.[4]

It is true that the strikers immediately began to go back to work in St Petersburg, but they were soon out again both there and in other cities, especially in peripheral regions such as Poland, the Baltic and Caspian littorals. And it was not just the workers who were aroused. Scarcely anybody from the meanest peasant to the grandest university professor (if he is at the opposite end of the spectrum of consciousness) was unaffected by the movement which swept throughout the length and breadth of the empire for the rest of the year and into the next. Even the tsar and his entourage, although not visibly moved by Bloody Sunday, were soon forced to shift their ground. After much hesitation the government took three significant steps in February 1905: a summons to all loyal Russians to rally round the throne; a declaration of intent to consult representatives of the people in the preparation of new laws; and an instruction to the Council of Ministers to consider seriously proposals for the improvement of the state's organisation and of social welfare.

Tsushima in May was an even more humiliating defeat for the Baltic and Black Sea fleets than the loss of Port Arthur had been for the remnants of the Pacific fleet in December 1904. The government was being driven towards peace with Japan in order to achieve it with its own people. But the people moved more quickly than the government. A new wave of unrest engulfed the centre of the empire and many of the nationalities near the borders, especially the Poles. The middle-class intelligentsia could not agree before 1905 on calling for a constituent assembly, or how to co-ordinate their organisations; now fourteen different groups came together in a Union of Unions which accepted the need for terrorism and urged Nicholas to rid himself of the 'gang of robbers' around him. The less radical *zemstvo* representatives had an audience with the tsar in June, only to find their conference, scheduled for July, banned. They conferred nevertheless, and echoed the Populists of the nineteenth century in calling for a movement to the people. By this time, the peasants had mobilised themselves, refusing to work or pay rent and resorting to various kinds of illegality on behalf of the bellies of their animals and their own. Giving his full support to the peasant movement, Lunacharsky a Social Democrat, also gave a warning: 'We must also fight against a Pugachevshchina; there have already been cases of "generals" appearing in various uniforms.'[5] Taking their organisation to a level higher than in that famous struggle of former times, at least some rural inhabitants had assembled with urban advisers to form a Peasant Union in May. Throughout the summer of 1905 industrial strikes continued, the troops being called out against one in Łodz while another in Odessa led to the famous *Potemkin* mutiny. While further disaffection from the armed forces was feared, the terrorists were still in action, assassinating a number of victims including the military governor of Moscow.

After such a season of discontent the government was forced to act again. The tsar was the recipient of much advice from those close to him. Many counselled firm discipline and diversionary tactics – more use of the knout and more pogroms, but he vacillated between severity and leniency in his policies. In August the procedure was announced for elections to the representative assembly promised in February, with countryside (supposedly conservative) heavily outweighing town (allegedly radical). Later in the same month the voice of academia was liberated with an unexpected decree restoring autonomy to the universities. Excited speeches, by no means all by professors or even students, filled the lecture halls, and the procedure for elections was given far from first-class marks.

If summer had produced considerable unrest, autumn brought forth utter turmoil. After a number of fluctuations, the strike movement became general with the encouragement of the railway union. The trains stopped in October, and almost everything else stopped too. One important movement began in the same month with the formation of the St Petersburg Soviet of Workers' Deputies. To some extent prepared by the agitation of radical politicians, by discussions in the universities and by organisations on the shop floor, the Soviet was something new. As Trotsky, one of its leading figures, put it:

> It was an organisation which was authoritative and yet had no traditions; which could immediately involve a scattered mass of hundreds of thousands of people while having virtually no organisational machinery; which united the revolutionary currents within the proletariat; which was capable of initiative and spontaneous self-control – and, most important of all, which could be brought out from underground within twenty-four hours.[6]

The Soviet was soon bringing out its own newspaper, *Izvestiia* (News), and acquiring wide authority.

Recognising that he was in danger of losing his own authority, Nicholas made further concessions, after being persuaded by Witte, who had just come back from concluding the Treaty of Portsmouth with Japan, that the only alternative was military dictatorship. Nicholas was wise enough to realise that to exert a military dictatorship he needed armed forces made of sterner stuff than those immediately at his disposal, and so he issued what came to be known as the October Manifesto. This broadened the franchise for the representative assembly, the State Duma, which was now to be consulted for its approval of every new law; and fundamental civil liberties were guaranteed. The October Manifesto was greeted with wild enthusiasm by many in the middle of the political road,[7] but those to the right showed their alarm by persecuting more Jews and other unfortunates, while those to the left believed that no genuine concession had been made. 'The proletariat . . . rejects the police whip wrapped in the parchment of the constitution', wrote Trotsky in *Izvestiia*.[8]

The government had done enough for the strike movement to waver. But the Revolution of 1905 came to an end not with a whimper but with a bang. Rural areas within the Empire were subject to widespread and more violent disturbances towards the end of the year, while the Peasant Union met in Moscow in November to voice there the aspirations of the tillers of the soil, augmented and adapted it is true by revolutionary intellectuals whose number had increased after the government had permitted the return of political exiles in the previous month. Now the government resumed its former firmness, declaring a 'state of emergency' in the Baltic provinces and elsewhere and arresting the Moscow leaders of the Peasant Union. It soon moved in on the Soviet, arresting the president of the St Petersburg Soviet, and then, after an inflammatory manifesto, all its deputies. A protest strike came to very little, and the torch passed to Moscow, where a Soviet of Soldiers' Deputies was set up. By mid-December all was over bar the shooting, when an armed uprising which had lasted for a week was crushed without difficulty by guards brought in from the newer capital. Other loyal troops had to be sent out to Siberia, where a section of the railway was in the hands of soldiers who had lost all semblance of good order and military discipline. The most famous of a series of acts of insubordination among the armed forces was a mutiny led by Lieutenant Schmidt in Sevastopol.

1906 saw the return of something like calm to the Russian Empire, and it would be wrong to suggest that even 1905 brought the threat of revolution to every single corner of the land. Had this been the case, the Revolution would probably have been more successful, although a further reason for its eventual failure was lack of co-ordination among its several parts. Its impact was certainly felt throughout the world, according to Trotsky, even at the beginning of the fateful year: 'Every Paris concierge knew three days in advance that there was going to be a revolution in Petersburg on Sunday, 9 January.'[9] We shall look more closely at the spread of the news and its influence in the next two chapters. Here we shall concentrate on its effect as far as the international revolutionary movement was concerned.

In the assessment of 1905 by Julius Braunthal, one of the historians of the International:

> It was an unforgettable experience, this first revolutionary uprising of the workers since the Paris Commune of 1871, and, for many contemporaries, the first experience of revolution. To some it seemed that they were living through a turning-point in world history and witnessing the start of a new epoch of European revolutions.[10]

Braunthal quotes from a letter from Victor Adler to August Bebel in December 1904: '. . . to me, the centre of gravity lies now in Russia. I simply burn of tension, and I believe that there our destiny will be, if not decided, in any case decisively influenced. . .'. He also tells us of the reception given to news of the tsar's October Manifesto at the Party Congress of the Austrian Social Democrats. As soon as the first paragraph was read out, conceding freedom of the press and of assembly, great cheers went up, and then the delegates stood to hear the rest of the manifesto 'gripped by an almost religious emotion'. At its end

> . . . the delegates instinctively found the appropriate way of expressing their feelings. Suddenly the hall rang with the sound of revolutionary songs. The Czechs and Poles were singing the *Red Flag*, whereupon the Germans responded with the *Marseillaise*.[11]

The choice of song may have been an indication of attitude concerning one of the big questions that was occupying the international socialist movement at the time – the general strike. German socialists tended to see it as a shield, while others saw it as a spear. Experience of workers in Belgium, Holland and Italy and elsewhere in Europe had so far been conflicting; and in the end the new evidence from Russia could lend support to either side in the debate. In the longer perspective that is available to us we can see one of the beginnings of the split that was to tear the Second International apart.

One of the leading figures in that disruption, Lenin, was absent from the revolutionary arena until after the amnesty for political exiles in October 1905. But before then, of course, as he heard of the events he was ceaselessly subjecting them to his searching analysis. And he did not talk of Europe alone. On 1 January 1905 he published an article in the periodical *Vpered* entitled 'The Fall of Port Arthur', in which he emphasised that:

> A progressive and advanced Asia has inflicted an irreparable blow on a backward and reactionary Europe. . . . Military writers say that in strength Port Arthur was equal to six Sevastopols. And behold, a small hitherto universally despised Japan took possession of this citadel in eight months, whereas England and France together took a whole year to seize one Sevastopol.

Already Lenin sensed the implications of the Japanese victory and of the domestic sequel to the Russian defeat; by 1927 the Soviet writer M. Pavlovich was prepared to give the internal disturbance precedence over the international upset, writing:

> The Russian Revolution of 1905 made an even greater impression on the peoples of the East. In the life of the Asian peoples the Russian Revolution played the same tremendous role as the great French Revolution formerly played in the lives of the Europeans.[12]

In many ways the war and the Revolution are inseparable; neither can be understood without some examination of the other, and they both stand out more clearly when placed in a wider context. What is beyond all doubt is that between them they stimulated the movement for socialism in Asia as in Europe. (See also Chapters 5 and 6).

For the moment we must move on towards February. Of course between the first and second of the Russian Revolutions there were many significant developments rendering the nature of the events in early 1917 considerably different from those of 1905, and there has been a considerable quantity of interesting historical discussion about them. But since our major purpose here is to look at the Revolutions themselves and at their international impact, we will not be able to subject the intervals between the three of them to anything more than the most summary scrutiny.

The 1905 Revolution did bring about the creation of the State Duma, but this did not mean the introduction of parliamentary democracy into Russia, or even of constitutional monarchy. For most of what Nicholas and his entourage had granted with one hand they quickly seized back with the other. The unabashed penchant of the tsarist government for autocracy was to some extent consolidated and mirrored by the inclination towards 'Bonapartism' of the chief minister during the years following the Revolution of 1905, P. A. Stolypin. Perhaps rendered too self-conscious and premeditated a policy in the interpretation of some Soviet historians, his balance of one socio-political force against another did enable Stolypin to make some progress towards the solution of some of Russia's continuing problems, especially that of rural Russia. But like other strong men before him, Bonapartes and Bismarcks, Stolypin did perhaps develop too great a confidence in his own judgement and power, and he was already on the decline when assassinated in 1911. Where Stolypin had failed, lesser men were hardly likely to succeed. Moreover the political arena in which he and his less able successors operated was separated from the world of most inhabitants of the Russian Empire, even if his and their policies certainly affected their fellow-countrymen's contentment and prosperity. Above all, the landlord and industrial–commercial groups, the upper and middle classes and their political representatives, were involved in the debates of the Duma. But meanwhile outside the Duma, the extremist parties were building up support, if by no means in a smooth progression, and were preparing themselves, if by no means with the ruthless precision sometimes attributed to them, for the leadership of large-scale unrest should it ever flare up again.

For political consciousness was undoubtedly spreading among the 'dark people', as was demonstrated in the works of such writers as

Maksim Gorky[13] and such investigations as that carried out by the Socialist–Revolutionary Party among the peasantry in 1907–8 which found that: ' . . . whatever form the peasant mood might take, one thing is indubitable from the replies – their attitude towards the landowners and the authorities is everywhere sharply negative.' Gone completely was the 'naive monarchism' that had acted as something of a restraint in pre-1905 days: 'The attitude of the peasants to the tsar is to a high degree unanimous. There is literally not a single reply which does not indicate that faith in the tsar among the masses either "is declining" or has already "completely disappeared".' And the attitude towards active opposition, including violence, was favourable. For example one group of respondents said: 'We shall drive all the masters out, and some will go to St Petersburg, and some will go to England, and the land will be left to us.' The report on the investigations concluded: 'The field is ploughed. Now it is up to the sowers.'[14] Although the peasantry constituted by far the largest class, the industrial proletariat possessed a significance well in excess of its small numbers, and it too was more radical than before in the years after the 1905 Revolution, causing a threat of considerable although disputed proportions to social stability in the towns as the peasantry had to the countryside.[15] Significant stirrings could be detected among the armed forces[16] and the nationalities,[17] too.

It is still a question of debate whether or not the arrival of the First World War brought forward or made inevitable the Second and Third Russian Revolutions. There are those who argue that the outbreak of hostilities provided a safety-valve for internal pressures and gave Nicholas some respite as differences with him were forgotten in a renewed and strengthened patriotism. Others believe that, had it not been for the war, the tsar would have been able to survive the adjustment to modernisation that his régime was belatedly but successfully making. To omit the war, however, would be rather a huge step even in counter-factual analysis. And if the war in the short run produced relief for the tsar, in the course of the following two and a half years it added enormously to his difficulties. His own foolhardy decision to take personal command of the army in the late summer of 1915 certainly compounded his predicament, as did his compliant attitude to his wife's interference in matters of governmental policy. But the social dislocation which overtook Russia by late 1916 was too great for even the firmest actions of a 'strong tsar' whom many apprehensive people were calling for, by that time, to restrain and overcome.

Not that the story of imperial Russia in its last days is exclusively one of despondency and decline. At least twice, at the very beginning

of the war and again in 1916, action by the Russian army on the eastern front probably saved the situation for the sorely pressed armies
of the Allies on the western front. The outcome of the Battle of the
Marne and the first Ypres, of Verdun and the Somme, might well
have been different had the Russian troops not pulled 'the chestnuts
out of the fire' for their French and British comrades. As late as the
end of 1916, the percentage of deaths in the German casualties on the
eastern front and the number of Germans captured there were higher
than to the west. Nor was this always a case of poorly equipped Russ-
kies pushing back the Fritzes by bravery alone – the imperial war
machine was by no means as primitive as has often been suggested.
For example, by September 1916 Russia could produce $4\frac{1}{2}$ million
shells a month, not so far behind the 7 million of Germany. True, the
communications network left more and more to be desired and the
guns and shells did not always arrive where they would best have finished the job.[18]

Behind the lines, too, production was not often an insuperable
problem; the difficulty lay increasingly with distribution and
exchange. There were probably enough foodstuffs being grown by
the peasants, even with the sharp reduction in available fertiliser and
machinery, but they were not getting through to the progressively
hungrier inhabitants of the towns. Also distressed by steep inflation
and fuel shortages, the industrial workers (many of them recently
uprooted peasants) and their families were becoming dangerously
restless by the beginning of the year 1917.

More than coincidentally, that fateful year opened with an energetic demonstration on 9 January, the anniversary of Bloody
Sunday, the event which had triggered off the first Revolution in
1905. More than coincidentally too, the second Revolution of
February actually commenced on the 23rd of that month (8 March
New Style), which was another anniversary, International Woman's
Day. Thus the necessity of considering the fall of tsarism in a wider
context, both chronologically and geographically, is strongly indi-
cated, although the centre of attention must be February in
Petrograd.

Towards the end of 1916 the police department compared the
situation in the new and old capitals with that to be found there ten
or so years before, and concluded that 'now the mood of opposition
has reached such extraordinary proportions as it did not approach
by a long way among the broad masses in that troubled time'. Rumblings were heard in the provinces too. The root of all these troubles
was clear enough to the Empress Alexandra. 'Dissolve the Duma
immediately', she wrote to her husband in December 1916. 'Quietly
and with a clean conscience before all Russia I would send Lvov to

Siberia. . . . (So it has been done for far less important actions.) . . .'[19] Prince Lvov and the other Duma leaders, to whom Alexandra would have meted out a like fate, were in fact among the best friends of tsarism, if not of Nicholas and Alexandra. They would certainly have been happy with some reduction in the prerogative of the tsar and certainly of the tsarina, and a growing number of them would have welcomed an abdication, but a change of incumbent upon the throne rather than the throne's destruction.[20] Their strongest criticisms were reserved for Rasputin and other 'dark forces' in the tsarist entourage, although even the assassination of 'Our Friend' in late December did not markedly increase sympathy for the royal couple. But the most complete opposition to the régime came from members of the proletariat and, although weakened by exile and imprisonment, from the radical political parties, especially the Mensheviks and Bolsheviks. Guarded support for the strike on 9 January 1917 came also from the Worker Group of the Central War Industry Committee, which shared the fundamental philosophy of the Duma leaders.

The Bloody Sunday anniversary demonstration brought out 300,000 workers in Petrograd, according to the calculations of the Social Democrats. As an accompaniment to it there were meetings with speeches and revolutionary songs; in places the Red Flag was unfurled and anti-tsarist slogans shouted. While the police noticed with satisfaction that the demonstration went off peacefully, the executive committee of the Petrograd Social Democrats observed that the turn-out was the highest of the war and that 'the mood in the factories is very bright, politically conscious and opens up wide revolutionary possibilities'.[21] While the mood was most energetic in Petrograd, there was some animation in Moscow and signs of it in provincial towns, too.

From January to February the strike movement developed in the direction of revolution, particularly in the capital. Still using the experience of 1905, the workers of Petrograd had now moved twelve years on in their tactics and were also now in a position to take advantage of a much more promising military situation. While there were about one million men under arms, most of them away in the Far East, at the time of the first Revolution, there were fifteen times that number mobilised for the First World War, and nearly a third of a million in and around Petrograd, two and a half times as many as in peacetime, and a significant proportion of them workers and peasants.

Armed revolutionary bands as in 1905 would not now be enough; the soldiers had to be won over. An important means of achieving this vital end was demonstration in the streets, but just how consciously such an approach was formulated by the beginning of 1917 it is difficult to say. There has been much discussion concerning the 'spontaneity' of the February Revolution, and direction and leadership were certainly not as visible then as they were in October. But too much emphasis on 'spontaneity' would render impossible any form of explanation, and many of us find it very difficult to imagine how events just happen without origin or cause. And, while the moderate and radical leadership might both have been somewhat without clear purpose as the revolutionary movement got under way again, the rank and file and local committees of the SRs and SDs, particularly the latter, appear to have been conscious enough of what they were doing as strikes turned into demonstrations.[22] Moreover, for their part, the Petrograd authorities had little doubt that the matter of insurgency was coming to a head in the new year.

The women who came out into the streets on 23 February were not exclusively bent on joining in festivities to celebrate their international day; indeed most of them had little inclination towards such commemoration, but were much more concerned to make a protest against the hardships being imposed on their families, particularly the bread shortage.[23] Strikers, especially from the Putilov works in the south-west of the city, and other workers, particularly from the Vyborg district in the north-east, gave solidarity to the demonstration, which centred on the Nevsky Prospect, and came to number 100,000 and more. The police made some effort to stem the flow, but were not successful. The moderate members of the Duma still hoped that peace could be restored to the streets without any great political upset; some of the members of the radical parties were already thinking of reviving the institution characteristic of 1905 – the Soviet.

On the next day, Friday 24 February, the number of demonstrators probably doubled, their slogans became more extreme and their clashes with the authorities intensified. And on Saturday 25 February there was a further deterioration or improvement in the situation, depending on the observer's point of view. The way was prepared for yet another Bloody Sunday. The first activity came during the night from the tsarist police, who clearly showed their disbelief in 'spontaneity' by arresting those whom they considered responsible for stirring up the troubles. A quiet morning appeared to vindicate their policy, but by afternoon the crowds were out again on the Nevsky Prospect. The point of no return was reached both individually by a few hundreds of the demonstrators who were shot down by rifle or even machine-gun fire, and generally by the Revolution, which could not now turn back. Some middle-class politicians believed that it was still possible for the tsar to create a ministry of trust; the radicals in touch with the people knew better, especially when troops started to defect. And when the crowds stormed the Peter and Paul fortress and other prisons on Monday, Russia's 14 July had come on 27 February. The chorus of the Russian version of 'La Marseillaise' rose to a new crescendo, swelled by thousands of ex-prisoners, and, more significantly, by thousands of soldiers and sailors.

Nicholas II did not abdicate before 2 March, but by that time he must have been about the last to realise that his abdication was inevitable, and even then he did not accept that the three centuries of Romanov rule had definitely come to an end. The government set up in the place of tsarism, on the other hand, saw itself as no more than provisional, partly through deference to its predecessor and putative successor, partly from a realisation forced upon it from the very beginning that its hold on power by no means gave the appearance of completeness or permanence. As it set itself up in the Taurida Palace it was also conscious of another occupant there – a revived Soviet, with which it would have to share a 'dual power'.[24]

The Soviet might have been an even more formidable rival if it had been set up by the far left in the Vyborg district, as at least a few groups proposed, rather than in the Taurida Palace, where it was comparatively remote from the greatest centres of proletarian power. If it had been in the Vyborg district, it would have been near at hand for Lenin after his celebrated return to the Finland Station in Petrograd. There, in the speech that was to form the basis of his celebrated 'April Theses', the Bolshevik leader gave great emphasis to the international situation. The 'April Theses' themselves begin with the assertion that 'a predatory imperialistic war would have to be opposed as much as before because of the 'capitalist character' of the new government. And they end with a call for the revival of the International and the creation of a revolutionary International.[25] Here, as nearly always, Lenin gives emphasis in his analysis to the wider setting of the Russian situation. Throughout the war up to 1917 he had been struggling at least as much against the traitors of the Second International throughout Europe as against the defenders of tsarism. And so when on 9 January 1917 he made his oft-quoted (more often than not out of context) remark that 'We of the older generation may not live to see the decisive battles of this coming revolution',[26] he was probably not thinking of the crisis in Petrograd so much as about the development of the struggle to be faced throughout the whole world.

Meanwhile the new government under Prince Lvov, whom Alexandra would have sent to Siberia along with many of his colleagues, accepted without demur the full inheritance of the foreign policy of its predecessor. Not for them opposition to the war or even the adoption of a defensive attitude towards it, but on to 'a decisive victory' in conjunction with the other democracies, including the 'new Ally, the great Trans-Atlantic Republic'.[27] True, there was some modification of the language of imperialist expansionism when the Soviets made known their objections, but even they did not come out unequivocally for Russia's withdrawal from the war. But under Kerensky, as under Lvov before him, the Provisional Government remained firm in its determination to keep faith with the Allies (even though there was a diminishing amount of evidence that the Allies were keeping faith with it) and to fight on to a glorious end (in spite of vast numbers of Russian soldiers voting for peace with their feet).

Meanwhile Lenin kept strictly to his policy too. He would have nothing to do with that movement for socialist solidarity on an attitude towards the war which would approve of it as a protection for the working classes in the respective belligerent states. Soon after his arrival back in Petrograd and his enunciation of the 'April Theses', he declared:

'I hear that in Russia there is a movement towards unity, unity with the defensists. This is a betrayal of Socialism. I think that it is better to stand alone . . . one against one hundred and ten'.

He insisted continuously on the necessity for withdrawal from the war and the foundation of a new International, and would have nothing to do with the 'defensist' Stockholm Conference in the summer. In mid-October he was still thinking of how to promote what he believed to be a genuine socialist movement throughout the world:

Not until the proletarian revolution has triumphed in at least one country, or until the war has come to an end, may we hope for a speedy and successful movement towards the convoking of a *great* conference of revolutionary internationalist parties of various countries; nor for their consent to a formal adoption of a new program.[28]

The first of his desiderata was about to be realised, with the culminating Russian Revolution, that of October.

In retrospect October appears to have followed February almost as night follows day. And yet, just as the spontaneity of the second Revolution has been exaggerated, so has the planning of the third. Lenin was not taken completely by surprise in February, nor was he entirely expecting October. Certainly during the summer and autumn of 1917 the internal situation had been deteriorating in Russia while her international predicament grew sufficiently to turn domestic dislocation into utter chaos; Kerensky's ship of state was not so much sinking as disintegrating. Like Nicholas II before him, Kerensky was the last to realise what was happening, although he was to make a quicker getaway than his predecessor. The Allies put what trust they had left in a 'strong man', General Kornilov; *The Times* was at first optimistic about the chances for success of the revolt associated with his name, but after the revolt's speedy failure, was obliged to try to make do again with Kerensky.[29] And now that the strong man was revealed as powerless, what could be made of the weak?

Among those who had helped to forestall Kornilov's plans were the Red Guards, some thousands of workers armed partly at least by Kerensky himself to defend the Revolution. This kind of 'defensism' was attractive enough to the Bolsheviks, who felt their strength growing still more on 31 August, the day after the crushing of the revolt, when the Petrograd Soviet first passed a resolution put forward by the Bolsheviks, who now took over its control. On 5 September the same development took place in the Moscow Soviet, and during the remainder of that month the Bolsheviks achieved majorities in a number of other towns. A slogan from the period after February which had fallen into desuetude was now revived with a new fervour – 'All Power to the Soviets!'

With mass desertions from the armed forces, proletarian strikes and peasant land seizures, centrifugal pressures from many of the former empire's many nationalities, and no firm support for the government from any quarter, the prospect of a new comprehensive change was presenting itself with ever greater clarity.[30] On 29 September Lenin could write in an article entitled 'The Crisis Has Matured' that the end of the month marked 'a great turning-point in the history of the Russian revolution and, to all appearances, of the world revolution as well'.[31]

But again we must emphasise that 'Great October' was as yet far from cut and dried. Lenin was becoming more confident, but he still had to persuade his colleagues in the Bolshevik Central Committee that his estimate was correct that the majority of the people were behind the Bolsheviks, and that the time had come for the preparation of an armed insurrection. On 12 October a Military Revolutionary Committee (MRC) was set up in Petrograd by the Soviet under the chairmanship of Trotsky. It was to defend the Revolution with the help of the Red Guards, and its members were soon coming round to the idea that the best form of defence was attack. On 16 October a Military Revolutionary Centre was organised as a Bolshevik caucus

within the MRC and, not without hesitation, demur and even opposition from some comrades, plans for the seizure of power were now
drawn up.

On Tuesday 24 October the implementation of the plans was set in
motion, not entirely because of prior decision, but to a significant
extent as a result of anti-Bolshevik activity. Military cadets were
authorised to close the offices of the party newspaper, while the Provisional Government raised the city's bridges for tactical reasons at
the same time as reinforcing the defence of the Winter Palace, which
had become its principal seat. Such forces as Kerensky could still
command were poised for an attack on the Smolny Institute, which
had become the headquarters of the MRC. To counter such moves,
the MRC gave orders for the expulsion of the young officers from the
newspaper offices and for the assembly of the Red Guards along with
sympathetic soldiers and sailors at Smolny. The cruiser *Aurora*,
whose crew had come over to join the revolutionaries, broadcast
radio messages to all revolutionary units in the vicinity of Petrograd
to deny pro-government forces access to the capital. And Red sailors
from the base of Kronstadt some miles out of town were mobilised
for action, too.

Lenin came out of hiding at about midnight on 24/25 October. By
that time the Red forces had seized such strategic points as all the
bridges across the Neva and two important telegraph offices. The
telephone exchange, railway stations, power stations and banks were
taken over during the night as Lenin assumed personal control of the
revolutionary activities. By morning the Provisional Government
was beleaguered in the Winter Palace and a few other official buildings. Kerensky made a few last desperate efforts to acquire more
military support and then left Petrograd hurriedly in an official car
from the American Embassy. He just missed the address of Lenin to
the citizens of Russia that was issued by the MRC at about 10 a.m.
and which declared:

> The cause for which the people have fought, namely the immediate
> offer of a democratic peace, the abolition of landed pro-
> prietorship, workers' control over production, and the estab-
> lishment of Soviet power – this cause has been secured.

During the rest of 25 October the cause was made doubly secure until
only the Winter Palace remained as a centre of opposition to the
MRC's forces. The historic storming of the Winter Palace was completed by the early morning of 26 October.[32]

Immediately the new government set about issuing decrees that
fulfilled the promise of Lenin's address of 25 October, the first few of

them being passed by the Second All-Russia Congress of Soviets which was then in session. Soon, with the euphoria of victory barely tasted, the Communists (as they were to call themselves soon after their transfer of the capital back to Moscow to distinguish their party from discredited Social Democrats) ran into many grievous problems, including several connected with the all-important question of peace.

First we should look at the constitutional problem, the least in Lenin's eyes, but one that has been much discussed in the West. For Lenin, the ratification of the seizure of power by the Second All-Russia Congress of Soviets was enough; for others at the time and since, the ultimate authority should have been vested in the Constituent Assembly, which the Bolsheviks along with most political activists had been calling for throughout the earlier part of 1917, and which was now at last going to convene, the elections having taken place without Bolshevik interference. As Western historians have pointed out in detail, the Bolsheviks won a smaller total of votes than the Socialist Revolutionary Party, and should therefore have given up the government to their rivals.[33] But, apart from the fact that there are few if any examples of a revolutionary régime handing over the power that it has just seized, especially during a disastrous war, and the further fact that the Socialist Revolutionaries formed a party in little more than name and could not easily have taken up the reins of power, there was the further countervailing circumstance that, as an acute observer Arthur Ransome put it: 'The idea of a Constituent Assembly played a part in the Russian Revolution profitable at different times to different parties.'[34] Just after the February Revolution, it provided whatever cohesion the dual power possessed, since the agreement between the Provisional Government and the Soviets was formed on the basis of its temporary nature, with the promise of early resolution through the ballot box of the question of the more permanent nature of the state order, Arthur Ransome continues:

> As it was clear that immediate elections to the Assembly would have given an immense majority in the Assembly to parties represented in the Soviets, the parties on the Right desired to postpone it, while the demand for its immediate summoning became a useful lever against them in the hands of the Bolsheviks. As the Soviets became more Bolshevik the postponement of the Constituent Assembly became less desirable except by those who hoped that it would be possible by some military coup to suppress the parties of the Left before the elections. When, after the failure of the Kornilov adventure, these hopes were dashed, the Constituent Assembly became in the minds of the anti-Bolshevik parties a means of

drowning the extremist vote of the towns in the slightly more moderate votes of the peasants, and active preparations for the elections were at last begun.[35]

After the October Revolution, the Bolsheviks now looked upon the Constituent Assembly 'as unnecessary and even dangerous since it might mean what was to them a retrograde step from the hegemony of the towns to a democracy in which the towns would be outvoted'.[36] Although they argued that Soviet power was of a more advanced form than the bourgeois parliamentary form, the Bolsheviks were 'a little hampered by the momentum of the agitation they had carried on formerly against its postponement'. And so:

> They decided to hurry on the elections, to split the peasant vote and simultaneously to declare that the Soviets were, in a revolution, a higher authority than any assembly in which the possessing classes could take part. If by hook or crook they could get the Assembly to confirm the authority of the Soviets, well and good. If not, they would use the methods of Cromwell.

When the vote went against them, they allowed the Constituent Assembly to meet, but as use began of it as a mouthpiece for opposition to Soviet power, its guards told it to go home as it had talked enough. Lenin and his supporters made no effort to keep it in session, and the Constituent Assembly now became 'a watchword used indiscriminately by all the anti-Bolshevik parties'.[37]

As Lenin put it in his 'The Constituent Assembly elections and the dictatorship of the proletariat' written in December 1919:

> ... the experience of Kolchak and Denikin 'democracy', about which every hack writer in Kolchakia and Denikia shouted in every issue of the whiteguard newspapers, showed the peasants that phrases about democracy and about the 'Constituent Assembly' serve only as a screen to conceal the dictatorship of the landowners and capitalists.

Lenin believed that the peasants came in the end to see that their real friends were the Bolsheviks, although after the end of the Civil War, Maksim Gorky was not so sure, writing of the peasants:

> They will develop a good historical memory and, remembering their recent tormented past, in the first stages of building a new life they will be rather distrustful of, if not outright hostile to, the intelligentsia and the workers who cause various disorders and revolts.

Enough of them must have been in favour of the Bolsheviks, however, or indifferent to them or at the very least not actively opposed
for the Reds to emerge the final victors in the Civil War. And if the
main strength of the Bolsheviks was clearly shown in the elections to
the Constituent Assembly to lie in the towns and the armed forces,
returning servicemen or other propagandists could make some impression on the SR strongholds of the rural areas, a task facilitated
by the government's adoption of a significant part of the SR land
programme, and its immediate Decree on Peace.[38]

To take that all-important matter further, negotiations were to
begin at Brest–Litovsk just after an armistice had been signed there
on 5 December 1917. The Bolsheviks, wanting to give their policies
maximum publicity, tried to set the negotiations up elsewhere,
ideally in a neutral capital as Stockholm, but the Germans insisted
on continuing in their frontier fortress and held the whip hand on this
and later decisons. After a ten-day adjournment aimed at involving
other powers in the discussions, the two sides met again face to face.
Their bargaining position made even stronger by the willingness of
one of the Ukrainian factions to make a separate peace, the German
representatives grew even less accommodating, as Trotsky, the
leader of the Russian delegation, made a somewhat desperate appeal
to the German troops over the heads of their leaders. Communist
rhetoric and delay led to a deterioration in the terms that the Germans were prepared to offer. At first, Lenin's arguments that Russia
needed a breathing space attracted only minority support among his
colleagues, but when Trotsky himself abandoned his 'neither war
nor peace' formula and went over to Lenin's side, the harsh terms of
the Treaty of Brest–Litovsk were finally accepted by March 1918.
A large slice of the former Russian Empire was now lost, the
Baltic Provinces as well as the Ukraine and pieces of Transcaucasia. A wedge driven in as far as the environs of Petrograd could
now serve as a useful springboard for intervention in the Civil
War.[39]

To counter threats from outside and even more from within, the
All-Russian Extraordinary Commission for the Suppression of
Counter-Revolution, Sabotage and Profiteering, or Cheka as it
was known after its first two Russian initials, was formed soon
after the October Revolution and became the main agency of the
Red Terror which accompanied the Civil War along with a White
Terror. As it became clear that this war was going to be more than
a brief and minor affair, the Red Army was formed from a number of different sources, including the Red Guards and former
tsarist troops and officers.[40]

So great was the potential of the White forces and their interventionist allies that the odds against Red survival soon appeared to be formidable.[41] But, as Arthur Ransome pointed out, such an assumption did not allow 'for that strange, incalculable x of revolutionary enthusiasms which, in Russia in the twentieth century as in France in the eighteenth, continually provided miracles for the discomfiture of logicians.' Moreover, adversity was turned to advantage. As Ransome puts it:

> Throughout the Civil War the Communists adopted the opposite method to that of rulers who exaggerate victories and minimise defeats. Huge maps were set up on boardings in the streets of the towns with a thick black line to mark the encircling front. Day by day during the White advances the black line was moved nearer to Moscow. Defeats intensified instead of disheartening the defence, in spite of the appalling conditions in the besieged camp. In this war few of the wounded could hope to survive, for the blockade did not allow the importation even of anaesthetics or the necessary drugs. Outside the territory of the Soviets to be a member of the Communist Party was a crime punishable by death. Captured Communists were shot at once. Yet at the worst moment, October 1919, when White forces were within striking distance of Moscow and of Petrograd, thousands of working men poured into the party.[42]

An additional boost to the morale of the Red Army and its supporters came from the belief that the events in Russia were of much wider, even global significance, a view shared by many of the backers of the White armies and the Interventionists.

For as one world war was coming to an end, another was beginning. The statesmen coming together to draw up the peace treaties were very conscious of this new development, of imperial Germany's grasp for world power being succeeded by Soviet Russia's attempt at world revolution. As Ray Stannard Baker put it:

> The effect of the Russian problem on the Paris Conference was profound: Paris cannot be understood without Moscow. Without ever being represented at Paris at all, the Bolsheviki and Bolshevism were powerful elements at every turn.[43]

The delegates were all too conscious of such threats from Lenin as that in *Pravda* of October 1918: 'The time is not far off when the first day of the world revolution will be celebrated everywhere.'[44] At that time, just before the conclusion of the Armistice, governments throughout Western Europe were apprehensive, and not without cause, as we shall see in the next chapter. When their representatives convened in Paris in January 1919, the apprehension had grown rather than diminished. Some of the voices heard in the Western world at that time, such as those of Churchill and Foch, were in favour of the instant crushing of the Revolution. Others, such as Woodrow Wilson and Lloyd George, took a somewhat less implacable stance. Wilson went so far as to recognise that Bolshevism was 'a protest against the way in which the world has worked'. His 'Fourteen Points' had been issued at the beginning of 1918 to a considerable degree in response to

> ... the voice of the Russian people. ... a voice calling for these definitions of principle and purpose which is, it seems to me, more thrilling and compelling than any of the moving voices with which the troubled air of the world is filled.[45]

Lloyd George, not so charitable or so hypocritical (depending on how one is affected by Woodrow Wilson's pious utterances), shared no illusion about the harmful potential of Bolshevism, but feared that the cause might be advanced rather than retarded if intervention were to be stepped up and Soviet sympathisers in Western Europe were mobilised. Agreeing with Wilson that the new League of Nations might guarantee the kind of order that Western statesmen were seeking, he gave the following warning in a memorandum of March 1919:

> The whole of Europe is filled with the spirit of revolution. There is a deep sense not only of discontent, but of anger and revolt amongst the workmen against pre-war conditions. The whole existing order in its political, social and economic aspects is questioned by the masses of the population from one end of Europe to the other. There is a danger that we might throw the masses ... into the arms of the extremists whose only idea for regenerating mankind is to destroy utterly the whole existing fabric of society. These men have triumphed in Russia.[46]

Just as Allied attitudes towards Soviet Russia varied between complete opposition and at least some measure of accommodation, so there was some difference among them as to the question of how to negotiate with her, if at all. Lloyd George gave some support to the invitation drafted by Woodrow Wilson for all the belligerents in the Russian Civil War to be represented at a conference at Prinkipo Island in the Sea of Marmora (later the home for several years of the exiled Leon Trotsky). This venue was chosen because Clemenceau, to some extent listening to White Russians in Paris, refused to invite Bolsheviks to come there. The Soviet government accepted the invitation which had been broadcast to them and their opponents by radio and offered to discuss the question of financial obligations and of timber and mining concessions. But the anti-Soviet voice prevailed, and the Prinkipo Conference never materialised. As a new means of making contact with Moscow, Woodrow Wilson sent a member of his delegation – William Bullitt – on a special secret mission to the Red capital. Once again Lenin and his associates were prepared to come more than half way to meet their opponents, but some of their die-hard enemies would not budge an inch, particularly since a new strong man, Admiral Kolchak, was enjoying outstanding success in his push westwards through Siberia. So the Bullitt mission, too, ended in failure. A third means of contact with the Reds, through famine relief organised by Herbert Hoover and Frijdthof Nansen, was viewed with suspicion on both sides and came to nothing in 1919.

And so the Allies settled on a policy of mainly passive anti-Bolshevism, including the blockade and isolation of Soviet Russia accompanied by support for White armies and non-Russian nationalities aspiring to independence. A lot of their money was still on Kolchak, who was addressed by the Supreme Council of the Conference on 27 May as 'Supreme Ruler of all the Russias', although some was also placed on the Balts, the Poles, the Rumanians and Caucasians. Kolchak indicated his determination to rule Russia on a 'democratic basis' just before being thrown back by the Red Army across Siberia. And by this time, isolated though they were from the governments of the outside world, the Communists in Moscow did not feel themselves cut off from many sympathisers there. For in March they had set up the Third or Communist International, the Comintern, partly as a fulfilment of Lenin's long-held aspiration, partly as a more immediate counter to 'the danger that the alliance of capitalist states that are organising themselves against the revolution under the hypocritical banner of the League of Nations will strangle the revolution'.[47] At its First Congress an appeal was sent out to the workers of all countries for their support, and Lenin declared: 'Comrades present in this hall saw how the first Soviet Republic was established; they now witness the establishment of the Communist International and they will see how a World Federative Republic will be founded.'[48] More will be said of the Comintern below.

For their part, the Entente and its clients were increasingly disturbed, although, as during the cold war, many groups and factions played the 'Communist bogey' for all it was worth in order to get the recognition and support of the major powers. Representatives from Poland and Rumania emphasised how much they needed sustenance in their fight against Red Russia and Red Hungary; Italians stressed the need for help against domestic upheaval, and so on. As the various treaties came to be signed in 1919 and 1920, the effectiveness of much of this special pleading was clearly revealed. For example, the Treaty of St Germain of September 1919 with Austria made Poland into a powerful independent buffer against Bolshevism. By the Treaty of Trianon with Hungary in June 1920 Transylvania and Bessarabia were incorporated into a southern buffer – Rumania. To the north help of all kinds was given to the Baltic states (that is to the régimes set up in them under German patronage) until their independence from Soviet Russia was guaranteed. Lloyd George believed that they might offer 'a means of peaceful penetration'.[49]

Lenin denounced the treaties in July 1919 as 'this unworthy repressive peace' which was 'winning us friends throughout the world every day'[50] as it revealed the true nature of imperialism. The May Day Manifesto of the Comintern in 1920 declared:

> Conscious workers throughout the world know perfectly well that the so-called League of Nations is in fact a League of bourgeois robbers for the oppression of nations, for the division of the world, for the enslavement of workers, for strangling the proletarian revolution.[51]

For a few months in 1920 the spectre of communism attained its greatest proportions as the Red Army pushed the Poles back to Warsaw, the fall of which was widely seen as the prelude to the fall of Berlin. But the Red Star gave way to the White Eagle and the Treaty of Riga of March 1921 followed an armistice arranged in October 1920 and guaranteed a large Poland with a considerable amount of territory to the east of the line previously drawn up on its behalf by Lord Curzon. With such a central bastion for its *cordon sanitaire*, the Entente could now breathe more easily and contemplate some normalisation of relations with the Soviet Union. From the Communist point of view, now that the blockade had been lifted and the last of the serious White threats was coming to an inglorious end, normalisation was welcome too. And so with the Anglo–Russian Trade Treaty of March 1921 the 'shooting war' for world revolution had come to an end.

Having established the context for the creation of the Third International by a brief examination of its anti-thesis the Paris Peace Conference and the League of Nations, we must now take a closer look at the specific origins of the Comintern and its first two congresses. Just as Woodrow Wilson's views were outstanding in the great meeting of the representatives of the capitalist world, so were Lenin's at the first assemblies of the advocates of world communism. As Trotsky said, these two leaders were the antipodes of their time. Ever since the 'treason' of the majority of European socialists in 1914 had meant for him and a not inconsiderable number of others the death of the Second International, Lenin had been thinking of the creation of another International more consistently dedicated to the cause. He referred to it immediately after his return to Petrograd in the 'April Theses' and then in his 'Letter to the Workers of Europe and America' in January 1919 he wrote that:

> ... when the Spartakusbund called itself the 'Communist Party of Germany', then the *foundation* of a really proletarian, really international, really revolutionary Third International, a *Communist International*, became a *fact*. Formally this foundation has not yet been made secure, but in fact the Third International now already exists.[52]

The formalities were to follow just a couple of months later.

After a few smaller conferences to which foreign representatives were invited, and many preparatory discussions among members of the Soviet government, fifty or so delegates came to Moscow at the beginning of March 1919 for the formal foundation of the Third Communist International and its First Congress. Most of the delegates were European, particularly from Russia and its neighbours, and the language used was German, but there were 'consultative' emissaries from China, Persia and Korea. One of the two German delegates objected to such a small gathering taking it upon themselves to adopt a constitution:

> Real communist parties exist in only a few countries; in most, they have been created only in the last few weeks; in many countries where there are communists today they have as yet no organisation. . . . What is missing is the whole of Western Europe. Belgium, Italy are not represented; the Swiss representative cannot speak in the name of the party; France, England, Spain, Portugal are missing; and America is equally not in a position to say what parties would support us.[53]

Nevertheless the meeting carried out its transformation into a congress by unanimous vote, and soon drew up both a programme and a manifesto. Zinoviev was made president of an executive committee, and Karl Radek (at that time in a German prison) its secretary; the committee was to look after the Comintern's affairs between congresses. Lenin was of course the principal speaker, and devoted his remarks to a defence of the Communist message, including the dictatorship of the proletariat, and an attack on 'bourgeois democracy', vilified adherents of which were members of the discredited Second International. Lenin appealed to workers everywhere to oppose intervention and to render whatever assistance was within their power to the beleaguered Soviet republic, the first home of true, proletarian democracy. The Congress dispersed in a mood of bold optimism, Trotsky writing on May Day 1919:

> Moscow is the centre of the Third International, tomorrow – we are profoundly convinced – this centre will move to the west: to Berlin, Paris, London. However joyfully the Russian proletariat welcomed the representatives of the working class of the world in the walls of the Kremlin, it will with even greater joy send its representatives to the second congress of the Communist International in one of the Western European centres. For an international communist congress in Berlin or Paris will mean the complete triumph of the proletarian revolution in Europe and, probably, in the whole world.[54]

Tomorrow did not immediately come, and the Second Comintern Congress met again in Moscow in July 1920. But the assembled delegates were far from downhearted. Indeed, with the Red Army deep into Poland and almost up to the gates of Warsaw, Berlin and even Paris did not seem so far away at all. The mood of the meeting was well caught by its president, Zinoviev:

> In the congress hall hung a great map on which was marked every day the movement of our armies. And the delegates every morning stood with breathless interest before this map. It was a sort of symbol: the best representatives of the international proletariat with breathless interest, with palpitating heart, followed every advance of our armies, and all perfectly realised that, if the military aim set by our army was achieved, it would mean an immense acceleration of the international proletarian revolution.[55]

The number of these excited delegates was two hundred or so, four times the attendance at the First Congress, and thirty-five countries, including a much better coverage of Europe and a less inadequate coverage of Asia, were represented. The general confidence was reflected in the smaller amount of attention given to appeals for support and the larger concentration on qualifications for membership and correct strategy for the spread of revolution rather than last-ditch defence.

Indeed the most striking document to come out of the Second Congress of the Comintern was the so-called 'twenty-one conditions' for membership. These called for 'iron discipline' and the strict avoidance of compromise with basic principles. The 'dictatorship of the proletariat' was not just 'a current formula', but a concept to be continually advocated in such a manner that ordinary working people could understand it. 'Reformists of all shades', 'petty-bourgeois elements' and 'social-patriots' were among class enemies to be opposed outside the ranks of the Party and ruthlessly purged from inside. Special attention was given in Condition 8 to the necessity for 'a particularly explicit and clear attitude on the question of the colonies and the oppressed peoples' in the Parties formed in imperialist states. Lenin declared that 'The imperialist war drew the dependent peoples into world history', and that their insurgency must now be fostered wherever and whenever possible. But even with anti-colonial movements, there would have to be purity of motive. 'The reactionary, medieval influence of clergy, missionaries and other such elements' was denounced, but so were movements such as Pan-Islamism and Pan-Turkism. 'Bourgeois democratic movements' in the dependent countries could only be supported if they genuinely opposed imperialist domination, and even this approach was only accepted after a passionate debate.[56]

Such attention given to the rest of the world did mean that the Eurocentric focus of the Revolution was now being widened to make its sphere of attention completely world-wide. Good news was recognised as coming from the Caucasus as well as from Poland; with the Black and Caspian Seas being opened up to the Red forces, Asia could well now lie open to the influence of October. To mark such a broadening of emphasis, the First Congress of the Toilers of the East was held in Baku in early September 1920. Zinoviev reached new heights of oratory:

The real revolution will blaze up only when we are joined by the 800,000,000 people who live in Asia, when the African continent joins us, when we see hundreds of millions of people in the movement . . . . When in 1914–1918 they spoke of a 'holy war', that was a monstrous deception. But now, comrades, you who have for the first time assembled in a congress of peoples of the East, must here proclaim a real holy war, against the robbers, the Anglo–French capitalists. Now we must say that the hour has sounded when the workers of the whole world can arouse and raise up tens and hundreds of millions of peasants, can form a Red Army in the East as well, can arm and organise a revolt in the rear of the British, can hurl fire against the bandits, can poison the existence of every insolent British officer who is lording it in Turkey, Persia, India and China.[57]

The hour turned out not to have sounded, but as we shall see, there was some basis for thinking so in the year 1920 and even beyond. By 1921, however, 'normalisation' of relations, which would mean in the East continuance of empire, was more to be found in both Asia and Europe than the continued threat of world revolution. A breathing space was made necessary by domestic events too, notably the Kronstadt Revolt,[58] although as Lenin argued, the internal and international situations were inextricably connected.[59] And so, the Third Congress of the Comintern meeting in Moscow in July 1921 was not so much a congress of victors as of hardened and somewhat chastened warriors who realised that they were in for a long struggle before the high hopes of 1919 and 1920 were finally realised. And at the First Congress of the Toilers of the Far East that met in Moscow and Petrograd in 1922, there came the reminder from such speakers as Katayama Sen that, if the support given to the Kronstadt Revolt by Miliukov and his associates in Europe constituted a threat to Soviet Russia from the West, the Washington Conference had confirmed Great Britain, France, the USA and especially Japan in their intention to persist in their harassment from the East.[60]

5   The Western World

In this chapter we shall consider the impact of the three Russian Revolutions, especially that of October, on the Western or industrialised world. While the core of this world is Europe and North America, included in it will also be the offshoot settlements of the Southern Hemisphere – South Africa, Australia and New Zealand – and Japan, an even more anomalous exception to prove the rule.

Bloody Sunday aroused immediate protests from many parts of this Western world, the way having already been prepared by widespread revulsion not only against the treatment of dissidents including the Siberian exile system and the Jewish pogroms but also by sympathy for the 1896 strike in St Petersburg, about which Felix Volkovsky wrote in *Free Russia* (the London-based journal of the Society of Friends of Russian Freedom (SFRF)):

> It is evident that the main struggle for personal rights in Russia will develop mainly on the basis of the workmen striving for the bettering of their lives. In this context, strikes will be the most powerful means, and a means which international sympathy and pecuniary help can strengthen to a tremendous extent. . . . Thus the way that lies before the Friends of Russian Freedom is obvious. When the Russian workers are driven into another strike we should be found armed and ready to assist them in a few hours. We must have ready cash in hand and good connections with all important British labour organisations to be set in motion on the first notice.[1]

On 1 February 1905 at Queen's Hall, London, one of many protest meetings against Bloody Sunday was duly convened by the SFRF in conjunction with the Social Democratic Federation, the London Trades Council, the Fabian Society and other organisations. A Russian Strikers Relief Fund was set up and nearly a thousand pounds raised in Britain by the end of May. In addition various kinds

of underground work were undertaken, including travel arrangements to and from Russia for revolutionaries and probably some gun
running.[2] Here were sentiments and actions beyond the 'Christian
universalism coloured by a self-confident belief in the bounty of
English liberty . . . a morality born of the buoyancy of Victorian
capitalism' which typified the outlook of many of the Friends of
Russian Freedom. The pressures of imperialism and of the growing
working-class movement were beginning to act on erstwhile liberals
in their ranks as well as socialists.[3] And after the defeat of his party in
the January 1906 General Election, the Conservative leader Balfour
declared: 'What is going on here is the faint echo of the same movement which has produced massacres in St Petersburg, riots in
Vienna, and socialist processions in Berlin.'[4]

The impact of 1905 was indeed similar elsewhere in the Western
world. Meetings of support for the Revolution were held almost im-
mediately after its outbreak in Germany, France and the United
States, to give but three examples. The *Leipziger Volkszeitung* of 23
January 1905 declared: 'A Russian victory is a German victory, is a
European victory, is an international victory.' Later in 1906 Rosa
Luxemburg enlarged upon this theme, writing:

> It would be completely mistaken to view the Russian Revolution
> as a fine spectacle, as something specifically 'Russian', and to
> enthuse from afar at best about the heroism of its fighters, in other
> words, about the external accessories of the struggle. It is much
> more important to teach the German workers that they have seen
> in the Russian Revolution *their own cause*, not only in the sense of
> international class solidarity with the Russian proletariat, but
> above all *a part of their own social and political history*.

At the Jena Party Congress of September 1905 and at the Congress
of the Second International in Stuttgart in 1907 she helped to promote resolutions supporting such a view, which was also supported
in strikes of hundreds of thousands of workers in Berlin, Hamburg
and other German cities. But Eduard Bernstein was not without a
considerable measure of support for his belief that working-class
agitation should be for reform rather than revolution. In France
the influence of developments in Russia combined with internal
pressures such as the Dreyfus Affair to bring about the formation
of a united socialist party under Jean Jaurès, although here, too,
cohesion was difficult to maintain between those who favoured the
parliamentary and those who favoured the more radical roads.[5]

In the United States Eugene Debs, Daniel De Leon and Bill
Haywood supported a resolution calling the cause of the Russian

workers the cause of workers everywhere at the inaugural meeting of the Industrial Workers of the World (IWW) in the summer of 1905. But reformers to the centre and right were more cautious, Teddy Roosevelt the trust-buster being concerned about the deterioration in the Russian situation and partly for that reason using his influence to bring about a non-punitive conclusion to the Russo–Japanese War.[6] Other governments reacted in a more positive manner, Germany putting a whole squadron of warships at the disposal of tsarism in the Baltic and Austria–Hungary concentrating three army corps on the Galician frontier.[7]

News of the February Revolution was slow to penetrate the outside world because the tsarist censorship was still in operation. The major events had already taken place in Petrograd and Nicholas had already abdicated when intimation of the beginnings of the great upheaval was at last getting through. Partly because it was already an accomplished fact, the Revolution was welcomed by the Western allies and their newspapers. At the same time there was a considerable variety among the interpretations given to February, although nearly everybody was able to find something in it to satisfy personal predilections. By and large the Revolution was attributed to the Duma and the army, sometimes to the 'people', but hardly ever to the workers and the left-wing politicians. Sympathy was often extended to Nicholas: George V sent a personal message of condolence;[8] and Lloyd George, although welcoming the abdication, wrote warmly about the tsar to Prince Lvov, the Duma leader.[9] Newspapers of right-wing persuasion advised the tsar to exercise restraint so that the future of the dynasty would be assured. On the other hand more liberal organs wrote that the Russian people themselves were perfectly capable of choosing for themselves that form of government which would best assure their liberty and ultimate victory.[10]

The new Provisional Government in its first telegrammed message to the world, it will be remembered, emphasised the determination of the united people to fight on to a glorious conclusion of the war. Western politicians and press saluted the Russian determination to fight with renewed energy and more complete efficiency. *The Times* of London declared on 16 March 1917:

It is still too soon for entire confidence in the issue, but the general trend of events and the attitude of the army and the more important elements of the population justify the Allies of Russia in optimism. They may well hope that she will emerge from the ordeal she has undergone strong with the new strength of a united people who are led by a constitutional Government of their own choosing under the auspices of their historic dynasty.

More aware of what had actually happened, the French and British ambassadors, Paléologue and Buchanan, sought assurances that the Russians were indeed determined to carry the fight to the enemy, and these Miliukov duly gave them. Thus reassured, the governments of the Entente proceeded to establish relations with the new régime on the same basis as with the old one, i.e. continuance of the war until a successful conclusion. The ambassador of Russia's more recent ally, David Francis of the USA, was also convinced by Miliukov, and urged his government to recognise the Provisional Government. On 9 March (22 March New Style), the USA, France and Great Britain, as well as Italy, duly communicated their decision to grant such recognition.[11]

But this positive step by the Allies and the continued eloquence of Miliukov could not engender complete mutual confidence. While the position of the Provisional Government did not appear completely certain, while the Soviets talked in a loud voice of matters other than of victory, even of a more immediate peace, was the 'anarchy' of the revolutionary days indeed suppressed, and were the 'extreme left-wing elements' really under control? The Provisional Government's representatives in London and Paris, K. Nabokov and A. Izvolsky respectively, reported that there was profound uncertainty and concern about these questions in the Western capitals, and the Japanese leaders in the Far East seemed worried, too. A former American ambassador asserted that the situation had deteriorated to the point where only Witte could control it. The British General Knox and other military attachés were doing all they could to instil martial vigour into the detachments with which they came in contact, but sometimes such strength was found where it did not exist.[12]

The Central Powers could also be guilty of wishful thinking, but in their case aspiration more closely matched reality, for they rightly saw the overthrow of Nicholas as an indicator of a weakening rather than strengthening of the will to fight on to the end. The likelihood had grown of a separate peace, which would eliminate the necessity of a war on two fronts. Listening to the ringing declarations of the Provisional Government, however, the German authorities began to entertain the suspicion that the Allies had deliberately engineered the February Revolution for their own militaristic ends. Fraternisation at the front allayed fears of a new threat on the Eastern front to some extent, but also raised the question of the subversion of the German and other armies of the Central Powers – the overthrow of one monarchy could after all lead to that of others, even of the monarchical principle as a whole. Kaiser William was worried, and conservatives in the Reichstag began to contemplate the unthinkable, namely concessions to the democratic aspirations of their own people in order to protect their power and that of their emperor.[13]

German Social Democrats, on the other hand, gave a less qualified welcome to the February Revolution, as did socialists in German-occupied Eastern Europe. To the West William Gallacher later remembered the joyful reception given to the event by himself and his friends in Scotland, with banners proclaiming 'Free Russia' going up in street demonstrations in Glasgow.[14] Italian socialists, like their comrades elsewhere, could now give their support to the idea of a war for democracy.[15]

The leader of the Japanese socialists, Sakai Yasaburo, wrote that 'The Russian Revolution is indeed a very great joy', and a colleague considered that 'the speed of movement of revolutionary thought through the whole world, thanks to the Russian Revolution, will alleviate our position and create a more favourable moment for our own revolutionary movement.'[16]

While the welcome given to February by the left everywhere was warmly enthusiastic, there was widespread disagreement about its significance, particularly as far as the war was concerned. Most liberals and right-wing socialists sent fraternal greetings to the victors in Petrograd together with a call to joint efforts in the common struggle right up to the final victory. But a minority of Labour leaders in Britain put the emphasis on 'the cause of democracy and peace in Europe and throughout the world'[17] French colleagues voiced similar sentiments. And so, to give a boost to sagging spirits as the Provisional Government began to run into difficulties, the British and French governments both encouraged socialist delegations to visit democratic Russia, hoping that the war effort would thus be encouraged.

However left-wingers from the Entente nations talked of the Russian Revolution as a powerful blow struck for proletarian solidarity against the imperialist war. Antonio Gramsci wrote in April 1917: 'We are persuaded that the Russian Revolution is proletarian in character, as it has been so far in its deeds, and that it will naturally result in a socialist régime.'[18] The newspaper *Avanti* said in a leading article of 6 April:

The French Revolution led in our continent to a change in the political order. It may be hoped that the Russian Revolution will lead to a change in the social order. In the nineteenth century free institutions gradually spread from France to other European countries. In the twentieth century a new social order spreads from Russia to all Europe.

G. Serrati, the editor of *Avanti*, asserted that the Russian Revolution would not be completed until the land belonged to the peasants and the factories to the workers. A celebratory meeting in Paris in April produced cries from the hall of 'Long live the Third International', 'Down with war' and 'Long live peace'. In London the *Daily Herald* talked of the necessity of setting up Soviets in Great Britain, and of welcoming the great events in Russia with a British sequel.[19] Lloyd George reflected the anxiety that such declarations produced in his *War Memoirs*.[20] Meanwhile a speaker at a meeting in Winnipeg told his Canadian hearers that now that the autocracy had been overthrown and Nicholas had abdicated, the people must move ahead from the Provisional Government to a government of workers and socialists, while Eugene Debs and others voiced similar sentiments in the USA. The Norwegian socialist leader M. Tranmael summarised the situation thus:

It must be hoped that the spark that has ignited with such a bright flame in Russia will also flare up everywhere in Europe and America and that this revolution which initially took on the character of a struggle for bourgeois freedoms will culminate in a socialist revolution.[21]

In Germany the Social Democrats who had at first voted for war credits because the struggle was against tsarism were now caught in a dilemma, although their newspaper *Vorwärts* pointed out that they did not want civil strife during time of war. At the beginning of April 1917 dissident left-wingers in the Workers Group convened the initial assembly of the Independent Social Democratic Party (USPD). The delegates came out for the cessation of the war and the democratisation of the German state order, albeit through peaceful parliamentarianism rather than revolutionary violence. Hugo Haase and other leading figures charged the members of the Reichstag not to delay reforms lest the masses begin to act together in the Russian manner. The more extreme leaders of the Spartacus League (a fraction of the USPD) were in prison at the time, but Rosa Luxemburg was able to write to her comrades outside in April 1917:

The miraculous events taking place in Russia are acting upon me like the elixir of life. What is going on there is for us all a tonic piece of news. I fear that you do not value it highly enough, do not sufficiently accept that what is winning there is our own cause.

Another Spartacus leader, Fritz Heckert declared: 'The red banner which is being unfurled in Petersburg over the Winter Palace is for us an inspiring symbol. Turning to the Russian proletarians, we exclaim – we will do the same.' The kaiser would have to go the same way as the tsar, and events soon occurred which gave some indication that he might indeed be about to do so. Mass strikes in April provoked by a cut in the bread ration were a mighty portent: 300,000 workers came out in Berlin; and in Leipzig proclamations specifically said: 'The Russian workers have given us an outstanding example. Follow their example. Yielding to such pressure, William II talked in his Easter message of electoral reform in Prussia, and the parties in the Reichstag began to talk more earnestly of internal change and of international peace, thus laying the foundations for the coalition of the Weimar period.[22]

As the year 1917 wore on and the revolutionary momentum gathered speed rather than slowed down in Russia, agitation grew rather than diminished in many parts of the Western world. In Great Britain the United Socialist Council which had been revived under the influence of the February Revolution promoted in June a Convention at Leeds where, according to John Paton (the Aberdonian who was to play an important part in the formation of the Independent Labour Party), the delegates 'spent a deliriously happy weekend in bold talk of what they hoped to do. There had even been mention of the new Russian device of Workers' and Soldiers' Council.'[23] As the Convention opened, a message was read out from a unit in the Royal Army Medical Corps stating that

We should very much like to see the establishment of a society on lines similar to those of the Council of Soldiers' and Workmen's in Russia, for we are quite convinced that the great majority of men in the Army are in sympathy with the Russian aims.[24]

The fourth resolution passed by the Convention did indeed set up such a council, with Ramsay Macdonald and the twelve other conveners as its central committee, but none of these would give much support to William Gallacher, whose speech was briefly reported in the *Daily Herald* for 9 June thus:

This conference seems to be agreed that the Russian Revolution is definitely settled. But is it? No. The Russian workers' and soldiers' delegates have the biggest fight on, not against the capitalists of Russia, but against the capitalists of other countries who are determined that they have to be beaten back. Give your own capitalist class in this country so much to do that it won't have time to attend to it.[25]

The tension between the reforming and revolutionary impulses was personified by the seconder of the fourth resolution and one of the conveners, W. C. Anderson, who now spoke in fiery-enough terms but had used very different language in the House of Commons barely a month before. At Leeds Anderson declared:

> If a revolution be the conquest of political power by an hitherto disinherited class, if revolution be that we are not going to put up in the future with what we have put up with in the past, we are not going to have the shams and poverty of the past, then the sooner we have revolution in this country the better.

But at Westminster he had said:

> What you are now doing by coercive laws, by repressive laws, by the penal side of the Munitions Act, and so on, is to try to dam up all the current of discontent, but that current will not be dammed up. I do assure you you will be astonished, and unless you are very careful you will bring the country to the very verge of revolution. Only a week ago, I saw 70,000 people – the estimate was made not by any labour people, but by one of the local newspapers – march through the streets of Glasgow with bands and banners, every one of the members of that procession wearing the revolutionary colours. That is an amazing thing to happen in a city like Glasgow. I say that to a very large extent it is the policy of the Government that is responsible for that. Now you have to choose whether you are going to apply increasing repressions to these men, or whether you are going to try to establish confidence and a sense of freedom. That is really the issue. I hope that in what I have said this afternoon I have avoided anything that would increase passion, anything likely to make matters worse. I do hope the reply we may receive from the Government Front Bench will be an answer that will help to tone down or to remove that unrest that undoubtedly now exists.

The tension was there already right enough, but before the year was out it was to become much more strained. As Ralph Miliband rightly puts it:

The Leeds Convention had fortuitously brought together the revolutionaries and the constitutionalists. But the gulf between them remained as profound as it had ever been and the instauration of the Bolshevik regime in November 1917 only served to widen that gulf.[26]

After the November instauration or October Revolution, the Russian Communists, like Marx and Engels in 1848, turned their attention 'chiefly to Germany', and largely for the same reasons:

... because that country is on the eve of a bourgeois revolution that is bound to be carried out under more advanced conditions of European civilisation, and with a much more developed proletariat, than that of England was in the seventeenth, and of France in the eighteenth century, and because the bourgeois revolution in Germany will be but the prelude to an immediately following proletarian revolution.[27]

Lenin would want to add that Germany was also more advanced than Russia and its proletariat similarly more developed. As the German autocracy neared collapse, so there loomed up the prospect of a German February, to be followed inexorably by a German October.

Such a scenario appeared to be unfolding when, after orders from its admiral on 28 October and again on 30 October, the High Seas Fleet refused to put to sea from Kiel for one last expedition against its British enemy. The mutineers put forward radical demands: an end to the war, the abdication of William II, the abolition of martial law, the extension of the suffrage to all adults, and the release of sailors arrested in the earlier mutiny of 1917. The trouble soon spread throughout Kiel; a general strike of dockers ensued immediately, and on 4 November elections took place of workers' and soldiers' councils, which promptly assumed control of the city and of the garrison. By 6 November the insurgent movement spread to Hamburg, Bremen and Lübeck, and within days down from the north to nearly all of the major cities, as far as Bavaria.

The revolt had begun and spread 'spontaneously', but as in the case of the Russian February this 'spontaneity' needs to be defined and qualified. Not only February itself but also October had certainly made a considerable impression on the minds of German workers and servicemen. Delay of peace with Russia had already caused a munitions strike in January 1918. Moreover, towards the end of 1918 there were uprisings of various kinds throughout Central Europe, heavily involved it is true with the nationalist issues that had long constituted a powerful centrifugal force in Austria–Hungary, but also more than a little tinged with the Red wave sweeping westwards from Petrograd. In Prague there had been Czech nationalist action with socialist overtones throughout October. A republic – whose significance was variously interpreted according to political persuasion – was declared in the same month, and the empire of the Habsburgs appeared to be nearing its final dissolution. This threatened collapse could not avoid being of dire import for the Hohenzollerns too. The position of the kaiser was not helped by American proposals for armistice which gave a strong pointer towards abdication. Similar thoughts were already occurring to members of the Reichstag, who passed fairly sweeping constitutional reforms in October, but were still wondering if they had gone far enough. The new chancellor, Prince Max von Baden – who was now responsible to the Reichstag – and his cabinet strove to hold the parliamentary régime together with the assistance of the moderate political parties. These included the SPD, whose leaders, according to *The Times* of 6 November 1918, 'have issued a leaflet urging comrades and workers not to neglect their work during the next few days and not to demonstrate in the streets as they have been urged to do by unsigned leaflets and verbal instigations'. Even most members of the USPD were for restraint, the all-important exception being the Spartacus League led by Karl Liebknecht and Rosa Luxemburg. Both in the longer term, at least from 1905 onwards, and now in the shorter, after their release from custody along with other political prisoners in October, Liebknecht and Luxemburg and their comrades did all they could to bring socialist revolution in Germany, looking for a model and a lead chiefly to Russia. Now, particularly, they were agitating among the shop stewards for an intensification of the movement that had begun in Kiel at the end of October.

The shop stewards were somewhat hesitant, mostly because their trade-union consciousness was deeply engrained by an historical experience differing considerably from that of their Russian counterparts. Some analysts of the German situation in 1918 and the immediately following years would call such an interpretation of the hesitancy of the shop stewards unnecessarily fatalistic. At the beginning of November 1918 and at other crucial moments, they would argue, the irresolution of their leaders betrayed the workers and their cause. But to attribute to any given group an inordinate amount of what is in any case an unquantifiable, even indefinable characteristic is to defy rational explanation. Such qualities as 'determination' and 'courage' have to be given equal distribution throughout mankind if there is to be a sensible discussion of their application. We cannot say, unless we wish to be racialist, that German workers' leaders lacked in 1918–19 something that their Russian comrades possessed. Moreover, although again differences of historical development are reflected here, the ideology of the Spartacists differed significantly from that of the Bolsheviks, and the type of political direction that Rosa Luxemburg for one was prepared to offer explicitly rejected the specifications of Lenin. True, the Spartacists also rejected the parliamentary road completely and believed in progress exclusively through the dictatorship of the proletariat. As one of their declarations put it on 7 October 1918:

> The struggle for real democratisation is not concerned with parliamentary franchises or parliamentary ministers, or similar swindles; it is concerned with the real basis of all enemies of the people: ownership of land and capital, and power over the armed forces and over justice.

But Luxemburg had long rejected Lenin's concept of the Party as leader and preferred to regard the self-conscious masses as the spearhead of revolution. Possibly her experience of the German Social Democrats was as responsible for her antipathy towards the bureaucratic control of a political party as her disagreement with the arguments of Lenin's *What Is To Be Done*? The Spartacists were also somewhat restrained in their attitude towards another of Lenin's recommendations, the use of force as prescribed by him in another of his works, *The State and Revolution*. In late 1918 they talked of the necessity for the 'formation of a Red Guard with the workers as the active part of the militia for the permanent protection of the revolution against counter-revolutionary attacks and intrigues.' 'Defence of the revolution' had been one of the principal avowed intentions of the Russian Red Guards, too, but Luxemburg and especially Liebknecht drew back from resorting to violence in a manner which would have been foreign to both Lenin and Trotsky. The fastidiousness of the Spartacist leaders combined with the restraint of the shop stewards to make the chances of success for the German Revolution not very high from the beginning.

They were further reduced by the essential cohesion of the parties in the Reichstag, offering a united front to the threat from outside the parliamentary framework. When mass demonstrations began in Berlin on 9 November Prince Max von Baden began immediate arrangements for the abdication of the kaiser, the setting up of a Regency and the election of a German Constituent National

Assembly. This was showing a spirit similar to that of Prince Lvov, the leader of the Russian Duma. But unlike that body, the last imperial German government already had socialists in its ranks, the two SPD leaders, Scheidemann and Bauer, who had been brought in when Hindenburg and Ludendorff, the virtual military dictators, had recognised the virtual impossibility of victory and had urged the kaiser to form a coalition in October 1918. So now, as the kaiser abdicated, Prince Max could give an impression of legality and continuity by his appointment of Friedrich Ebert, chairman of the SPD, to the position of chancellor and regent.

Soon Ebert found himself in a Kerensky-like 'dual power' predicament, for while to the army, bureaucracy and middle class he was legally appointed head of state, to the Berlin masses he was leader of a revolution. In the second of these two capacities, Ebert yielded to popular pressure and to demands from Liebknecht for 'all power to the Soviets' sufficiently to participate in a meeting of workers' and soldiers' councils hastily brought together under joint SPD–USPD sponsorship. A Council of Peoples' Representatives was set up with a Social Democrat and an Independent Social Democrat appointed to control between them each Reich ministry. Unlike their Russian colleagues, the bureaucrats were reconciled to the new arrangements, recognising in them a restraint on more deterioration in their position and trusting with some justification in their ability to keep the politicians in check. Ebert himself went to the War Ministry, adding another title to that of chancellor and chairman of the Council of Peoples' Representatives. It was in his new capacity that Ebert was able to resolve Germany's 'dual power' situation by doing a deal with the army. In a famous telephone conversation of 10 November with General Groener, who had taken over as quartermaster-general from Ludendorff, and who spoke with the approval of the supreme commander, Hindenburg, Ebert agreed to give the army his government's full recognition in exchange for military support in the suppression of Bolshevism and maintenance of domestic stability. The Independent Socialists were not happy with such a direction in policy; and the Spartacists, together with some of the shop stewards and left-wing workers, were moved to reverse it.

The showdown came after a Reich Congress of workers' and soldiers' councils in December. Ebert had reluctantly acquiesced to the Congress in the more radical of his roles, but did all he could to stop the councils from arrogating to themselves the power and function of the Reichstag. The success of his efforts was reflected in the closing resolution of the Congress:

The Reich Congress of workers' and soldiers' councils in Germany, representing total political power, hereby transfers legislative and executive powers to the Council of Peoples' Representatives until such times as the National Assembly make other arrangements.

The majority SPD representation at the Congress had been able to restrain the extremist handful. Nationalisation of industry had been rejected on the grounds that it would make easier Allied assessments for reparation purposes, collectivisation of agriculture on the basis of the disruption it might cause at a crucial point in the farming calendar. On the other hand, a more sweeping stand had been taken on the army – replacement of the standing force by a people's militia, election by the other ranks of officers, and the assumption of the supreme command by the Council of Peoples' Representatives. But all this could be reversed by the National Assembly after a Constituent Assembly had met in January 1919. And neither the army nor the extreme left was prepared to stand idly by to wait and see.

At first the Spartacists and their allies appeared to be gaining the upper hand. The USPD withdrew from the Council of Peoples' Representatives after Ebert had used troops to suppress an insurrection of a 'peoples' naval division' in Berlin in late December 1918, and the militants among them – the Spartacists and other groups from Berlin and Bremen in particular – came together to form the Communist Party of Germany, the KPD. The troops had found it difficult to overcome their ill-organised opponents, and the way now seemed open to the new Communist leadership to press home their advantage. But appearances were deceptive, for if the remnants of the old army lacked organisation and will-power, a freshly levied body, the *Freikorps*, was to show more than enough of the appropriate fighting qualities. The *Freikorps*, which has been called the private army of the SPD, was put together by the Social Democrat Gustav Noske, a new member of the Council of Peoples' Representatives after the withdrawal of the USPD. Noske, who had already made something of a name for himself as a mediator during the Kiel insurrection, now managed the assembly in Berlin suburbs of various volunteer units composed partly of ex-soldiers and partly of raw recruits. Ebert gave his support, and General Groener promised reinforcements from what was left of the regular army – the resulting combination constituting more than enough to defeat the threat from the left.

The revolutionaries for their part also possessed some armed detachments, and, for all their widespread pacifism, did not in the end shrink from violence to the good of their cause. In early January 1919 confrontation between the opposing forces grew much nearer as, following the dismissal from the post of Berlin chief of police of a USPD sympathiser, the masses took again to the streets and a revolutionary committee was created headed by a three-man presidium including Liebknecht. Rosa Luxemburg and the Soviet emissary, Karl Radek, were dissentient voices as the others decided that the moment had come for the German October. But there was no German Military Revolutionary Committee and no Red Guard. After some savage street fighting, the *Freikorps* was triumphant, and thousands of their opponents were killed; Liebknecht and Luxemburg were brutally murdered, ostensibly while trying to escape. (Radek was arrested, and kept alive in custody.) The German Revolution came to a virtual conclusion by the middle of January 1919, although there was another flare up in March. There was some support from the rest of Germany. Bremen sympathisers rose up in January, but were promptly crushed by the *Freikorps*. In Bavaria, where the USPD leader Kurt Eisner had dominated the Munich Workers' Council, a Soviet Republic was declared in early April, but by 1 May – ironically – troops reoccupied the city, and there was little or no support from the rural hinterland, although some in Augsburg. And the Bavarian alignment was more or less repeated in the other German states: there were peoples' representatives in the administration, but only a small minority of would-be revolutionaries – many more Eberts and Scheidemanns than Liebknechts and Luxemburgs. And extremist workers were also small in number.

In January 1919 the Constituent Assembly was elected, with the socialist parties forming the biggest single group but not winning outright. Meanwhile the radical left had to try to put itself back into shape. The KPD was affiliated with the Third International, but its membership was minute, barely more than 30,000. As for the USPD, its ranks swelled during 1919 from about a third of a million to nearly a million, and it still talked of moving away from parliamentary representation, of striving for the dictatorship of the proletariat. There was much debate within the party about the advisability of leaving the Second International for the Third, the decision in favour and a consequent split in the party coming in October 1920 at the annual conference under pressure from Zinoviev and Radek. The USPD left now aligned itself with the KPD, and battled on against opposition from the armed forces and from the government. The humiliation of Versailles meant reverses for the SPD in elections to the Reichstag in April 1920, and a coalition of the centre now took over the government, but the extreme left held its own in the elections and showed its strength in the previous month when organising a general strike in opposition to the rightist Kapp *putsch*. If Germany was not to have an October, neither did its would-be Kornilov get any further than the original.

So the Weimar régime carried on its middle-of-the-road way resisting threats from right and left. Hitler's 'beerhall' *putsch* came to nothing in Munich in 1923; the KPD got nowhere in the March action of 1921. Lenin, it is true, was hoping for more during the more successful periods of the war against Poland than his denunciations of the *putschist* tactics of Zinoviev and Radek would sometimes suggest. But he was also coming round to the understanding that, as world revolution was failing in the short run at least, the two great powers excluded from the Versailles Conference were being pushed together, and that some accommodation would have to be reached between the Soviet Republic and Weimar. Not only would this *rapprochement* bring some stability and security to a Central Europe which had experienced more than its fair share of the ravages of war and internal discord, but it would also be of mutual advantage to two ravaged economies. Soviet Russia could offer some agricultural surplus and vast mineral deposits, Weimar Germany machinery and technological expertise. Moreover the German forces could train in the remote depths of the Russian steppe far away from the inquisitive eyes of the Allied War Control Commission. The agreement was realised with the Treaty of Rapallo of April 1922, and the KPD now resigned itself to building up its formal strength in a manner strongly reminiscent of the vilified SPD in the later nineteenth century.[28]

In this somewhat bare account of developments in Germany at the end of the war and during the years immediately following, there has been insufficient attention paid to its context, to the feverish expectations and anguished apprehensions that swept throughout not only Germany but the whole of Europe in this hectic period. This deficiency might be partially rectified as we turn to look at the continental setting of the rise and fall of the principal Communist hopes for the explosion of world revolution from a Russo–German nucleus. An important link was of course the conflict between the Reds and their opponents in Poland, the Baltic provinces and the Ukraine which have received mention in the previous chapter. Almost as central to the thoughts of Lenin and his associates for at least a few months were the events taking place in Hungary.

The junior partner in the Habsburg dual monarchy was of a somewhat brittle social structure even before the onslaught of the war. The chief source of tension was between city and country. Budapest was not only the most industrialised centre but also the home of much of its non-Magyar population – German, Italian and especially Jewish. The Jews of Budapest not only predominated in industry but also controlled most of the city's newspapers and were very active in cultural life in general. The countryside was Magyar and Catholic, anti-semitic and landlord-dominated. Something of a representative form of government had developed in the capital, but was not very discernible elsewhere, when in October 1918 Hungary, like Germany and Russia, adopted a liberal democratic form of government as the imperial régime was collapsing. Count Michael Karolyi was appointed prime minister by Franz Josef in his role as King of Hungary, but already crowds in Budapest were proclaiming the arrival of a republic. In January 1919 there were more demonstrations in the capital favouring social reforms and opposing the demand of the Entente powers for the cession of Transylvania to Rumania. Unable to provide much satisfaction on either issue, Karolyi resigned in March; and the United Socialist Party, which had been one of the members of his coalition, proclaimed on 21 March the creation of the Hungarian Soviet Republic.

The Hungarian United Socialist Party was hampered by an imperfect structure produced by the unbalanced social foundations. Although aspiring to mass and widespread support, it had a following of about three quarters of a million workers, nearly all from Budapest. Its leadership was mostly Jewish, and mostly from the younger generation of wealthy industrial families, and fanatically Marxist, with the Communist Bela Kun fresh from Moscow as the Hungarian Lenin. But Bela Kun and his associates lacked the tactical flexibility of Lenin and the Bolsheviks. To give the most important example, they made no concerted attempt to win over the peasants, advocating a policy of total nationalisation and collectivisation rather than at least a transitional phase of small-scale individual landholding. The peasants – who often found that their former owners were appointed as state farm managers, who were intensely suspicious of a new currency being introduced, particularly since the introducers were the 'Jews of Budapest' – presented a solid front of sullen opposition to the new régime. In Budapest itself revolutionary zeal took the form of a widespread Terror which brought about the loss of much former support, and the government increasingly depended on outside aid and the promise of it. Partly because of the new international dimension, and partly because of the old strategem of relieving social tensions through a vigorous foreign policy, the Hungarian army struck out into Slovakia, where there was a large minority Hungarian population and where links could be strengthened with Soviet Russia. The Hungarian troops moved in during May 1919 and were given an enthusiastic welcome; and in June the creation of a Slovakian Soviet Republic was proclaimed under their protection. This fresh addition to the Communist brotherhood lasted less than a month. The Czechs, who were for national self-determination more than the spread of communism, especially as they came to identify the hated Hungarians as the main agency for such a development, opposed it. The Slovaks themselves were less than happy at being pressed into the Hungarian army. And the Entente powers pressed with a blockade for a withdrawal accompanied by the *quid pro quo* of Rumanian withdrawal from Hungary. The invader army duly left Slovakia before the end of June, and the Soviet Republic duly collapsed, soon to be followed by its Hungarian instigator. With the Rumanians still encroaching rather than moving back and the Red grasp even on Budapest no longer sure, the white Admiral Horthy, with strong peasant support, was soon able to assume power and to hold it until 1944 – a long command of a state instead of a non-existent navy.[29]

Some kind of stability soon returned to the rest of Eastern Europe. At the heart of the old Habsburg Empire, Austria itself, a somewhat rootless Weimar-type government emerged – a coalition between conservatives and social democrats but, now that they had lost their imperial responsibilities, aspiring for the union with Germany which the Allies had ruled out.[30] States previously within the orbit of the two other deceased empires, the Hohenzollern and the Romanov – Poland and the Baltic states – we have glanced at in the previous chapter, but some attention remains to be given to the Balkans. Here, the stability was no more than comparative, more assured than before the war but always threatened by potentially explosive disputes, fuelled by fervent nationalism and much coloured by the possibility of Red revolution. At the centre of the area and of the problem was Macedonia, split between Yugoslavia and Greece with some of its people placed under Bulgarian rule. A passionate and terroristic Macedonian nationalist organisation agitated for independence from Yugoslavia and Greece and a merger with Bulgaria. Its activities resulted in the assassination of the head of the Bulgarian government, followed by a savagely crushed Communist attempt at takeover in Sofia, and subsequent fruitless raids on Yugoslavia and Greece. Yugoslavia was also rent by the rivalry between Serbs and Croats, but put into some semblance of order with the imposition of a monarchical dictatorship in 1929. Greece, on the other hand, became a republic in 1924 and managed to survive domestic problems, such as nearly a million and a half refugees, along with a number of frontier disputes, notably with Turkey and Albania (the latter being ruled officially by Ahmed Bey Zogu, from 1928 King Zog I, and unofficially for much of the time by Italy). And so the powder keg of the Balkans did not ignite after the First World War as it had done before, even though the Red flag was now raised to fan the flames of nationalism. There and in the rest of Eastern Europe new states were formed out of the ruins of old empires and the devastation of war without any lasting expansion of communism beyond the Soviet Russian borders. On the other hand enough support had been given to such a spread for a movement to be built up which would experience much greater success after the Second World War in the all-important presence of the Red Army.[31]

Taking a similarly long view, we could say that the shape of things to come after the Second World War was revealed after the First World War in Western Europe, too; in other words, that the origins of what has become known as Eurocommunism are to be found to some extent in the manner in which the various Communist parties first came to be formed. The precedent in this direction was set in Germany by the merger of the KPD 'intelligentsia' with the USPD 'proletariat' in December 1920; both French and Italian political developments soon went along similar lines. The French Socialist Party had been wondering for some time before this whether or not to affiliate with the Third International when the 21 conditions came to be debated at a party congress which met at Tours towards the end of December 1920. Emissaries returning from the Moscow Congress were in favour, and Clara Zetkin smuggled herself in to plead for the good of the Comintern cause. There was opposition, notably from Léon Blum, but the anti-Communist trade union leadership had no weight at the congress, and so the proposal was accepted by a considerable majority and the French Socialist Party was renamed the French Communist Party. The moderates formed their own party, and a year later the trade union movement split between the two parties. In early 1921 the Italian Socialists got together at Livorno. Delegates from the Comintern were present, as was G. Serrati, leader of the Italian delegation to its second congress. A strong left wing emerged, for unconditional acceptance of the '21 conditions', and a passionate right-wing view, almost as strongly opposed to acceptance. Serrati was spokesman for the largest group, the centre, which came out in favour of the acceptance of the '21 conditions' but also, in clear contradiction to the 21st, of continued co-operation with the socialist right. The contradiction finally led to a vote in favour of the secession of the Italian Socialist Party from the Comintern, with A. Bordiga, who had first proposed the 21st condition in Moscow, leading the left wing to the formation of the Italian Communist Party. Of course more immediately significant events than the socialist split were occurring in Italy in 1921, to a considerable extent encouraged by it. The former socialist, Mussolini, was building up the strength of his movement to defeat that of the workers after the March on Rome in 1922 and the formation of the Fascist government. The Italian left was to be suppressed until the end of the Second World War, by which time it had learned some lessons about the consequences of its own disunity. The French left, although sometimes successful at elections and never persecuted, was also divided, too much so to rule.[32]

In Italy and to a lesser extent France, the years 1917–21 were disturbed and often violent, reflecting not only the chaos attending the conclusion of the First World War and the years immediately following it, but also the impact of the Russian Revolution. Perhaps the Iberian peninsula, although not deeply involved in the war and most remote from Moscow, experienced the greatest amount of social dislocation in Western Europe, but there was a radical, even would-be revolutionary upsurge in the Low Countries as well, partly because of their contiguity with Germany. In Holland, for example, according to the historian Pieter Geyl writing in *The Encyclopaedia Britannica*:

> Mr. Troelstra, the Socialist leader, his imagination fired by the spectacle of the German revolution, toyed with the idea of imitating it among his own people. The attempt was a ludicrous failure. The Government took strong measures and the people rallied to them, and after an excited week quiet was restored on 21 November 1918. The Socialist party, which had been far from unanimous about this adventurous policy, re-entered the path of constitutionalism, and Mr. Troelstra, who resigned the leadership in 1925 owing to ill-health, never regained his old prestige.

To the north, in newly independent Finland, all the firmness of General Mannerheim was called for to maintain order, while there was a wave of unrest throughout adjacent Scandinavia, in, for example, the 'revolutionary' railway strike of December 1920 and national strike of May 1921 in Norway.[33]

Across the sea, in Great Britain, October also made its impact. Although the violence involved was on a much smaller scale than in many parts of Europe, the 'battle' of George Square in Glasgow in January 1919 appeared to be the beginning of a British or at least a Scottish communist revolution to some observers, although some opponents might have been more certain than many supporters. One of the major participants, William Gallacher, wrote in his autobiographical *Revolt on the Clyde*:

> We were being isolated and encircled with enemies, but we had possibilities of winning great new forces to our side if we had only the necessary revolutionary understanding and audacity. Revolt was seething everywhere, especially in the army. We had within

our own hands the possibility of giving actual expression and leadership to it, but it never entered our heads to do so. We were carrying on a strike when we ought to have been making a revolution.[34]

More confidently the secretary of state for Scotland said that 'it was a misnomer to call the situation in Scotland a strike – it was a Bolshevist rising', and he and his colleagues in the War Cabinet, still in existence, kept troops in readiness on a war footing in case the situation should deteriorate.[35]

If the revolutionary aspirations of John Maclean and others were not realised, the British workers did make a considerable contribution to the consolidation of the first Communist state through the 'Hands Off Russia' movement which grew in early 1920. Later on in the same year a Council of Action was formed in London with affiliates elsewhere to arrange an immediate strike to stop the interventionist war. The successful White defence of Warsaw reduced the apparent threat of the export of Red revolution, and the capitalist British and Soviet Russian governments were soon talking about a more peaceful form of commerce. Meanwhile, in August 1920, the Communist Party of Great Britain was formed from a number of radical groups, its initial membership being small but dedicated and including several participants in the councils of action.[36] By 1922, hopes for mass support for the CPGB or for Soviet Russia were fading and the Party journal *The Communist* lamented on 17 June:

> Four generations of industrial capitalism have bred a class so pathetically loyal to existing institutions that almost any crime is regarded with less abhorrence than attacks upon the framework of society. Every thinking capitalist is amazed at this stolid conservatism, however much he secretly rejoices. It is worth battalions of riflemen and parks of artillery to a governing class otherwise very shaky about its future prospects.[37]

In John Bull's other island, with the Civil War still raging, the situation was much more turbulent. Lenin had been excited by the Easter Rising of 1916, writing in July of that year:

> A blow of identical strength, delivered against the power of the British imperialist bourgeoisie by a rising in Ireland, has a hundred times greater political significance than one in Asia or Africa. . . . The misfortune of the Irish is that they rose prematurely – when a European-scale rising of the proletariat had not yet matured.

At the Second Congress of the Comintern in the summer of 1920, Roderick Connolly, the son of James, echoed Lenin in his assertion that:

> If we consider the international situation as a bitter struggle between the centre of the world revolution, Soviet Russia, with the small states grouped around Russia on the one hand, and the League of Nations led by British imperialism on the other, then Ireland, that constant hearth of revolution in the heart of the empire, which keeps an English army of 200,000 men permanently occupied, is of great importance for the international revolutionary movement.

Although Connolly was by no means alone in such a belief, and although Soviets of various kinds were formed in Ireland in 1921, long-term hopes for close association between the Irish and Soviet republics were not realised. In the shorter run, there is no doubt, the British government's anxieties about Ireland compounded those concerning security nearer home and further away. *The Times* reflected the wider concerns, which will be looked at more closely below, in an editorial of 23 January 1920:

> Supposing that the Bolshevist successes were to affect our security in Asia, or that the Russians were to attack Poland or any of the other political arrangements made by the Paris Conferences, what in that case would our policy be? It is an issue quite distinct from any that has yet been decided. It is no longer a question of supporting military operations in Russia, but of the defence of India, which is as much British territory as Ottawa or Melbourne or Kent. It is no longer at issue whether Russians shall be well governed or ill, but whether we shall govern ourselves as we wish or others may choose to dictate.[38]

As we move finally to consider the impact of October in the rest of the Western world, we leave Europe and cross the Atlantic to become remote from the main cockpit, but also to find much excited talk and no small amount of action. In the USA, long the home of great enthusiasms, there were those who were carried away by the news of the Revolution, for example, William M. Brown, who gained considerable notoriety by resigning as Bishop of Arkansas to become the self-styled 'Episcopus in partibus Bolshevikium et Infidelium'.[39] Debate among the politicians of the extreme left was rather more down to earth. At a convention in Chicago in September 1919,

differences of national origin as well as some doctrinal disputes
going back into the nineteenth century produced two breakaways
from the Socialist Party – a Communist Labor Party and a Communist Party of America – although under the influence of the
Comintern, a united Communist Party of North America was formed
in May 1921.[40] Discussion had now moved from down to earth to the
underground, for the Communist Party had been made illegal, held
its founding congress in secret and had to make use of various front
organisations. As for the trade union movement, it was often antipathetic to Bolshevism, certainly when its spokesman was Samuel
Gompers, head of the American Federation of Labor. Although the
IWW was still strong and there were many strikes in 1919, with
'Soviets' being set up in Butte, Montana, and Portland, Oregon,[41] the
spread of the 'Red menace' among American workers was greatly
exaggerated, notably at the time of the General Strike in Seattle in
1919, when Mayor Ole Hanson made himself into a national hero by
his firm action and sentiments such as the following:

> Bolshevists believe in destruction of nationalism, loyalty and
> patriotism and the adoption of a sentimental, sickly, unworkable,
> skim-milk internationalism. Loving no country, they excuse them-
> selves by saying they love all countries alike. Polygamous men
> have ever used the same excuse. . . . Bolshevism would disarm and
> Chinafy our great people. . . . Bolshevism teaches and its votaries
> practise immorality, indecency, cruelty, rape, murder, theft,
> arson.[42]

Hanson's views were widely shared, as the 'Red scare' built up in
1919 with the encouragement of the attorney-general, A. Mitchell
Palmer, demonstrated. Any kind of agitation was suspect; the mai-
ling of a few bombs and the explosion of even fewer was interpreted
as part of a concerted attempt to subvert probity and good order.
Many innocent people lost their jobs and some their lives in the wave
of hysteria that swept throughout the USA. And to counter the all-
pervasive threat, new emphasis was put on the patriotism that had
already been stirred up by the war. The Joint Committee of New
York State Legislature investigating seditious activities under Clayton R. Lusk asserted that:

> . . . steps are being taken by the public school authorities with the
> cooperation of the legislatures of almost every state in the United
> States to make Americanization and citizenship training as vital
> and integral a part of the public school curricula as the universal
> teaching of the justly famed three r's. They seem to subscribe to the

belief that if we could give children in their early youth a real and sympathetic appreciation of American ideals and a respect for the institutions through which these ideals find realisation, their patriotism will be deep-rooted and lasting and their loyalty to this nation so strong that it will withstand the influence of subversive propaganda.

But sometimes, the Committee warned, 'subversive activities masquerade under the name of Americanization', two alleged examples being lectures on psychoanalysis and on Henrik Ibsen. The Joint Committee also quoted with approval the approach to problems of Americanisation of A. W. Coffin, of the War Civics Committee, East St Louis, Illinois:

> Too often the superintendent, the foreman, the employer and the native-born workman miss a great opportunity to be the foreign-born workman's hero or his general or corporal instead of his task-master, through neglect to form a play fellowship with the new-comer. . . . If the Italians are present, buy some baccio balls and see what happens. If the Slavs are enrolled, make some parallel bars, and watch who uses them most during the noon hour. If there are English, Scotchmen or Canadians to be considered, have facilities for soccer and cricket.[43]

Problems of the great American 'melting-pot' were indeed at the root of much of the trouble in 1919 and the years following, particularly since the fusion process was not yet very advanced. And some extreme ideas had indeed been imported from Europe along with its huddled masses. These two sets of circumstances were clearly incorporated in the famous case of Sacco and Vanzetti, who were finally executed in 1927 because they were Italian radicals rather than thieving murderers, as Vanzetti said in his last statement to the court. But among the other motives probably spurring on some of the Americanisers was the realisation that patriotism could perform a useful service as a blanket cover for the dismantling of some of the liberal measures of the pre-war period. Certainly, the anti-Red tumult never died down completely as normalcy was restored in the 1920s, and was to rise up again in almost equally strident tones after the Second World War.[44]

Even across the northern border soccer and cricket were not enough to give Canada complete domestic peace at the end of the war. The Canada First Publicity Association purchased newspaper space in the summer of 1919 to advertise 'The Frozen Breath of Bolshevism. If Bolshevism comes to Canada it will do here what it has

done in Russia and what it seeks to do in Germany.'[45] Sources of the
icy halitosis were believed to be everywhere, especially in Winnipeg
and back across the ocean at a demobilisation camp in Kinmel,
North Wales. At Kinmel, the trouble appears to have stemmed from
delays in the return of soldiers to civilian life and the frightful camp
conditions as much as from radical impulses, although the leaders
certainly carried red flags in their demonstrations.[46] A correspondent
in the *Calgary Daily Herald* of 12 March 1919 wrote that conversation with all ranks had convinced him that:

> Bolshevism had no real place among the Canadian troops though
> the feeling is strongly entertained that Canada should carefully re-
> view her immigration policy and exclude Russian and other Euro-
> pean immigrants who are incapable of appreciating the benefit of
> Canadian institutions.[47]

In its policy of One Big Industrial Union the Western Conference
of Labor meeting in Calgary in March 1919 was believed in particular to be advocating the introduction into Canada of Bolshevism; it
did indeed declare itself in favour of proletarian dictatorship. When
another of its policies, the general strike, was adopted in Winnipeg in
May, there were newspaper reports of 'a military junta, which
attempted to establish a strikers' government in Winnipeg modelled
along the Leninist Russian monstrosity', and of 'a red guard of aliens
headed chiefly by imported English and Scottish anarchists'.[48] In fact
the most violent occurrence was a peaceful march (in defiance of the
mayor's ban) during the course of the control of which one person
was killed and about thirty were wounded. And with the leaders in
jail, the strike was called off as a royal commission was set up to investigate the whole affair; this found that the strike had consisted of
non-violent collective bargaining led by Canadian citizens rather
than by alien elements.[49] Nevertheless, without it reaching anything
like American proportions, the domestic 'Red scare' continued, and
the first convention of the Canadian Communist Party in 1921 had to
be held in secret in a barn outside Guelph, Ontario. Up to that point
Canadian socialism had contained a somewhat disparate mixture of
preachers of the 'social gospel', trade unionists, Marxist and non-
Marxist intellectuals and (particularly marked in such a widely
scattered and heterogeneous people) provincialists, regionalists and
nationalists (especially French Canadian). Even now, after 1921, the
lines were not clearly drawn, and the rise of the social credit movement added yet another element to the mixture.[50]

The principal characteristic of the situation across the Atlantic
ocean in the outpost of the Western world, South Africa, was of

course race. The foothold carved out of the Cape by the British and Dutch was still precarious enough in 1908 for Bill Andrews, a white union leader, to argue that the 'coloured races, if unchecked would rise to the top and endanger the state itself by reason of their numbers, vitality and low standards'. Another feature of the South African situation was the strong legacy of the Boer War, which meant continued, powerful antipathy to Great Britain and therefore to the First World War. S. P. Bunting, a prominent Labour politician, argued in 1915 that his colleagues had to choose between the Afrikaner vote and support for the war; there was with him little or none of the principled internationalism of some socialists. Even in 1917 Andrews was pressing for 'parallel' trade unions for coloured and Kaffir workers, and standing along with Bunting and others in all-white elections. When the Communist Party of South Africa was formed in 1921, Andrews was secretary–editor, Bunting treasurer, and the executive all-white in its membership and pro-white in its policies. Their outlook was well illustrated at the Rand strike in 1922 when a banner inscribed with the legend 'Workers of the World, Fight and Unite for a White South Africa' was carried along in a daily march with a band playing the 'Red Flag'.[51]

Across the Indian Ocean in Australia racism and anti-British feeling were also to be found, albeit in comparatively diluted form, since the aborigines were not as numerous as the Kaffirs and the antipodean Irish not as prominent as the Afrikaners. On the other hand, Australians were worried by the 'yellow peril', as they began to realise after 1905 and even more after 1914 that they were rather further from the old country than they had usually thought during the latter part of the nineteenth century. As a leader in the *Sydney Morning Herald* put it on 18 December 1917:

There is probably no centre of population in the world quite so open to attack from the enemy without and the enemy within. . . the forces of disaffection make it more like Petrograd than London or Paris. . . . The same implied threats of violence and disorder were offered to Lincoln when he forced his will upon the Northern States in the American Civil War.

These last remarks were occasioned by the fact that at the time of the October Revolution Australia was holding a referendum on a problem that had caused Lincoln much trouble – that of conscription. The same leader-writer, C. Brunsden Fletcher, had made no secret of his attitude in the *Herald* on 14 November: 'Self-respecting men cannot be expected to play the fool to please a populace only fit to be compared with the lunatics of Leninism – the poor pacifists of

Petrograd.' There were few 'lunatics of Leninism' at large in Australia at this time, although the fact that at least one of them – Peter Simonoff – was of Russian origin encouraged complaints of 'alien elements' and an upsurge of anti-semitism (since a clear majority of Australian Russians were Jewish). But Tom Barker, an IWW organiser and an energetic member of the band of socialists who were among the opponents of conscription, was more representative of the Australian extreme left in his later recollection that 'I'd never heard of Lenin or Trotsky but I had organised meetings in Sydney in support of the February Revolution, so I was able to tell . . . something about the struggles of the Russian people.'[52] The IWW not only welcomed October, but also spoke out against conscription and in favour of the One Big Union before moving with other socialists including seceding members of the reformist Labour Party towards the formation of the Communist Party of Australia, which was finally achieved in Sydney in October 1920.[53] The Australian Labour Party, (ALP) with strong union affiliations, remained little interested in ideology or internationalism, antipathetic to communism and preoccupied by economic motives. The prime minister, W. M. Hughes, a Labour politician but now heading a Nationalist government (since the bulk of the ALP had opposed conscription in 1917 while Hughes and thirty other MPs had split to support it) was able to argue in September 1919 that the war had achieved national security, White Australia and freedom from communism. 'Australia', he proclaimed, 'is safe.'[54]

Of apparently sterner stuff as well as less racist was H. E. Holland, a leader of the Labour Party across the Tasman Sea in New Zealand, who in February 1920 could still say that the light of the Soviet Russian achievements was destined 'to illumine the world and to leave Russia flaming like a star of the first magnitude in the constellation of nations'.[55] Earlier on 23 January 1918, equal enthusiasm had been shown by 'The Vag' (E. J. Howard of Christchurch), a columnist in the *Maoriland Worker*:

> It's coming, Brother! you can hear the coming of Democracy even in God's Own Country. Russia! Australia! China! America! Why not New Zealand? Get ready, comrades, get ready. Be ready to take over the mines, the mills, the ships and the factories.

The *Maoriland Worker* was to cool down by 4 August 1920, however, arguing that:

> In British communities it is idle to hope for a Revolution after the Russian method. Britons are hopelessly constitutional. . . . While,

therefore, we favour revolutionary principles, we recognise that methods in such a country as Maoriland must be a compromise between reformist and revolutionary'.[56]

And, in like manner, in the same month as he made the above remarks, Henry Holland also pointed out that 'the Social Revolution will achieve itself and be achieved through evolutionary processes'.[57] Poking fun at the similarly compromising approach of another Labour leader, Walter Nash, some irreverent colleagues sang:

> The people's flag is palest pink,
> It's not so red as you might think.[58]

Recoiling from such dilution of the revolutionary message, Thomas Feary, a young miner, and other enthusiasts, formed a New Zealand Marxian Association in 1918 which was to become the New Zealand Communist Party in the spring of 1921.[59] As for the first post-war government, its programme has been characterised as 'a shred of socialism, a patch of patriotism, a humanitarian thread, and an imperialist ribbon on the ragged conservative cloak'.[60] Problems and tensions there certainly were during its period in office – economic, racial and religious as well as political – but the 'Fish of Maui' continued to swim through the South Pacific without encountering unmanageably stormy waters.[61]

Moving up to the North Pacific, we arrive at our last port of call, the oriental outlier of the Western world, Japan. Here the October Revolution encouraged the government to decide on intervention, and by November the General Staff had already drafted 'The Plan to Dispatch Troops to Protect the Japanese Residents in the Russian-Occupied Far East'. The Japanese ambassador to Russia, Uchida, was greatly alarmed by such a policy, arguing that, whether Japan liked it or not, the Bolshevik régime was likely to last for a long time, and Japan would have to deal with it. He argued in favour of recognition rather than intervention, but was forced to resign in July 1918. More radical criticism of the government came from Ishibashi Tanzan, the liberal editor of *Toyo keizai Shimpo* ('The New Asian Economic Gazette'). After the October Revolution, Ishibashi rejected the notion that Lenin and the Bolshevik régime were puppets of the Germans, and argued that Lenin's policies succeeded only because they tried to meet the aspirations of the masses. In his view, the Soviets expressed the will of a previously suppressed people, and a new era which was opening would mean the death of imperialism. What was dangerous to Japan was not a German thrust into Siberia, nor the threat of Bolshevism, but rather the fact that, too preoccupied with the pursuit of narrow national interests, Japan was blind to the economic and political bankruptcy of imperialism. Like Uchida, he argued in favour of recognition and against intervention, and continued to do so even though incurring government censorship.

As for the Japanese socialists, they had been virtually silenced since an alleged attempt at regicide in 1912, but a small group of them still managed to put out 20 issues of a journal called *Shin shakai* ('New Society') during the period January 1917 to August 1918. To begin with, they were very ignorant of the great events of 1917, one of them Arahata Kanson explaining that:

> We knew nothing about the nature of the Russian Revolution, nor about the organisation of the Soviets, nor the political parties which formed the new government. We knew the differences between the SRs and the SDs, but the differences between the Bolsheviks and the Mensheviks only after the revolution. Nobody knew or had heard of Kerensky, Lenin or Trotsky.

Such ignorance stemmed basically from the circumstance that Japanese socialists had mostly been interested in gaining enlightenment from the works of Marx and Engels, and had paid little attention previously to developments in Russia.[62] But February and especially October made all the difference. In the estimate of Chitoshi Yanaga:

> The Russian Revolution came in 1917, at a time when the advocates of democracy were gathering strength and voices denouncing militarism were beginning to reverberate throughout the nation. The success of the Bolsheviks made a profound impression upon the mind of Japanese youth and had the effect of stimulating leftist thought and movement.[63]

Shin shakai made a considerable contribution to the discussion which aroused Japanese socialists but also split them in three directions, each represented by an outstanding individual. Takabatake Motoyuki became convinced that Bolshevism could be revolutionary only in Russia, and turned to a right-wing state socialism. Osugi Sakae was dismayed by the Bolshevik split with the SRs and the suppression of the Kronstadt Revolt, and was an enthusiastic advocate of anarchism until his assassination by the Secret Police in 1923. Yamakawa Hitoshi remained deeply committed to the October Revolution, and made a revaluation of Japanese socialist thought using it as a basis.

Along with all this debate, serious labour troubles developed for the first time in Japanese history. The year 1919 was one of great strikes in factories, mines and transportation, with thousands of workers jailed for their part in these disturbances. Reacting to this activity as well as to the inspiration of events in Russia, workers and intellectuals marched in the first Japanese May Day parade in 1920 and came together to form a Socialist Union in the same year. But the inaugural meeting was disrupted by the police, and the Union was dissolved in May 1921 at the order of the government. The Communist Party of Japan, formed about a year later by Japanese delegates to the Third Congress of the Comintern, had an equally difficult time from the start; its leaders, including Yamakawa Hitoshi and Arahata Kanson, were arrested in May 1923, and the Party virtually collapsed and then disappeared for some years.[64]

Concern for the general security of the Pacific as well as for that of its several parts was widely expressed in a number of different ways in 1917 and after. For example, headlines in *The Pacific Commercial Advertiser* published in Honolulu on 9 November 1917 ran: 'Kerensky's Fall Menace to Hawaii, say Congressmen. May Open Way for Germany to Establish Bases in Siberian Port for Raiders.' And what the Germans might begin a successful Bolshevik régime could follow. This was especially alarming to Hawaians because of their unhappy experience with Russian religious refugees just before 1914, of whom the *Advertiser* said, also on 9 November:

They demanded life, liberty and the pursuit of happiness without work. The world, they thought, owed them a living, but they failed to understand that they owed the world anything in return. So it seems to be with virtually the entire Russian nation.

Thoughts for the guarantee of Pacific security against the Red Star as well as the Rising Sun were in the minds of many delegates to the Washington Conference which met towards the end of 1921, as the exclusion of Soviet Russia (in spite of her vigorous protests) indicated.[65]

And before the Versailles Conference some two and a half years previously, General Smuts was no doubt thinking of more than the security of Europe in his recommendation of the restoration of Germany as a bulwark against Bolshevism and his fear 'that the Paris Conference may prove one of the historic failures of the world; that the statesmen connected with it will return to their countries broken, discredited men, and that the Bolsheviks will reap where they have sown'.[66] In these years immediately following the Russian Revolution, a vast number of writers discussed the global implications of

February and especially of October. Some were highly alarmed, such as G. Pitt-Rivers, who in a book entitled *The World Significance of the Russian Revolution* and published in 1920 expressed the wish that Russia 'would free herself from the crazy paranoiacs and parasites who are sucking her life's blood'.[67] Others were wildly enthusiastic, such as Frank Anstey, an Australian M.P., who concluded a work written in 1919 with the declaration:

'All Power' in its scope, the right of each locality to work out its own salvation, land, homes and industries, local action, direct action, action quick and on the spot; emulation, stimulation, rivalry in effort for the common good; the foremost a beacon to the backward. . . . The impatient world will wait no longer. . . . Capitalism listens with quaking soul to the drum beats of the Armies of Revolution. Those beats grow louder and louder – they draw nearer and nearer.[68]

To assess the extent to which the fears of the opponents of Bolshevism and the hopes of its supporters were justified, we must now turn from the Western world to find out how the drums were beating in the Third.

6   The Third World

There was no substantial part of the inhabited world completely unaffected by the immediate impact of the Russian Revolution. Even the most sparsely peopled region – the Arctic – was soon under the influence of the great event, largely because of its proximity to and partial inclusion in the Russian Republic, at least to some extent because of the belief of such an expert as Vilhjalmur Stefansson in, as he called it, *The Northward Course of Empire,* which was to lead him on to *The Adventure of Wrangel Island.*[1] While the uninhabited Antarctic remained outside the most immediate contention, it too was later to become a disputed region, the Soviet government basing its claims on the activities of prerevolutionary explorers.[2]

In this chapter, the focus of our attention will be on those parts of the world more firmly incorporated in the great global empires, whose subjects were rarely proletarian and not often bourgeois, but were nevertheless seen by Lenin and his associates as potential participants in the world revolution, even though the manner of their doing so was the subject of keen debate at the Second Congress of the Comintern. Should 'bourgeois nationalism' be encouraged, and to what extent and in conjunction with which other social forces? Such questions involved Lenin in considerable controversy.[3] Here, we take as a point of departure the observation of the geographer A. Supan quoted by Lenin in *Imperialism: The Highest Stage of Capitalism* and concerning development at the end of the nineteenth century: 'The characteristic feature of the period is . . . the division of Africa and Polynesia.' Supan pointed out that between 1876 and 1900 the percentage of territory belonging to the colonial powers rose by nearly eighty per cent in Africa and by over forty per cent in Polynesia.[4] We shall begin our survey by giving our attention to a remote part of Polynesia in order to demonstrate that even in most unlikely places only recently brought into the imperialist network the impact of October was palpably felt soon after the event itself.

The islands of the South Pacific presented an image on the face of it which was pre-capitalist and even pre-feudal, with hints of primitive communism. This was explicitly discovered by a New Zealand Parliamentary Commission visiting Western Samoa soon after the First World War and commenting:

> Unfortunately, the Samoans are communistic in their ideas of life, and this fact has an important bearing on labour matters. It is expected that the man who has should support the man who has not, and as a consequence the man who does work is preyed upon by the man who does not. It has been asserted that the Samoan is physically unfit to put forth sustained effort for any lengthened period, but this theory is difficult to believe. It seems more probable that the principle of communism rather than any physical unfitness is responsible for his unwillingness to work.

But as part of its investigations, the Commission discovered that, in some parts of the South Pacific at least, something like the feudal stage had been passed. Makea, an *Ariki* or chief in Rarotonga in the Cook Islands, pointed out that formerly he and his fellows had held absolute power over the land, and 'the tenants had to render certain services in return, including military service. . . . Tenants failing to render their obligations were dispossessed.' Later, however, a land court had shared out a portion to each individual, 'exactly the same as in New Zealand'. So, in quite a short space of time, some inhabitants of the South Seas had been pushed through a complete historical phase.[5]

Were any of them anxious to move further, to socialism? Certainly, they would have found it difficult to follow the lead of the Russian revolutionaries, even to know what such a lead was. South Pacific newspapers, often weekly rather than daily and without much information from the world outside, were often misinformed. For example, the *Samoa Times* reported on 17 November 1917 that 'Kerensky is reported to have defeated the Bolsheviki, the majority of the troops having joined the premier', while the *Fiji Times* announced on 28 November that 'Bolsheviki is the latest to secure the alleged control of the army and navy, Kerensky, Lenin and others having been relegated to somewhere behind the scenes.' Some of this news was probably distorted as relayed through Hawaii, the above misunderstandings may partly have been suggested by the *Pacific Commercial Advertiser* of 12 November which stated that the fall of the Russian radicals was believed to be only hours away, and of 14 November, which contained the headline 'Bolshe-Viki Bands are Reported To Have Committed Terrible Excesses and Made Conditions in Russian Capital Intolerable.' News travelling in the other direction, from the South Seas outwards, may have been distorted, too, but if not, an item in the New York radical newspaper The *Liberator*, in September 1919, answered the question posed at the beginning of this paragraph in the affirmative. This was a dispatch from Papeete, Tahiti, which ran as follows:

A sort of communist republic has been set up in the island of Mauke by soldiers who returned recently from the battlefields of France. Mauke is one of the Cook group of islands west of Tahiti. Reports from Mauke say the soldiers have taken entire charge of the island, displaced the government resident, assumed direction of the trading stores, set prices on the goods for sale, and established government by committee.

Here, obviously, is a case that merits closer investigation, for it could encourage excited exclamations indeed. C. E. Russell in Indianapolis had probably read his *Liberator* when he wrote about Lenin and Bolshevism:

From what might be called a student's cell in the city of Cracow, Austria, to the utmost Orient and the islands of the South Seas, taking in much territory between, and all in these few months – wonderful is the flight, all must admit it to be so! The creed of one man become already the creed of millions and still going on to other millions and to others.[6]

To what sort of place had the message apparently come? Discovered by the explorer whose name they bear in 1777, the Cook Islands were not proclaimed a British protectorate until 1888. In 1890 a general legislature was set up along with an executive council of which the *Arikis* were members. The whole archipelago was annexed by the Governor of New Zealand in 1901.[7] Although their total number was not many more than 6000, the Cook Islanders were keenly prepared to do their bit when the news of the outbreak of the First World War came to them. On Niue, a western outlier of the group, £164 was collected and sent to Wellington along with the offer of 200 young men and the following message: 'To King George V, all those in authority, and the brave men who fight. I am the small island of Niue, a small child that stands up to help the King to stand fast.'[8] The Rarotongan Company (named after the most important island of the group) of the Australia and New Zealand Mid-Division duly found its way to Egypt, where it was involved in the handling of ammunition and other such duties. Its Captain – G. A. Bush – noted that its discipline was generally good from April 1917 to December

1918[9]; but it may well have been in contact with other troops whose behaviour was less exemplary in Egypt during roughly the same period and who had taken the bold step of forming their own councils.[10] Meanwhile, back home, a Cook Islands Act was passed in April 1916 to clear up some serious anomalies in their constitutional position, a leading role in the work being taken by Dr Maui Pomare, a Maori member of the New Zealand Cabinet closely involved in the affairs of his own people and those of their island cousins.[11] On the face of it, the way was prepared for a peaceful demobilisation of the returning troops, but Captain Bush's charges were not to maintain their record for keeping good order.

When we turn to look at the official records of the incident noticed in the *Liberator*, we can have little doubt that it seemed very serious to the government's man on the spot. The Telegraph Office in Christchurch, New Zealand, regretted to inform the governor-general, Lord Liverpool, on 11 March 1919 that it had intercepted the following radio message:

> To Governor Papeete. Serious disturbances here by returned soldiers who are taking charge of settlement. Require armed assistance. Can you send warship or other assistance. Fifty armed men at least required. Signed – Platts, Resident Commissioner, Rarotonga.

The next day, 12 March, the acting prime minister of New Zealand, the Hon. Sir James Allen, was able to give the governor-general a fuller account:

> A communication was received late last night from the Resident Commissioner Rarotonga as follows. Begins. Soldiers out of hand raided three stores. Looted contents. Two serious assaults. Captain Bush advised immediate appeal for help. Sent message Governor Tahiti for warship. Sent another independently passing troopship. Today High Court convicted two ringleaders. Heavily sentenced. Expect attempt to break gaol tonight and other stores. 'Flora' arrives Wednesday. Please arrange without fail Union Company remove Atui and Mauke men who are chief offenders by 'Flora' on Wednesday. Captain Bush says assistance man of war imperative. Organising Europeans, natives special constables. Ends.

To this communication Sir James Allen added the note that arrangements had been made with the Union Company for the *Flora* to remove the Atui and Mauke men to their respective islands, and on the first despatch another administrator added the comment that the job was too much for Platts, the commissioner. Whether or not Captain Bush was also finding his responsibilities inordinately heavy was not discussed, but both men were obviously seriously alarmed. Still on 12 March Allen informed the governor-general that he had received from the commissioner in Rarotonga the news that thirty-five white special constables and fifty reliable native troops had prevented the threatened disturbance the previous night. Platts considered that the crisis was over and the position was improving. He also reported that complaints of overcharging by the traders had been one of the causes of the disturbance, and that shopkeepers had made claims of £1500 to cover the losses that they had incurred from looting.

Twelve days later the governor-general received confirmation of the return of calm to the Cook Islands from Sir James Allen. A telegram dated 22 March from the commissioner at Rarotonga had said that three offenders had been convicted and that the police, military officers and *Arikis* all agreed that there was no cause for further anxiety as to a fresh outbreak. On 24 March the acting prime minister also sent the governor-general news of other telegrams which it did not appear advisable he should send over the wires, namely:

> Public meeting requests public enquiry into system administration operating Cook Islands giving special consideration events preceding disturbances. Enquiry should include Island industries and commercial conditions. Unsatisfactory economic position held largely responsible present unrest. Future causes grave position unless conditions improved. Signed – Russell Chairman.

And a second telegram explained the first:

> Russell's message to Premier is entirely a Progressive Association move. That body is trying to make political capital of soldiers disorder, hence application for enquiry into scheme of administration operating in these Islands. Have nothing to fear from any enquiry. Enquiry into causes of outbreak might be useful. Suggest one you await report etc. per 'Moana' before reply to Russell two you come down yourself and decide what enquiry if any desirable. No risk further outbreak. First one is being effectively dealt with. Signed – M. Pomare.

Sir James Allen told Lord Liverpool that he had telegraphed Dr Pomare to ask when he would return to Wellington as the matter would have to be considered by the cabinet.[12] The atmosphere of the incident is well suggested for us by the name affixed to a communication dated 9 May 1919 from their man in Rarotonga to the London Missionary Society: 'The returned soldiers caused a little disturbance but everything is quiet now. Bond James.'[13]

A month or so after Bond James had sent in his report, the governor-general himself was making a tour of the South Pacific Islands. At Mangaia, in the Cook group, he noted:

When addressing the people, I took the opportunity of impressing the men who had lately been demobilised of the advisability of laying to heart all the good lessons which they had learned while under military discipline, and I told them that we looked to them to assist materially in fostering the interests of their Island. Some of the men had been in Egypt where, unfortunately, they had witnessed certain acts of insubordination perpetrated on the traders, and there was just a possibility that they might be inclined to do something of the same kind on the few White traders if their terms did not meet with approbation.

About Mauke, the governor-general was less communicative, unfortunately:

Here it also appeared to me and to Doctor Pomare that we should say a few words to the returned soldiers as regards their behaviour, as Mr. Cameron [the resident agent] told us there had been an inclination on their part to get out of hand.[14]

The whole matter was finally, if not completely, cleared up in the following year with the *Report of the Commission to Inquire into the Conditions of Trade between New Zealand and Fiji, Tonga, Western Samoa, and Cook Islands* published as an *Appendix to the Journals of the House of Representatives of New Zealand, 1920.*[15] It was probably to a considerable extent in order to influence the findings of the Commission that the merchants, planters and traders of the Cook Islands also published in 1920 the following pamphlet: *Cook Islands Administration: An Arbitrary Autocracy: Denial of Justice: A Serious Crisis: An Impartial Inquiry into the Causes of Declining Trade and Growing Discontent: Also An Appeal to the Parliament and People of New Zealand.* The anonymous author began by revealing a clear political attitude as well as something of a literary flair, and his first paragraph merits quotation at length:

It is generally conceded that good administration is of far greater importance than the particular form of Government that may be in vogue in any country – that a 'benevolent despotism' is much to be preferred to a hideously cruel and tyrannical régime of State Socialism such as the Bolshevists have established in Russia. This must not be taken as an unqualified endorsement of Alexander Pope's dictum:

> For forms of government let fools contest;
> Whate'er is best administered is best.

The form of Government under which people live is a matter of very great moment. It is especially desirable that Governments should be of representative character, so that, in the event of any failure to deal out even-handed justice to all, there should be a ready means of obtaining redress or of securing a change of administration. The axiom, 'No taxation without representation', should have as its corollary 'No representation without taxation'. Grievances caused by maladministration may arise under the most democratic system, but the people in such case have the power to demand justice. When, however, the people have no such power – when an autocratic Administrator, by whatever name he may be called –

> . . . dressed in a little brief authority,
> Plays such fantastic tricks before high Heaven
> As makes the angels weep –

and those who suffer from his caprice, corruption, incompetence or malevolence have no effective means of protest – when, in short, justice is denied and appeal is futile, an intolerable situation is created. It will thus be seen that, when maladministration is allied with a bad form of Government, conditions are created that are tyrannical and oppressive, and against which the people are justified in employing the forces of Revolution.

Here was an explicit appeal for a Cook Islands 1776 or 1789 or even February 1917, although on behalf of the merchants, planters and traders rather than the native people. As the remainder of the pamphlet confirms, in the view of its sponsors the resident commissioner was indeed carrying on a 'benevolent despotism' on behalf of the Islanders themselves. Island Councils set up in 1915 gave the appearance of constitutional government, but they were a sham since the native representatives accepted his every suggestion. And when the returning soldiers rioted in 1919 the resident commissioner attempted to throw the blame on 'profiteering' tactics by the traders. Furthermore:

It is alleged, on the testimony of many eye-witnesses, that a drunken soldier entered the Commissioner's office, armed with a bar of iron, and threatened mischief if two of his friends who had been arrested were not at once released from gaol. This is denied by the Commissioner; but confirmation of the story is afforded by the report that the agent of the London Missionary Society took the offending native in hand and made him apologise to the Commissioner, the upshot being that no prosecution followed.

This was not only another exploit for Bond James but also, as far as the pamphleteer was concerned, a revelation to the natives of the weakness of the resident commissioner. They had been led by him to believe that 'the Administration is standing between them and a band of selfish exploiters'. This was far from the case, but if not properly led, the Cook Islanders might become like Samoans and relapse into 'habits of indolence and lack of ambition'.

The Parliamentary Commission, for its part, formed a somewhat different impression of the enterprise of the Cook Islanders, receiving many complaints that the traders were exploiting the natives and making vast profits out of the sale of fruit to New Zealand. For this reason a serious attempt was being made among the natives to form a co-operative association in the fruit trade, and the Commission believed that encouragement should be given to such an aspiration. Their Report also stated:

We are informed, however, that notices were posted in public places asking the Natives to deal only with the Native Committee, and were signed 'By order'. The traders contended that many Natives were under the impression that 'By Order' meant by order of the Administration, and as a consequence were afraid to sell or consign their fruit through the traders. As a matter of fact the Administration had nothing whatever to do with the publication of such notices: they were issued by the Native Committee. This may be a comparatively small matter to mention; nevertheless we think that the person or persons who issue such notices should be compelled to sign them.

A small matter indeed, and yet a further illustration of the Parliamentary Commission's attitude, in favour of moderate encouragement of the Cook Islanders and a certain amount of restraint on the traders, including persistence with at least some form of the 'benevolent despotism' of the resident commissioner. This kind of attitude led to some further mild reform, attempting to placate both Europeans and natives. The Cook Islands Amendment Act of November 1921 gave the Europeans their representation on the

Island Council, but removed their exclusive privilege of obtaining alcoholic liquor by introducing absolute prohibition. In June 1922, Dr Pomare was created a Knight Commander of the British Empire, which no doubt pleased his supporters in the Islands, even if they were not legally able to celebrate this honour by drinking Sir Maui's health.[16]

Unfortunately the Cook Islanders did not live happily ever after. Jackson Webb writes in *The Times* of 2 December 1977 of 'The so-called civilisation that is strangling the Cook Islands'. He complains that fruit companies and tourism have done much social and ecological damage, and goes on to lament that:

> Since the early 1880s, there has been no looking back for Polynesia. It is an old tragedy. The past has been annihilated by greed, imported diseases and religious bullying. Today, there are simply no precedents. Economically pinioned from the outside, with its cultural backbone broken and rich artistic and ritualistic sources of life cut off by the missionaries, what can the Cook Islands people do but turn completely, desperately to the bleak present, while their integrity and communal spirit dwindle to extinction.

Jackson Webb also makes the shrewd point that 'Ironically, it is the small outlying places of the world, like the Cooks, which seem to register most violently the aberrant currents of the time.' That which applied to 1977 arguably applied to 1919, too. Like their comrades in other parts of the world, the Cook Islands soldiers came home wanting homes fit for heroes, and were prepared to take action when they did not find them. While their ideas cannot be precisely determined, their general direction seems clear enough. Moreover, their enemies' enemies would have been looked upon by them as their friends, and these, they would have discovered from the Progressive Association's pamphlet if they did not know it before, included the 'Bolshevists'.

Radical ideas certainly passed through the head of the leader of a strike in 1920 to the west of Polynesia in Fiji, although that began in January for 'increase of wages in view of the high cost of living'. Alarm spread quickly enough for New Zealand to send 50 men and 200 rifles and Australia a gunboat with 50 ratings at the beginning of February. On the tenth of that month, 'Loyal Indians British subjects' asked the Governor for protection 'from interference by political agitators' and he – C. H. Rodwell – wired the Secretary of State for the Colonies that 'Indian unrest is assuming appearance of racial outbreak.' Five days later, the Governor could be reassuring, now that the nominated member of the Legislative Council the

Honourable Badri Mahraj had arrived 'and rendered excellent service by addressing meetings and warning Indians against mischievous and seditious propaganda which has nothing to do with stated grievances namely cost of living and rate of wages', and then, after another three days, 'All have returned to work' and 'Complete order prevails.'[17]

Reporting to Milner at greater length on 12 March 1920, Rodwell wrote that on 5 February he had been shown a draft of an address just given at a meeting of the strikers, which consisted mostly of a 'long résumé of political complaints and aspirations'. He added:

> It was in fact a clear proof that the economic grievances, on which the leaders had induced the labourers to strike, had been relegated to the background, and that the movement had been converted into a political agitation.[18]

The chief culprit was singled out as Dr Manilal, who had arrived in Fiji in 1911 from Mauritius, to which he had gone in 1907 at the request of Mahatma Gandhi.[19] Manilal and his associates themselves indicated that Rodwell had not been scaremongering, sending to Milner on 13 March a petition in which they argued that 'repressive legislation . . . has been so practised as to terrorise and emasculate [sic] all Indians' and that 'the world is moving towards democracy and the vested interests in Fiji cannot stem the world tide reaching Indian labourers.' On 2 April Manilal wrote to the Colonial Secretary 'God save the Fiji government from the retribution due to their underlings or their exploiters the capitalists', and then on 10 April wrote to him again, putting his ideas and complaints in a more explicit context:

> 1. . . . I happened to read *Red Europe* by Frank Anstey MP Melbourne during this my exile and I am profoundly affected and arrive at the conclusion that the true place of every Indian must be in India and that there is no hope of gaining anything from European civilisation. In India, we must fight tooth and nail this European civilisation by the revival of our old spiritual life; otherwise Indians will be swallowed up like the rest of the world in the abysmal chaos of Capitalism or Imperialism, and God only knows, where that may lead.
>
> 2. I am charged with having said things, which Frank Anstey in his book charges against all governments concerned with the war – I am exiled, while he is re-voted into the Commonwealth Parliament.
>
> 3. Frank Anstey does not spare the highest and best in British

politics and I am condemned for raising my voice against certain occurrences in a small place like Fiji.[20]

So, according to his own testimony, if still more Gandhian than Bolshevik, Manilal was certainly aware of the Russian Revolution and influenced by it. Whether or not it was he to whom the New Zealander Thomas Feary made the suggestion in late 1919 of a Pacific association of Marxist organisations cannot be ascertained, but Feary undoubtedly communicated with an individual in Fiji as well as with groups in Canada, the USA and Australia.[21] Manilal was now to have the chance of talking to Feary (although whether or not he did so is unknown), for it was to New Zealand that he was deported on 15 April after a petition in favour of his release with 1500 signatures was rejected.[22] The persistence of revolutionary ideas in Fiji after his departure appears unlikely, and they were not likely to have been present in a strike in Rabaul, New Britain, still further to the west in Melanesia in 1929, even though the Administrator General E. A. Wisdom thought that the instigator might have been 'a religious fanatic or Bolshevik influence'.[23]

When we move from the South Pacific to the other area recently incorporated into the imperialist network, namely Africa, we find that pre-revolutionary Russia was among those involved in the great rivalry. Tsarist interest in the dark continent went back at least as far as Peter the Great, although it really gathered momentum towards the end of the nineteenth century along with the race for empire involving nearly all European nations. Yet Russia did not seek so much to establish colonies in the fastnesses of Africa as to prevent rivals, especially Great Britain, from establishing a stranglehold there. Initially aimed before this period at hindering the Turks or helping to establish trade routes by sea to the Orient, tsarist policy from the 1880s to about 1905 was concerned, in the words of a contemporary, 'to establish an Ethiopian Empire as a fortress and bulwark against Egypt, and to prevent the English colonies of Africa from becoming united . . .'. Influence in Ethiopia would be a restraint on Great Britain's monopoly control of the Suez Canal route and a hindrance to the implementation of her Cape to Cairo scheme. Thus Russia gave support to the Boers, as Nicholas II himself explained to his sister in 1899:

It is pleasant for me to know that the ultimate means of deciding the course of the war in South Africa lies entirely in my hands. It is very simple – just a telegraphic order to all the troops in Turkestan to mobilise and to advance towards the frontier [of India]. Not even the strongest fleet in the world can keep us from striking

England in that, her most vulnerable point.

Some of his advisers wanted to go even further, the former Boer general, Pinaar-Joubert, believing that the tsar and his government could establish a hold over the whole of Black Africa. 'Russia must be willing to declare itself suzerain of South and Central Africa', he maintained in 1905, putting forth the alluring prospect of 'a precious stone to add to the crown of Russia'. Economic and political realism prevailed, for Russia was hardly in a position in 1905 to embark upon an adventure far away from home with an adversary even stronger than the Japanese. But the British government for its part certainly took the Russian interest in Africa seriously enough for it to weigh heavily in calculations concerning world-wide imperial strategy. For example, as Winston Churchill pointed out later, a policy of conciliation towards Russia in China was followed in 1898 in order 'to influence the impending conflict on the Upper Nile and to make it certain, or at least likely, that when Great Britain and France should be placed in direct opposition, France should find herself alone'.

With the world crisis looming up towards 1914, Anglo-French and Anglo-Russian rivalries were pushed into the background and priorities given to African problems were placed much lower than before. But the First World War and the Revolutions of 1917 were by no means to end the Russian concern with tropical Africa. In the view of the author of a scholarly Western work on the subject:

> . . . in determining its political objectives in Africa and in choosing the means of achieving these objectives, the Soviet government was to repeat to a remarkable extent the experience of its predecessor. The opportunism of Czarist approach, the intensity of opposition to British colonial power, the recognition of the disruptive potential of indigenous nationalist movements, and the exploitation of Negro discontent were all to find their echo in postrevolutionary Russian policy.[24]

Of course, there were also important discontinuities, too, especially from the ideological point of view; the aims and beliefs of Soviet communism and of Western democracy were not completely in the same category as those of pre-First World War empires even if, as in all historical mutations, there are some untidy overlaps and indistinct borderlines. Moreover, in the years immediately following 1917, the weak Soviet Republic was hardly capable of embarking on a clear, energetic policy towards Black Africa; even if there was no shortage of arguments pressing in that direction, there was no social movement on the spot calling for prompt action.

Some sources suggest that there was no consciousness at all of the Russian Revolution in certain parts of West Africa. Dispatches from the Gold Coast in 1919, for example, talk of racial tension, criminal activity and even of civil disturbances. In February, our man out there reported unrest among local civil servants, who along with other complaints including the shortage of false teeth and hammocks, had objected to one of their British seniors as a 'Negrophobist'. Our man, Hugh Clifford, wrote that 'the Native Public Service . . . must be cleansed, I consider of the scum which is present at the top'. In May, he recommended that 'Owing to an increasing number of outrages by armed criminals strengthening of European staff is an urgent matter', and later in the year referred to civil disturbances, but without giving any details.[25] In none of these dispatches is there any suggestion of 'Communist' influence. Indeed although saluted by Soviet commentators as progressive, the political writing and activity in the Gold Coast at this time appears to have been nationalist rather than Marxist–Leninist. Finding a voice in what an early Soviet writer called a 'radical, indigenous press', West Africans wrote in the first number of the Gold Coast Independent in June 1918: 'There is a distinct public opinion taking shape in West African affairs today; it may be crude, rough-hewn, but it is growing and developing vigorously.' They asserted: 'The war has proved our loyalty, our equal sacrifices in lives and money.' Already in the second number, the Gold Coast Independent journalists wanted to know 'whether we shall develop as a free people under the Union Jack or be made hewers of wood and drawers of water'. What they themselves called a 'growing tide of public indignation' had led by March 1920 to the formation in Accra of the National Congress of British West Africa (NCBWA). The first modern organisation in African politics, the NCBWA was moderate and constitutional in its approach, sending a delegation to King George V in 1921 to ask why Africa had been excluded from the extension to his subject peoples of the right of self-determination, and another to the Council of the League of Nations with self-determination again in view. Here the spirit was predominantly that of Woodrow Wilson's Fourteen Points, from which one delegate extensively quoted, going on to say that the principle of self-determination had 'brooded over almost the whole of our continent' and was also 'the energising force which has brought into being the NCBWA'. But at least one commentator, discussing the part played by British Negro Africans in the war, suspected something more than the spirit of Wilsonian liberalism among them, talking of 'dangerous revolutionary tendencies'.[26]

None of these, if they existed, can be readily identified either in the Gold Coast, which we have chosen here for our specific example, or in Nigeria and the rest of British West Africa. The picture changes somewhat when we turn to consider British West Africa's French neighbour. There, although the prevailing spirit was less that of 1917 than of 1789 – a tradition arguably originating in the late eighteenth century when the cry of 'Vive Robespierre' went up in these colonies as well as in the metropolis –[27] we can also discover at least some positive evidence and more suggestion that the Communist message did quickly penetrate to Francophone West Africa. The carriers were the soldiers and other colonials, for the most part brought over to Europe to help with the winning of the war but to a minor extent making their way for other reasons as had Ho Chi Minh and Chou En-lai, two other more famous revolutionaries. Over tens of thousands of soldiers were recruited from French West Africa, and battalions of them made a contribution to the ultimate victory at Verdun and elsewhere. At the front and especially behind the lines they were exposed to political influences. Even such innocent occasions as the 14 July celebrations could not help but make an impact, but according to some observers, there were more sinister influences at work. The military censor in the Bordeaux region, for example, complained in 1916 of 'anarchist thoughts' among the Senegalese troops stationed locally, and Blaise Diagne, a collaborationist Negro parliamentary deputy, called one of the colonial officers in the French forces of occupation in Germany 'a Bolshevik Mahdi'. More significantly several hundred Senegalese and Algerians were sent along as part of the French interventionist force to Odessa and Sevastopol at the end of 1918. The story goes that several Blacks were converted to Bolshevism and went over to the Red side, one of them reputedly meeting a hero's death in a cavalry charge against the Whites. Boris Kornilov in his poem 'My Africa' describes this unknown warrior making his sacrifice 'in order to deal a blow to the African capitalists and bourgeoisie'. Others less adventurous took back home with them something of the message of October, including revolutionary songs. However, there was no immediate upsurge of activity in any way emulating October in French West Africa, nor indeed many 'African capitalists or bourgeoisie' to strike out against. Many of the swelling ranks of colonial *évolué* intelligentsia, if attracted to thoughts of opposition at all, warmed more to non-Communist movements such as Garveyism and Pan-Africanism, Black nationalist or internationalist in their composition. A much smaller number were attracted by the explicitly Marxist Union Intercoloniale, set up in Paris in 1921 by the future Ho Chi Minh, with the assistance of members of the French Communist Party and on behalf of all those from French colonies throughout the world.[28]

As in the case of tropical Africans, many Vietnamese made their acquaintance with socialism in the factories and trenches of the First World War, about 100,000 of them being sent to France at this time. Not only Ho Chi Minh but other leaders also served a revolutionary apprenticeship there, Ton Duc Thang becoming involved in a French naval revolt against intervention at Odessa and Nguyen Ai Quoc working towards the arguments to be contained in *Le Procès de la colonisation française*, including a powerful tribute to the lead and support of the Russian revolutionary régime. It was not until about ten years after October, however, that the desire for emulation began to take firm root in Indochina itself.[29]

In most of the rest of South-east Asia the movement would develop later, too. The major exception was the Dutch Indies, where the older faith of Islam joined the newer – Marxism – in a powerful combination by 1920. Nationalism was present along with Islam in the formation of the first political party, the Sarekat Islam formed in Japan in 1912. Two years later a group of Dutchmen, notably Sneevliet and Baars, attempted to set up for local radical workers the Social-Democratic Association of the Indies (ISDV) with its own journal, *Het Vrye Woord* ('The True Word'). This party was successful enough to alarm the colonial authorities, particularly after the Russian Revolution, and they sent Sneevliet into exile in 1918. Under the alias of Maring, he was the representative at the Second Congress of the Comintern of the Communist Party of the Indies (PKI), which Baars had helped to form from the ISDV in the spring of 1920. At first, the PKI operated within the ranks of the Sarekat Islam, but was able to gain a large measure of independence through securing the following of tens of thousands of workers, especially in the trade union movement. But the denunciation of Pan-Islamism at the Second Congress of the Comintern did it no good, and contributed to the failure of an attempted coup in 1926 and the subsequent destruction of the PKI. In any case somewhat foolhardy, the local Communists had not yet fully learned the lesson that they would have to take more notice of the traditional beliefs of their countrymen in their attempts to inculcate revolutionary ideology. The point was argued forcefully at the Fourth Congress of the Comintern in 1922:

At present, Pan-Islamism is a national-liberation struggle, because Islam for the Moslems is everything: not only religion, but also the State, the economic system, the food, in fact everything. Thus, Pan-Islamism now means the fraternity of all Mohammedan peoples and the liberation not only of the Arabian, but also the Indian, Javanese and all other oppressed Mohammedan peoples.

This fraternity is called the liberation struggle against the British, French and Italian capitalists, consequently against world capitalism. . . . This is our new task, and just as we are willing to support the national war, we shall also support the liberation struggle of the very active and energetic 250 million Mohammedans, who are subject to the Imperialist powers. Therefore, I ask once more if we should support Pan-Islamism in this sense, and in how far we are to support it.[30]

The question may have been of most pressing importance as far as Islam was concerned, but it had also to be considered when the other major religions of the world were involved, as well as when the equally powerful force of nationalism was at work. Such a consideration stands out clearly when we turn to look at the development of the Communist impulse in the great sub-continent of India. In this case, four major trends of development have been discerned. First there were the leaders working from abroad during the First World War and immediately afterwards, among whom the best known was M. N. Roy. Secondly there were the members of the Pan-Islamic Khilafat movement, some of whom also went away from home during the war. Thirdly there were Sikh and Punjabi migrant workers in the USA who under the influence of the IWW formed themselves into the Ghadar Party before the war, and staged an unsuccessful rising in their native land in early 1915. And fourthly there were left-wing members of the National Congress, of the Khilafat and other movements who stayed in India and searched for the organisation of a revolutionary party on the model of the Bolsheviks after the success of October. Moslem motives combined here with others – Hindu, Sikh, Christian and socialist.[31]

The Indian intelligentsia, that is an intelligentsia concerned with Western ideas, had been in existence since the early nineteenth century. Predominantly Bengali and Hindi, it had been receptive from an early date to the ideas of Paine and Bentham, and had debated these and others in such organisations as the Society for Acquisition of General Knowledge formed towards the end of the 1830s. A specifically socialist element entered the thought of the Indian intelligentsia at about the time of the Paris Commune. Also in 1871 an application was made from Calcutta for membership of the First International (see the *Eastern Post* of 19 August). Permission was granted on 5 September to the applicants, some or all of whom may have been Europeans. Shivanath Shastri, already a member of the Brahmo Samaj group, formed about five years later an Egalitarian Group whose aim was the creation of 'communism'. Great writers such as Bankin Chandra Chatterji and Rabindranath

Tagore discussed questions of socialism as well as nationalism in a manner which could loosely be called populist. Under their influence many members of the intelligentsia rediscovered their own people through personal contact and through the revival of classics such as the *Bhagavad-Ghita*. The state of mind among young intellectuals was well represented by a nephew of Tagore's who gave his support to a strike among Bombay railway signallers in 1899 and was soon afterwards writing about his aversion to industrialisation in general.[32]

As elsewhere in the Third World it was the Russo-Japanese War and the closely linked Revolution of 1905 that gave the first real impetus to the independence movement in India, breathing unprecedented vigour, for example, into the National Congress which had begun a fairly moderate campaign for constitutional reform twenty years earlier. At the opening of the Congress of 1906 the moderate 'grand old man of India' Dadabhai Nairoji asked:

At the very time that China in East Asia, and Persia in West Asia, are awakening, when Japan has already awakened, and Russia is struggling for liberation from despotism, is it possible for the free citizens of the British Empire in India – the people who were among the first to create world civilisation – to continue to remain under the yoke of despotism?

From the other side, Sir Valentine Chirol posed the following question concerning the Russo-Japanese War: 'If the young Asiatic David could smite down the European Goliath, what might not 300 million Indians dare to achieve?' But it would be wrong to single out that war as a great stimulus separate from or superior to the other sources of inspiration for these 300 million. Moslems were excited by developments in the Ottoman Empire, and the burgeoning of Arab as well as Persian political consciousness, which in turn were all connected with events in other parts of the world, including the vast northern neighbour Russia. Moslem and Hindu alike were fired with enthusiasm by the Revolution of 1905, opposition to the tsarist régime 'opening the floodgates of the people's movement'. Now 'the people of India began to realise that the English would not be influenced in the least by the academic debate and discussions that were carried on by the Indian National Congress'.[33]

Among the 300 million, members of the intelligentsia would be more aware than others of the course that history was taking in various parts of the world, but in India itself a new excitement managed to communicate itself to at least some members of the small industrial working class and the vast rural peasantry. A key figure in this conjuncture was Bal Gangadhar Tilak, 'the real symbol of the new age' according to Jawaharlal Nehru. Tilak stood for a distinctive blend of Hindu culture with modern political action – the best means of achieving independence and a true rebirth of that culture. In his newspaper *Kesari* Tilak made frequent comparison between tsarist rule in Russia and British rule in India, and stressed the consequent necessity for the opposition to the latter to take up the approach of the opposition to the former. Arrested for his agitation in 1908, he declared: 'Once the Government resorts to repressive measures in the Russian spirit, then the Indian subjects of England must imitate, at least in part, the methods of the Russian people.'[34] Strikes of sympathy for Tilak in Bombay showed that his words were not going unheeded, and the news of them reached as far as Lenin, who wrote:

The Indian masses are beginning to come out into the streets in defence of their native writers and political leaders. The despicable sentence that the English jackals passed on the Indian democrat Tilak (he was sentenced to a long term of exile and in reply to a question in the House of Commons, it was revealed that the Indian Jurymen voted for his acquittal whereas the conviction was passed by the votes of the English jurymen!), this act of vengeance against a democrat on the part of the lackeys of the moneybags gave rise to street demonstrations and a strike in Bombay. The Indian proletariat too has already sufficiently matured to wage a class-conscious and political mass struggle and that being the case, Anglo-Russian methods in India are played out.[35]

Unrest, including violence and terrorism, continued down to the First World War, many of those involved owing their allegiance to 'Maharishi Marx'. But yet again as in Russia and many other parts of the world it was the outbreak of world war in 1914 that constituted the next important step in the development of the Indian revolutionary movement. M. N. Roy put the subsequent situation thus:

On the outbreak of the First World War in 1914, Indian revolutionaries in exile looked towards Germany as the land of hope and rushed there, full of expectations. By the end of the year, the news reached us in India that the Indian Revolutionary Committee in Berlin had obtained from the German Government the promise of arms and money required to declare the war of independence. The news spread like wildfire, to affect the Indian soldiers of the British army also. Revolution was round the corner, although we had the vaguest possible idea about the things to come; in any case independence was within reach. The imagined imminence of the attainment of the common goal induced several secret revolutionary organisations to compose their traditional feuds. Clandestine conferences led to the formation of the general staff of the coming revolution.[36]

Even in 1914 the Committee in Berlin insisted in its agreement with the German government that: 'If our revolution is successful, we shall strive to establish a communist republic in India and the Austro-German powers shall have no right to interfere in our efforts.'[37] There was no clear view about what shape this 'communist republic' would take, and no unanimous agreement that it should be set up at all, but there were certainly centres of Indian revolutionary activity not only in Berlin but also in Constantinople (after Turkey came into the war on the side of the central powers), Kabul in Afghanistan (for many years a centre of anti-British activity), and Stockton, California, USA (the headquarters of the Ghadar Party). From Constantinople attempts were made to infiltrate the Indian army detachments fighting the Turks in the Middle East. In Kabul a 'provisional government of independent India' was set up, and support sought not only from local Pathan tribes, but also from Germany, the tsar of Russia and then Kerensky. The Ghadar Party staged an unsuccessful rebellion in the Indian army in 1915, and also tried to run guns in to support other anti-British action.

The February Revolution acted as a further stimulus to seditious activity. On 24 May 1917 the British ambassador to Sweden sent home the following confidential telegram:

Papers recently reported arrival from Berlin of certain Indian nationalists under the head of V. Chattopadhyaya who stated in an interview that he was not concerned with peace propaganda but was working for self-government for India, independent of British control.
I was informed today that a nationalist conference will shortly take place instigated by Finns and representatives of various Russian nationalities, which these Indians will take part in.
Informant stated that Germans were behind it and that probably intention was to get Lenin or other anti-English Russian extremists to work up the Indian independence movement in Russia.[38]

Back home the Commonweal Office in Madras produced a pamphlet entitled *The Lesson from Russia: A Few Notes on the Effect of the Russian Revolution on the Problem of Home Rule for India*. The preface declared: 'What moral grit the stricken peasant of Russia displayed will be an inspiration to the equally if not more stricken peasant of India.' And later in the main part of the pamphlet there was the ringing assertion: 'The Sun of Liberty rose for the children of Nippon a few years ago; it has been rising for waking China; it is now rising for the Russians. Our hour is approaching – India too shall soon be free. . . .' Having learned more of the agitation abroad at Stockholm and elsewhere and the continued dissatisfaction in the subcontinent itself, Lord Sydenham felt bound to write in the *Sunday Times* of 21 October 1917: 'During the last three years we were threatened with the most dangerous and desperate Indian revolution since the great Mutiny of 1857.'

This was before the October Revolution, which would produce even greater levels of excitation among both Indian radicals and their opponents. The pro-government *Statesman* was soon proffering its view that:

> The Acts of the Russian Revolutionary Committee now constitute in their collectivity what is certainly the most rapid and bids fair to be the most comprehensive movement of subversion of which any historical state has been subject.[39]

And the government itself responded to the new challenge with what has been called its traditional policy of the carrot and the stick. The carrot was the Montagu–Chelmsford constitutional reform of 1918–19 denounced by the Congress movement as 'Inadequate, unsatisfactory, disappointing'. The stick was the Report of the Sedition Committee which sat under Justice Rowlatt, and put forward the Rowlatt Bill which proposed 'a régime of draconic repression and complete suppression of elementary democratic rights and liberties'.[40] Even the stick appeared inadequate as the high prices and wage reductions of economic slump led to great strikes after the end of the war in Ahmedabad, Bombay, Calcutta and Madras, and widespread peasant disturbance. Mahatma Gandhi who was making his way on to the national stage, led the striking textile workers of Ahmedabad and the dissident peasants of Champaran, and called for a countrywide protest against the Rowlatt Bill on 6 April 1919. Support for this 'hartal' was fairly general, and an alarmed government responded with the machine-gunning of thousands of unarmed demonstrators and the consequent killing of about five hundred of them in Jalianwalla Bagh, an almost completely enclosed square in Amritsar on 13 April. Martial law was introduced into the Punjab, and an extreme tension threatened further violence. At the National Congress meeting in Amritsar in December 1919 proposals were made for sweeping land reforms, and the government's intelligence bureau pointed out that 'Russian pro-Bolshevik practice in the

matter of division of land' would appeal very much to the Indian peasants. Increasingly Congress members were coming to think that no
real possibility of such reforms would present itself until independence was achieved.[41]

Meanwhile there were important developments among the Indian
revolutionaries abroad. The Berlin Indian Independence Committee
was now wound up, and several of its members made their way to
Soviet Russia. Lenin was host to an Indian delegation in May 1919,
and told them to avoid the path of 'Tolstoyism':

> In our country too Tolstoy and others tried for the emancipation
> of the people by propagating religion, but nothing came of it. So
> after returning to India you propagate class struggle, that will clear
> the path of liberation.[42]

Differences of attitude such as this apart, the meeting between Lenin
and the Indian revolutionaries was constructive and strengthened
the ties between them as well as leading forward towards the formation of the Communist Party of India (CPI). The leader of the delegation and head of the 'provisional government' in Kabul, Mahendra
Pratap, went off at once – according to his own account – as com-
panion to the Soviet ambassador to Afghanistan which had just
declared its independence and therefore found itself briefly at war
again with Great Britain. The others were soon at work either in central Asia with political agitation or in Moscow helping with the activities of the Comintern.[43]

Between its Amritsar session in December 1919 and its next session in Nagpur in December 1920 the National Congress came fully
to its new resolve: *Swaraj* or independence through non-cooperation
led by Gandhi, as well as the righting of pressing wrongs in the
Punjab and elsewhere. A further feature of the Nagpur session was a
new spirit of unity between Hindus and Moslems. The Pan-Islamic
Khilafat movement was agitated not only by frustrations in India
but also by the dismemberment of the Ottoman Empire, which
threatened the sanctity of Mecca and Medina, the holy places. So
while the All-India Khilafat Committee gave its full support to non-
cooperation, it could not help giving much of its attention to events
vital to its religion in the Middle East.

Ironically under pressure from Kemal Pasha, and post-war
events, Khilafat motives were being downplayed in Turkey itself
and more secular aims placed to the fore. Undeterred by such circumstances, or possibly quite ignorant of them, thousands of Moslems from the Punjab and other areas joined in a holy movement –
Hijrat or *Hegira* – to join in the struggle for the protection of the

centre of their religion away from their home where it seemed that the Moslem faith was unable to be free. Vast numbers of emigrants arrived in Afghanistan in the spring and summer of 1920. Most of them returned to India before the end of the year, but a determined handful set off through Soviet Russia to join Kemal Pasha. They were captured and enslaved on the way by counter-revolutionary Turcomans, but were soon then left to fend for themselves in the desert. They managed to make contact with Red detachments and fought with them against the Turcomans. A few may finally have achieved their aim of breaking through to Kemal Pasha, but at least some stayed in Soviet Central Asia.[44]

Here they were able to join an 'Army of Liberation' being directed towards Afghanistan by M. N. Roy, who in the face of Lenin's scepticism had been able to requisition for his purpose two trainloads of men, arms, munitions and money. At the beginning of October 1920 these supplies were used as the basic equipment for an Indian Military School in Tashkent but also, in the words of M. N. Roy, were to lead to wider triumphs for Soviet power: 'Indian revolutionaries would carry the message of the Russian revolution to their countries, which would surely inspire the Indian masses to undertake heroic actions for overthrowing the British rule.'[45] The British government was alarmed at the news, and Lord Curzon wrote a passionate protest in December 1920,[46] while the rupture of the Anglo-Russian trade talks then in progress could be used as a threat. But the failure of the Indian Military School was both the result of the inadequacy in numbers and aptitude of its students and the hostile attitude of the Afghan government, which Lenin had predicted:

> King Amanullah was not a revolutionary. He was shrewd enough to see that he could profit by pretending to be anti-British. But the opportunist policy would ultimately lead him to a deal with the highest bidder, and the British could pay more. Then, there was the decisive consideration that, in the last analysis, King Amanullah had more in common with the British rulers of India than the Russian Bolshevik regime.[47]

So although Amanullah addressed Lenin as the 'High-Born President of the Great Russian Republic' and Lenin greeted Amanullah with a compliment to Afghanistan as 'the only independent state in the world', relations between the two were never as close as optimists such as Roy had hoped. But nor was Afghanistan the puppet of the imperialists. Rather, as treaties were signed with the Soviet government in February 1921 and with the British government in November of the same year, there was the gradual realisation from both London and Moscow that 'an independent Afghanistan might serve as a barrier and a buffer, rather than as a bone of contention between them'. Chicherin attempted to reassure the still highly suspicious Curzon of this emerging stalemate at the Lausanne Conference in December 1922:

> You are uneasy because our horsemen have reappeared on the heights of the Pamirs, and because you no longer have to deal with the half-witted Tsar who ceded the ridge of the Hindu Kush to you in 1895. But it is not war that we offer you, it is peace, based on the principles of a partition wall between us.[48]

The Indian Military School at Tashkent was a failure as such, but it did produce several of the first members of the CPI, which numbered no more than ten in its ranks at the time of its foundation in Tashkent in October 1920. Roy was very much involved in the formation of the CPI, but was not its chief or sole instigator; Moslem emigrants and other Indian revolutionaries were also involved. Before this time the government already had at its disposal 'officers specially appointed for counter-propaganda, co-ordination of intelligence, both internal and external, and organisational measures to keep Bolshevist emissaries and propaganda out of India'.[49] To some extent, these appointments were made as part of the campaign of intervention, with emissaries and propaganda being sent into Soviet Russia. Moreover, an energetic attempt was made in the pro-government Indian press to blacken Bolshevism.[50] Such activity notwithstanding, the *rapprochement* of the National Congress with Communist elements already detectable in 1919 became more pronounced in the early 1920s. At the Gaya session of the National Congress in December 1922 Singaravelu, the Madras labour leader, declared:

> Comrades, first and foremost we have one thing to do – that is we have to attain Swaraj and the method which we can use in attaining Swaraj is non-violent non-cooperation. That method has been disputed by our fellow Communists abroad. I told them that we have adopted this method as a practical necessity and that I believed in that method. . . . We, the Communists in India differ from our fellow Communists in this fundamental method.[51]

In 1923 Singaravelu formed a political party both attached to the National Congress and adhering to the principles of communism – the Labour Kisan Party.

And throughout the 1920s, while the government reacted and

over-reacted to any suggestion of a Bolshevik conspiracy in India, discussions among worker and peasant opposition alike led towards the setting-up of the Communist Party in India. While relations with the National Congress were by no means always harmonious, the Communists were widely recognised as playing an important part in the struggle for *Swaraj*, Jawahalal Nehru himself writing in his *Autobiography*:

> It is difficult to be patient with many Communists; they have developed a peculiar method of irritating others. But ... I have always admired their great courage and capacity for sacrifice ... the real understanding Communist develops to some extent an organic sense of social life. Politics for him cease to be a mere record of opportunism and groping in the dark. The ideals and objectives he works for, give a meaning to the struggle and to the sacrifices he willingly faces. He feels that he is part of a grand army marching forward to realise human fate and destiny. . . .[52]

Conversely, as we have seen, at least some Indian revolutionaries were prepared to adapt their thinking to the 'Tolstoyan' religiosity of Gandhiism and to show respect for the Mahatma himself. Even the government gave some recognition to the chief proponent of *Swaraj* through *Satyagahra*. There may have been an element of political astuteness here, an advocate of passive resistance being patently preferable as the leader of an independent movement to the preachers of revolutionary violence. Yet colonial administrators, too, were capable of idealism as well as conscientious devotion to what they believed to be the best interests of the area under their jurisdiction. The framers of the Montagu–Chelmsford constitutional reforms at the end of the First World War were largely guided by their belief in the super-eminence of parliamentary government as were their successors during the inter-war period and after the Second World War.[53] And Gandhi himself believed in parliamentary government as well as in non-violent resistance as the best way of gaining it and independence.

From India we could move with equal ease and appropriateness to what the Western world has been accustomed to call the Far East or Middle East. This would still be so if we left India as we arrived, discussing Pan-Islamism. For even before 1914 that movement had reached almost global proportions. After the Russo-Japanese War students from Turkey went to Japan and helped develop the publication there of a Moslem newspaper, their heads full of the idea of a blend of their religion with the driving force of the conquerors of Russia. And China too was held up as an example for Moslems and the formation of an alliance with the Middle Kingdom was recommended, this argument gaining increased persuasiveness with the outbreak of the Chinese Revolution in 1911. Perhaps, although far more is involved here than the Pan-Moslem movement, we should first direct our attention towards Mecca.

In the Middle East, as well as new directions in the principal religion of the area, there was an upsurge in nationalism at the beginning of the twentieth century. And contiguity with Soviet Russia was to add an important further element to the sweeping changes taking place. When the sick man of Europe – the Ottoman Empire – died soon after its erstwhile largest neighbour and chief opponent – the Russian Empire – the time appeared to many to be ripe for revolution in Turkey and elsewhere in the Middle East. Already in 1905 there were strong-enough rumblings for a thorough political earthquake to threaten the régimes in both Turkey and Iran, to take just two examples.

For some years before 1905 the Young Turk movement had been kept firmly under control and the constitution of 1876 rendered a dead letter. Sultan Abdul Hamid II was determined to keep this satisfactory situation unchanged, and therefore did all he could to keep news of the inflammatory events from spreading through his empire, especially concerning those which had occurred on the other side of the Black Sea. He therefore took steps to make sure that the rebellious crew of the *Potemkin* did not take that notorious warship through the Straits. Coffee houses where rumours might be spread by word of mouth were closed, and journalists were prohibited not only from reporting the 'outrages', but even from mentioning the word 'Russian'. Special steps were also taken to stop the spread of revolution from Iran, including the dispatch of troops there.

For all the sultan's preventive measures, the insidious message did break through. Twenty-eight officers in the Turkish army and navy sent the following message of condolence to the family of Lieutenant Schmidt, the leader of the Sevastopol uprising, soon after his execution:

We too make a pledge to the great citizen Schmidt. We make a vow over his corpse, which is dear to us and to the Russian people. We swear that we will fight to the last drop of blood for sacred, civic freedom, for which cause many of our great citizens have perished. We vow that we will exert all our strength and means to acquaint the Turkish people with events in Russia, so that by our common effort we may achieve the right for ourselves to live as human beings.

(What became of the twenty-eight is unknown; certainly the letter was seized by the tsarist police before it reached the Schmidt family.) Moreover the rise of political consciousness among Russian Moslems in 1905 could not help but cross the frontiers of Turkey, especially since there was a considerable amount of human traffic across them. Again the sultan tried to seal off such pernicious penetration, but without success. By 1908 pressure within Turkey from the Young Turk movement, the Moslem leadership and more popular sources was so great that the Constitution of 1876 was revived, and in early 1909 Abdul Hamid was obliged to leave the throne in favour of his brother. But there was no unanimity among the opponents of the sultan. Some, like Mustafa Kemal, wanted the Ottoman Empire to be dismantled and a strong Turkish state set up; others, including émigré Russian Moslems, supported the idea of Pan-Turkism, which would involve the acquisition of parts of the Russian Empire; a few, mainly in Salonika and Paris, kept alive the belief in socialist internationalism.[54]

Meanwhile, in Iran, the Russian Revolution of 1905 'had a most astounding effect', according to a contemporary observer on the spot, who continued:

> Events in Russia have been watched with great attention, and a new spirit would seem to have come over the people. They are tired of their rulers, and taking example of Russia, have come to think that it is possible to have another and better form of government.

More than in the case of Turkey, migrant workers to Transcaucasia and Transcaspia brought back inflammatory views and supported opposition to the shah. The impetus for reform also came in the early stages from Moslem leaders who found the shah's policies infringing on their privileges. And so, after wide protests in 1905 and again in 1906, the shah granted a constitution including the election of a consultative National Assembly – the *Majlis*. This was enough for conservatives, but well short of sufficiency for liberals, 'the salt of the Assembly' centred in Iranian Azerbaidzhan, especially Tabriz.

The dénouement of the Iranian Revolution has to be seen in a wider context. First the Anglo-Russian Entente of 1907, whereby Iran was divided into spheres of influence, signalled the determination of two empires to stop subversion in the face of the threat of a powerful rival – Germany. Second, 'unofficially' supported by counter-revolutionary elements in Russia, a Persian Cossack Brigade (with Russian officers) blew up the *Majlis* in 1908. Tabriz held out with the support of Baku Social Democrats, and the tsarist government sent a force from the same city to break the siege in the spring of

1909. In July an insurgent march on Tehran led to the seizure of the capital and the overthrow of the shah, but the revival of the *Majlis* could not lead to much progress in the face of a threat of further Russian incursions and the Russian occupation of 1911 spelt the complete demise of the spirit of 1905.[55]

The presence of up to 17,000 Russian troops in Iran in 1914 led to a strained relationship with Turkey; then, in 1917 as in 1905, under the impact of war and revolution, more problems were posed. Turkey enjoyed mixed fortunes as ally to the Central Powers, but appeared to be doing very well with the Treaty of Brest-Litovsk, which handed over to it sections of southern Transcaucasia. With the collapse of the Central Powers however, British forces in the Middle East were able to restore a stability favourable to British interests. And Soviet Russia, publishing the secret treaties and disclaiming any legacy of ambitions for expansion from the tsarist and provisional governments, was able to appeal for Turkish friendship. In a radio broadcast to the 'workers and peasants of Turkey' on 13 September 1919 Chicherin declared:

> The way is open for England to seize on the Muslim states small and great, with a view to their enslavement. Already she is running things as she pleases in Persia, in Afghanistan, in the Caucasus, and in your country. Since the day when your government surrendered the Straits to the disposal of England, there has been no independent Turkey, no historic Turkish city of Istanbul on the mainland of Europe, no independent Ottoman nation.

Fraternal co-operation was offered and an invitation 'to expel the European robbers by simultaneous and combined force, and to destroy and render powerless those within the country who have become accustomed to build their fortune on your misfortune'.[56]

But the Bolsheviks were being overtaken by a new movement which had also stolen many of their clothes. Announcing his purpose in August 1919 and building up his strength in Anatolia where he had been army commander, Mustafa Kemal Ataturk soon acquired much support for his nationalist programme which also included many social reforms. A considerable number of his avowed aims, such as industrial and cultural revolution, recalled the programme of Lenin; some of them, such as the adoption of the Western calendar and a Western script, brought back memories of Peter the Great. The father of the new Turkey certainly leaned on Soviet support, but had no intention of succumbing to it.

Kemal and Lenin could co-operate to keep the imperialists out of their part of the world, but could not agree on how to divide it between themselves. Both had promised self-determination to minority peoples within their boundaries, but both were becoming reluctant to allow such a choice to be made in a world where departure from one sphere of influence would almost certainly mean entrance into another. As Kemal consolidated his power in Anatolia and moved towards British-occupied Istanbul, he could readily agree with Lenin that it was inimical to both their interests to acquiesce in the Allied plans for the unrestricted opening of the Straits into the Black Sea and the creation of buffer states in Transcaucasia. But where should frontiers be fixed? And could there be co-operation anyway between a Communist leader and a bourgeois nationalist?

The attempt of Kemal's rival, Enver, to secure the support of the Second Congress of the Communist International and the formation of the Turkish Communist Party in the summer of 1920 produced further embarrassments. Co-operation between Turkish Communists and nationalists was partly successful but mainly uneasy, and came to an end with the throwing into the sea of most of the leaders of the former in early 1921. Nevertheless, these problems and those of the frontiers were sufficiently solved for a Soviet–Turkish Treaty to be signed in March 1921, the same time exactly as the conclusion of the Anglo-Russian Trade Treaty and generally as the introduction of the New Economic Policy. A Greek invasion of Turkey with British support was sufficiently successful for the Soviet government at last to give help for the expulsion of the foreigners, but Kemal continued to show in negotiations concerning the integrity of Turkey and the opening of the Straits that he would not be the puppet of either the Western powers or of the Soviet Union. Indeed, he himself pulled some of the strings.[57]

Persia was occupied by British forces during the war, and accepted a thinly disguised protectorate in the summer of 1919. The Soviet government had renounced tsarist spheres of interest, but did not welcome such immediate advantage of the renunciation being taken by an interventionist. Chicherin made a declaration to the Persian 'workers and peasants' similar to that which he would make to their Turkish counterparts a month or so later. The first emissaries from Soviet Russia to Persia were turned back or shot, but a firm foothold was gained by Soviet troops in the northernmost province of Gilan in the spring of 1920 as they contributed to the establishment of a pro-Soviet republic under a colourful leader, Kuchik Khan. This wayward fanatic was more nationalist than Communist, but more hopes could soon be held out for the Communist Party of Persia set up under his protection in July. But as in the case of Turkey, Soviet support for local Communists was abandoned in favour of *rapprochement* with the bourgeois nationalists, this time with a group including

Riza Khan which seized power in Tehran in February 1921. Negotiations already in process with the preceding government were now concluded, and the Soviet–Persian Treaty was signed on 26 February 1921. Soviet hands would be kept off Persia as long as the hands of the British and others were kept off too. Some embarrassment was caused Moscow when Kuchik Khan marched on Tehran with the support of his local Soviet advisers in the summer of 1921; there was some relief when the attempted coup failed, and even approval when the republic of Gilan was re-occupied by Persian forces in October, and Kuchik Khan hanged. There was some ruffling of the waters over the question of Persian oil and concessions to capitalists and over that of how far the Red Flag might follow or at least influence the pattern of Soviet–Persian trade, but an amicable-enough resolution was achieved in both cases, for the time being at least.[58]

The Arab peoples were certainly in turmoil in the immediate aftermath of the First World War, but the influence among them of the Russian Revolution appears to have been less strong than that among their neighbours in the Middle East. This was partly because they did not share a frontier with Russia, as did Turkey and Iran, partly because some of their frontiers in general were still unfixed and the necessity for 'bourgeois nationalism' – here overlaid by Pan-Islamism or Pan-Arabism – was even greater than elsewhere in the region. Of course, there was some significant development. For example, in late 1920 three people from newly formed socialist groups came together in Alexandria to form what was to become the Communist Party of Egypt in 1922. A membership of hundreds rather than thousands (mostly Arabs) sent one of their number to the Third Congress of the Comintern and they accepted the '21 conditions' of affiliation to it. An early appeal to the 'manual and non-manual workers of the world' attacked the 'brutal aggression by which British militarist and colonial officials have replied to the sacred demands of Egypt' and promised that 'the Egyptian intellectual proletariat will cease all collaboration with the oppressors'. There were 'bourgeois nationalist' overtones here which would prevent the Party from being completely orthodox, but it was considered dangerous enough for it to be driven underground in 1924. Elsewhere among Arabs there were no greater signs of activity before that date.[59]

We must move over Asia to what the Western world was accustomed to call the Far East and, having already considered briefly Japan as an outlier of the Western world, we must now concentrate on China. This sleeping giant had begun to stir itself at the middle of the nineteenth century, to a considerable extent in response to the prompting of an increased amount of foreign incursion. The Taiping

Rebellion (1851–1864) was at once a millenarian movement and something more down to earth in such features as: the replacement of Confucianism by a mixture of Christian and indigenous beliefs; the advocacy of agrarian communism, especially collective cultivation of the land; and the espousal of enlightened doctrines (sex equality and the prohibition of concubines, arranged marriages, foot-binding and opium-smoking). The Taiping Rebellion was followed by restoration and reaction, but the continuance of imperialist pressures and the rapid defeat of China by Japan in the War of 1894–5 led to the movement of the summer of 1898 known as the Hundred Days Reform, and then to the Boxer Rebellion which reached its peak in 1899–1900, a more popular if less enlightened movement than the Reform.[60]

The westernised intelligentsia seized its chance again after the defeat of Russia by Japan, which was much more popular in China around 1905 than a decade before or, indeed, a decade later. For, taking its chance in 1915 with the notorious '21 demands' undermining China's very independence, Japan was to receive as much execration as the imperialist powers of the West. Sun Yat-sen said later in a speech in 1924, that in 1905, 'We regarded the Japanese victory as our own victory. It was indeed a happy event.' Returning to Tokyo from Europe in that year, he formed what has been called 'the first league of Chinese intellectuals in modern times'. And, for Mao Tse-tung, 'The anti-imperialist, anti-feudal, bourgeois–democratic revolution in China, strictly speaking, began with Sun Yat-sen.'

That other great revolutionary leader, Lenin, considered that Sun Yat-sen was 'apparently wholly unfamiliar with Russia' and that his analysis of the problems confronting China was 'completely independent of Russia, of Russian experience, of Russian literature'. And yet the league's newspaper *Min-pao* published from 1905–10 included many articles on Russia, some by Sun Yat-sen himself. In the fourth issue, for example, a contributor declared:

> The revolutionary storm in Russia has profoundly shaken the entire world. . . . Although the peoples of Russia have not yet received freedom, the domestic policy has changed, and this in turn has exercised a great influence on the reform movement in China.[61]

Sun Yat-sen and his colleagues, it needs to be emphasised, were bourgeois nationalists rather than radicals, Kadets rather than Bolsheviks, yet their Revolution of 1911 was an important step forward in the political consciousness of the Chinese people, an echo of 1905, even if for Mao it was 'a miscarriage' rather than a 'dress rehearsal'.[62]

The Manchu dynasty had ended six years before the Romanovs, but the Chinese proletariat had not awakened as much as the Russian, nor was the intelligentsia keen to rouse it. A scholarly assessment of this élite concludes:

> As a class their interest lay in Westernizing reform, but the prerequisite for such reform was social stability. In 1911, their primary and immediate concern was the preservation of law and order. That would remain their primary concern so long as their power was threatened by popular forces in the army, the secret societies, or the urban masses. Yet the very nature of the urban elite's reform program virtually guaranteed that popular opposition would exist, and that opposition would be met with a repressive concern for law and order. It was a vicious circle which not only precluded the possibility of unity between the elite and the masses, but increasingly drove the elite to the right in its effort to secure its own power.[63]

Thus the élite soon put its trust in a 'strong man', Yuan Shi-kai, and when he fell in 1916 the way was open for the warlords, a succession of whom appointed their own civil governments.

No immediate threat was posed to China after the February Revolution, still less after its successor in October. Already before 1917 the Russian imperial government had been losing its grip on the Far East, and the ensuing disturbances loosened that grip still more. This process, which has already been examined in chapter 4, resulted in a much slighter immediate impact of the Communist message on the Far East than had been hoped. However loud and colourful the oratory in Moscow or Baku, it was only faintly heard in Peking. And yet the Bolshevik example did influence the nature of the formation of the Chinese Communist Party, and some useful contacts were made with its founders in very difficult circumstances by Soviet emissaries.

Soon after October the Soviet government was making overtures to China for the negotiation of new treaties to replace the old, but in March 1918, according to a later Soviet complaint, the Allies 'seized the Peking government by the throat', compelling it to abandon relations with that in Moscow. Continued announcements of goodwill from the Kremlin were listened to with more attentiveness after the Allies favoured Japan rather than China in their settlement at Versailles in the spring of 1919. With the Red Army now pushing the forces of Admiral Kolchak back into Siberia, a declaration was made that it would bring about 'liberation from the yoke of the foreign bayonet, from the yoke of foreign gold'. The unequal treaties imposed by tsarism were denied again, and the affirmation was made that:

> The Soviet Government returns to the Chinese people without any kind of compensation the Chinese Eastern Railway, and all gold mining, and forestry concessions, which were seized from them by the government of the Tsar by the Kerensky government, by the outlaws Horvath, Semenov, Kolchak, and the Russian generals, merchants and capitalists.[64]

The declaration was received with enthusiasm in China, even though it took eight months to reach there. But the course of Sino-Soviet relations did not run nearly as smoothly as these promising beginnings suggested. Problems connected with the Red Army's advance into Mongolia, delay in the transfer of the Chinese Eastern Railway and fear of Communist infiltration were of concern to a series of Chinese governments and were still not completely solved after the first top-level mission of Ioffe in 1922, even though American pressure for Japanese withdrawal from the mainland had given Soviet diplomacy some excellent opportunities. Ioffe was certainly given an enthusiastic reception, especially at Peking University, where the chancellor declared at a banquet in his honour:

> The Chinese revolution was a political one. Now it is tending towards the direction of a social revolution. Russia furnishes a good example to China, which thinks it advisable to learn the lessons of the Russian Revolution, which started also as a political movement but later assumed the nature of a social revolution. Please accept the hearty welcome of the pupil to his teachers.[65]

Against a background of limited rapprochement, was the Chinese revolution making the kind of progress estimated by the Peking University Chancellor? He may well have been influenced in his judgement by the circumstance that it was at his institution in the winter of 1918 that a group of students encouraged by some outstanding liberal professors launched a new journal called *New Tide*, a title expressly defined in an early number as the October Revolution and its wider implications.[66] But students at Peking University were as much nationalist as communist. This was clearly shown by the May Fourth Movement launched there in 1919 in protest at the transfer by the Paris Peace Conference of Germany's rights in Shantung to Japan rather than China. This movement came to involve a renewed and more penetrative attack on the old ways. An offshoot from it was the Communist Party of China, which held its first congress in

Shanghai in the summer of 1921, and which was at first neither uniformly pro-Soviet or even completely Marxist, but, like the May Fourth Movement, predominantly formed by intellectuals with a wide range of views.[67]

A new element appeared to come into the situation with the first genuine mass strike in Chinese history, in Hong Kong during the early months of 1922. The Communist Party was far from being the most important at this time; although the strike did increase its strength and influence to some degree, Sun Yat-sen's Kuomintang – itself partly influenced by the Bolshevik model – was considerably more powerful. And so the Chinese Communist Party entered into its fateful alliance with the Kuomintang, the way prepared by Sneevliet and confirmed by Ioffe, who with Sun Yat-sen issued a joint statement in early 1923, including the following explanation:

Dr. Sun Yat-sen holds that neither the communistic order nor the Soviet system can actually be introduced into China, because there do not exist here the conditions necessary for the successful establishment of either communism or Sovietism. This view is entirely shared by Mr. Ioffe who is further of the opinion that China's paramount and most pressing problem is to achieve national unification and attain full national independence; and in connection with this great task, he has assured Dr. Sun Yat-sen that China has the warmest sympathy of the Russian People and can count on the support of Russia.[68]

If China was not ripe for proletarian revolution, its neighbouring states such as Korea and Outer Mongolia could hardly be expected to be more mature, although the foundation of the Communist Party of Korea and the Mongolian People's Party in 1920 pointed the way forward to later Red harvests.[69] Everywhere throughout Asia October's influence had been felt. As K. M. Panikkar puts it:

That the Russian Revolution quickened the pulse of the peoples of Asia no one would deny. That it also helped to awaken the masses, to create doubts in the minds of thinking people about the validity of many things which they had accepted without question from the West, could not also be doubted. Equally it would be accepted that its general effect was to weaken the hold of the West on the peoples of Asia.[70]

Panikkar goes on to point out that the impact would vary from one section of the continent to another. Nobody could argue with this either, although it would take some years before the differentiation became clear. In great countries and in others not so great, the Communist movements were often small, even minute, yet in the fevered atmosphere of the post-war world their potential was often exaggerated by themselves and their opponents. In the longer run, Communist confidence and capitalist concern both received ample justification.

Finally we move to Latin America, which was included by John Reed in a speech made by him at the Baku Congress of the Peoples of the East in September 1920:

> You, the peoples of the East, the peoples of Asia, have not yet experienced for yourselves the rule of America. You know and hate the British, French and Italian imperialists, and probably you think that 'free America' will govern better, will liberate the peoples of the colonies, will feed and defend them.
> No, the workers and peasants of the Philippines, the peoples of Central America and the islands of the Caribbean, they know what it means to live under the rule of 'free America'.[71]

True, John Reed was no longer in such a euphoric mood as he had been a year or two previously. Angelica Balabanova later recalled that on his return to Moscow, 'Jack spoke bitterly of the demagogy and display which had characterised the Baku Congress and the manner in which the native population and the Far Eastern delegates had been treated'.[72] Nevertheless, there is no gainsaying the circumstance that Central and even more South America would appear remote from Baku, Moscow and every other centre of the Russian Revolution in 1920. Broadly speaking we may accept the observation that in the early years the Soviet government and the Comintern 'concentrated their extra-European activities in the Asiatic and African territories of those Great Powers. The United States was at that time a minor foe, and so Latin America, the backyard of the USA, was considered of small importance'[73]

However, as in other remote areas, there could be some response from sympathisers with the Russian Revolution without any serious challenge to its opponents. Socialism had for some years been putting down its roots in Latin America, and, from such origins, five communist parties were formed in the years immediately following the Russian Revolution, in Argentina, Chile, Uruguay, Brazil and Mexico.

The nature of the party in Mexico was conditioned both by recent experience of a domestic revolution and the always significant contiguity with the United States. And so the Communist Party of Mexico first founded in 1919 soon took on a peasant–nationalist tinge graphically illustrated in the work of its most famous member, the painter Diego Rivera. Moreover, just as the American government had intervened on many occasions in Mexico's domestic affairs, so American radicals came to play an important part in the formation of the CPM – Linn A. E. Gale, Charles Phillips, Luis Fraina and Bertram D. Wolfe to name but four. In Mexico, too, there was most clearly evident the influence of other outsiders, all working on behalf of the Comintern – M. N. Roy, Katayama Sen and Michael Borodin (a Russian who had lived for some years in the USA). Not only might Mexico with a vigorous Communist Party appear as a possible springboard for revolution elsewhere, it could also continue to act as a thorn in the side of the United States and restrain that great power from continuance of intervention in Russia.[74]

Elsewhere in Latin America, communist parties tended to form where there were large immigrant groups among the population and enough urban industrialisation for labour organisations to take on some political importance. In Argentina before the First World War, the socialist movement's left wing had been against revisionism and compromise, and it could not be happy when, as the events of 1917 unfolded, the movement's newspaper labelled the Bolsheviks as the worst enemies of the Russian Revolution. In January 1918, therefore, a breakaway group founded the International Socialist Party, and this changed its name to the Communist Party of Argentina in December 1920. Although it protested strongly during the 'tragic week' of 1919 when strikers were shot down by the army, it possessed little worker membership of its own, and remained a small party in general. In Chile hopes were brighter because there was no split in the Socialist Workers Party. At the congress convened in December 1921 it voted unanimously to become the Communist Party of Chile and join the Comintern. It was very active in the trade union movement, and made some headway there in these early years. In Uruguay a majority of the Democratic Socialist Party agreed to become the Communist Party and to join the Comintern in April 1921. It also had some influence among the labour movement, publishing a newspaper with the title of *The Red Trade Union*. Brazil was a somewhat different case, since the radical movement there was anarchist more than socialist. Its newspaper carried a pro-Soviet appeal from Maxim Gorky in February 1919 and other sympathetic articles, but in March 1921 the Soviet government was denounced as the most brutal expression of authority. The Communist Party was formed in Rio at about this time but with only a handful of members. It enjoyed the further unique distinction of being the first Latin American Communist Party to be banned – in 1922.[75]

Apart from in these five countries, there was awareness of the

Russian Revolution throughout the rest of Latin America, including the Caribbean. But the major surge forward would come after the Second World War, notably with Castro's Revolution in Cuba. After the First World War, as in other parts of the world, Latin American governments were making an unofficial accommodation with the Soviet government in the shape of trade agreements. For example, as late as 1923, Argentina still recognised the tsarist diplomatic representatives, but commerce had been joined with Soviet Russia from 1921 onwards.[76] And so in the Third World as in the Western after some alarms and threats, at least a temporary rapprochement was being made between the citadel of world revolution and its principal opponents.

Part Three

Revolutions in Retrospect and Prospect

As Daniel Field has written:

> Professional historians produce in response to subjective and pro-
> fessional imperatives but also in response to demand. Society
> wants the historian's product because it seeks an affirmation of the
> cherished conception of itself and a rendering of the past for trans-
> mission to the young.

He adds:

> . . . the experience of Soviet life and culture has shaped their out-
> look, just as our society shapes ours, and the results are manifest in
> the works of historians in each country. [1]

In chapter 7, we shall be guided by these straight-forward yet far-
sighted remarks of an American scholar as we turn to an historiographical retrospect on revolution, concentrating on the practice on the
craft in the United States and the Soviet Union, especially as concerned with 1776 and 1917. For, although not completely apparent

as recently as 1945, the emergence of the two present super-powers and their huge influence in world affairs are all too obvious in 1978 and are likely to remain so for many years to come. That is, if there are many years to come, for the prospects of long-term survival for the human race do not appear any brighter at the time of writing than they have in the last thirty years or so. To the extent that the fateful clash stems from respective ideologies, the study of their historical roots and comparison between them are of outstanding importance. For American emphasis on individual rights and Soviet insistence on social justice both stem from revolutionary origins. Minor themes in this final chapter will be the 'totalitarian' view of the Soviet Union, especially in juxtaposition or even equation with Nazi Germany, and the attitudes towards other historiographical problems to be found in the West and the Third World. Finally, there will be some brief reference to the necessity for a future revolution; these concluding observations will emphasise that previous historical experience from the seventeenth to the twentieth centuries could be of service in preserving and reshaping the world of tomorrow.

6 Sixty Years After

All researchers operate in space–time, but the manner in which they do so varies considerably. Physicists work on a scale which varies from sub-atomic particles so small that their very existence is debated, to the whole universe too huge for the mind to grasp, from millionths of a second to millions of years. Meanwhile Western historians are reluctant to abandon specialisations which transcend national boundaries or more than a few decades. While they might to some extent be excused since the object of their enquiry, the development of human society, is so difficult to pin down, and the means of carrying out that task at their present disposal are so primitive, their timidity is often at variance with their aspiration. While they would widely agree with Marc Bloch that the only true history is universal history, many of them would argue that there must be a moratorium on such ambitious projects until the basic spadework, the collection of evidence and the refinement of technique, has been brought nearer completion. This is not so much a counsel of perfection as a confession of impotence, since in all fields of human enquiry, generalisation and supportive evidence advance together. Moreover there are pressing reasons for getting on with the job, as everybody knows. That tiny piece of the universe to which we attach disproportionate importance, the world, is in daily danger of self-destruction, and all its citizens need to do whatever they can to avert this local explosion. A few historians, much more assertive than their colleagues, argue that the study of their subject offers the most complete restraint on global fission. While most members of the guild appear to bury themselves in earlier centuries to avoid the twentieth, gaining a false confidence in the continuance of human life on the flimsy presupposition that there is no reason for it to cease what it has managed to do for so long, this small minority, agreeing with Shakespeare that what's past is prologue, believe that by unravelling the great knot of today's world into yesterday's more simple threads a comprehensive resolution may be achieved of our present complexities. A more moderate statement of such an approach would recognise not only that the exact isolation of every thread would be too demanding a task, but also that new lines or tangles might be introduced without obvious antecedents, thus accepting another argument with a different metaphor: 'The future grows from the past as a plant grows from a seed, yet it contains more than the past.'[1]

We have been talking so far of 'Western historians', by which we mean those who would be identified in other parts of the world as the 'bourgeois historians' of Western Europe, the Western and Southern Hemispheres and Japan. Socialist historians in the Soviet Union and Eastern Europe have no difficulty in pursuing a speciality at the same time as accepting an overall view of their subject which is at once scientific, progressive and universal. According to this view, world communism will take over from imperialism, that is, capitalism at its highest stage, as certainly as capitalism replaced the earlier feudal stage of human development. This, of course, is the Marxist view of history, and yet it should not be forgotten that Marx himself neither brought his own theory to the ultimate stage of refinement nor produced it in anything like its entirety out of the blue. Already in the eighteenth century and even in the seventeenth, the way was being prepared for the materialist conception of history. And later Lenin added his own gloss to Marxism, particularly appropriate for the stage of development reached in his own part of the world at a time of revolution, but also worthy of inclusion in the general corpus of Marxist theory.

In this book we have paid special attention to the Leninist arguments, to those which prepared the way for the Russian Revolution, and then gave direction to it. But it has been our first concern to give some account of the origins of the Russian Revolution and its context two centuries and more before the birth of Lenin. While not accepting the following argument of Miliukov we have agreed with him at least about the necessity of taking a longer view of the great event than is customary:

Just as a powerful geological cataclysm playfully casts down the crust of the latest cultural strata and brings to the surface long-hidden strata recalling the dim past – the ancient epochs of the earth's history – so the Russian Revolution laid bare for us all our historical structure, only thinly hidden by the superficial layers of recent cultural acquisitions. The study of Russian history in our day gains a singular new interest, because through the social and cultural strata displayed on the surface of the Russian upheaval the attentive observer can graphically trace the history of our past. What strikes the foreign observer of contemporary affairs, what is for him the first key to the eternal sphinxlike silence of the Russian people, has long been known to the sociologist and student of Russia's historical evolution. For the latter, Lenin and Trotsky lead movements far closer to Bolotnikov, Razin and Pugachev – to the seventeenth and eighteenth centuries of our history – than to the latest words of European anarchic-syndicalism.[2]

In our estimation 'European anarchic-syndicalism' had just as much to do with the Revolution as had the 'peasant wars' of the early modern period, since it contained within itself a formidable interpretation of world history as well as a recommendation for revolutionary change.

By no means all Marxists accept current Soviet interpretations of history; although they usually go along with what Lenin had to say, they often give more emphasis to the arguments of Trotsky, especially the 'combined development' assessment of Russian history as set out in the first chapter of his account of the Revolution. Most Trotskyists are to be found in the Western world, as are a whole range of other self-styled Marxists seeing themselves as the ideological opponents of the Soviet dogmatists. These sometimes follow the criticisms of Lenin made by such contemporaries as Antonio Gramsci and Rosa Luxemburg. A few, such as the Red Army Fraction in Germany and the Red Brigade in Italy, preach terroristic violence; a great many more in the revisionist Communist parties of Italy and France increasingly accept a peaceful, evolutionary view of human development and have at least begun to contemplate the abandonment of such central doctrines as the 'dictatorship of the proletariat'.

Meanwhile in the Third World the debate rages with at least equal ferocity. The Chinese world outlook, formed and fortified by the thoughts of Chairman Mao, is the strongest, or at least the best known, owing to the power that the Chinese Peoples Republic is able to exert. But there are many Third World leaders who do call themselves socialist, and more than a few who would accept the label of Marxist. In the case of newly formed nations, problems of historical interpretation are particularly pressing, since a convincing ancestry is as necessary for them as a credible attitude towards their place in the family of nations today.

In this final chapter we shall say something about each of the views forming such a wide spectrum. We will begin with and concentrate on a comparison of the outlooks not of the Third World, but of those to be found elsewhere. With the transformation of Europe from many states into two main blocs, at least some of the old quarrels have been settled and some of the old distortions put right. More generally J. H. Plumb has recently voiced a long-held aspiration that with the demise of the nationalistic history, to him false history, will come the dawn of universal, true history.[3] But how have historians responded to the call in the world's two most powerful states, the USA and the USSR? On the face of it, since their basic ideologies reflect respectively the universality of the eighteenth-century Enlightenment and of nineteenth-century Marxism, they should have produced work of a framework much wider than that of their European colleagues. To discover whether or not this has indeed been the case, let us consider American and Soviet historians first as they approach their own history, and then, as they approach each other's, giving special emphasis to problems of revolution and breadth of focus.

Perhaps the most striking characteristic of American historiography on the USA has been its heavy 'Whig' emphasis, its insistence that the American Revolution produced a new society of universal significance. The classical statement of this interpretation was made by George Bancroft, who was not only a thorough scholar but also a considerable patriot. A century or so after the great event he declared:

> When all Europe slumbered over questions of liberty, a band of exiles, keeping watch by night, heard the glad tidings which promised the political regeneration of the world. A revolution, unexpected in the moment of its coming, but prepared by glorious forerunners, grew naturally and necessarily out of the series of past events by the formative principle of a living belief.[4]

In such a view, the nearest approach to an individual saviour of mankind would be George Washington. Ludicrous though the tale of the felling of the cherry tree may now appear, the moral message contained in it and other anecdotes was real and earnest enough in its time to many of the contemporaries of George Bancroft. And the image of Washington as light of the world crossed the Atlantic sufficiently to arouse some stout defenders. To give a small but not insignificant illustration, one nineteenth-century reader of the University of Edinburgh copy of Aaron Bancroft's biography wrote as a marginal comment: 'The author of this book gives Washington by far too good a character, but there was an excuse for him as he was an American himself.' This aroused the following rejoinder of another reader: 'The writer of the above paragraph shows himself to be either an infernal idiot or an envious fool; for never was there a greater or a better man than George Washington, the *Founder* of the American Republic.' Washington's image may not shine so brightly two hundred years on, but, we are told, 'The drama that began in 1776 has not yet been played out'; the Revolution is still proclaimed as 'not an event in American history alone but a turning-point in world history, not a single crisis settled in a brief span of years but a broad movement of liberation which has not yet run its course'.[5]

Continued celebration has led inevitably to some distortion as well as exaggeration. The losers, the Tory Loyalists, were totally ignored when not maligned until towards the end of the nineteenth century, and have only recently been given anything like their scholarly due.[6] Because of the emphasis on a 'consensus' interpretation of the Revolution, the lower social orders, the city 'mobs' and the rank and file soldiers and sailors, have also not been examined in the manner they deserve until the last decade or so.[7] Most seriously in the context of the present discussion, the Revolution and American history in general were for too long looked upon as unique. A kind of Monroe Doctrine possessed the minds of historians in the USA; the New World should throw off the somnolent past of the Old as it rejected its political present. Paradoxically the people who had achieved its independence acknowledging that 'a decent respect to the opinions of mankind requires that they should declare the causes which impel them to the separation', increasingly believed in its 'Manifest Destiny' to conquer a continent irrespective of such opinions, the original universalist ideology becoming the cloak for a rampant nationalism.

Towards the end of the nineteenth century the classical Whig view of the American Revolution began to break up with the arrival of the so-called 'Imperial School' of historians. Coinciding with the arrival of the imperialist period in American development, and to some extent following on the 'frontier thesis' of F. J. Turner[8] – born of his realisation that possibilities of internal expansion had virtually exhausted themselves – this new school of historians were moved to follow the celebrated injunction of Admiral Mahan to look outward. In the works of Charles M. Andrews, George L. Beer and Herbert L. Osgood, the principal consideration was given to the Anglo-Saxon or English-speaking peoples, and the strong suggestion was made that the part played by them would continue to be of outstanding importance. For example, having defined imperialism as a 'new nationalism' based on the concept of a distinctive civilisation that was to be upheld and spread, Beer argued that in the late nineteenth century other Western powers realised that

> ... unless they themselves deliberately and methodically embarked on a similar course, their future part in the world was destined to be relatively unimportant, in comparison with the

seemingly assured destinies of the Russian and English-speaking peoples who had spread themselves over large areas.[9]

The resulting rivalry, including Germany's quest for her place in the sun, led to the First World War.

The next major stage in the expansion of the American historiographical framework occurred after the great watershed of the First World War and the Russian Revolution. The new *Wider Horizons of American History*, as described by Herbert E. Bolton, were to comprise the whole of the Western hemisphere, its Latin section now being joined with the Anglo-Saxon in what might be called a historiographical 'good neighbour' policy. In his presidential address to the American Historical Association in 1932 Bolton pointed out that

> A report by a recent committee of historians complains that many doctoral thesis subjects in United States history had been cultivated past the point of diminishing returns. A larger synthesis of American History, I am sure, would do much to relieve this rather pathetic situation.[10]

What Turner had achieved with his frontier thesis, Bolton now hoped to do with his concept of the 'Greater America'. If in the short run Bolton enjoyed nothing like the influence that was gained by F. J. Turner or C. A. Beard, views similar to his became widespread after the Second World War. (Neither Turner nor Beard widened the horizons of American history in the sense under discussion here.) Although Turner argued that 'local history must be viewed in the light of world history' and also considered briefly the question of possible sequels to the triumph in the USA of 'Bolshevistic labour ideas', his energies were concentrated on trying to account for, as Hofstadter says, 'not the evolution of modern democracy in general, but only the distinctive features of its American version.' Similarly, although considering class conflict, the Constitution and industrial revolution when examining the Civil War, Beard could be said throughout his work to be heading towards the 'American Continentalism' of his later years, for all the sentiments such as those voiced in his AHA presidential address of 1933, 'Written History as an Act of Faith':

> The supreme issue before the historian now is the determination of his attitude towards the disclosures of contemporary thought. He may deliberately evade them for reasons pertaining to personal, economic, and intellectual comfort, thus joining the innumerable throng of those who might have been but were not. Or he

may proceed to examine his own frame of reference, clarify it, enlarge it by acquiring knowledge of greater areas of thought and events, give it consistency of structure by a deliberate conjecture respecting the nature or direction of the vast movements of ideas and interests called world history.[11]

The first effect of the Second World War was the emergence of the idea of the Atlantic civilisation. Although this had some roots in the 'imperial school's' latter-day triumph in the shape of the Atlantic Charter and the English-speaking special relationship between Roosevelt and Churchill, it was more intimately connected with the alliance between the United States and Western Europe effected through the North Atlantic Treaty Organisation. Making specific reference to at least the Atlantic Charter in their contribution to the proceedings of the Tenth International Congress of Historians in Rome in 1955, R. R. Palmer and Jacques Godechot outlined the concept of a late eighteenth-century democratic revolution affecting the whole of Atlantic civilisation. They have since each developed the concept in a somewhat different manner, and encouraged others to conduct their researches according to their hypothesis.[12]

Another line of filiation stretching back to the 'imperial school' can be detected in the comparative studies of slavery and the slave trade that have been carried out since the Second World War, although the Bolton influence may also be seen here. A further relevant factor is the decolonisation movement and the burgeoning interest in their origins of black peoples both in Africa and the Western hemisphere. Thus one of the first books to trigger off discussion in this period was written by the Jamaican prime minister, Eric Williams, whose *Capitalism and Slavery* was first published in 1944. While Williams concentrated on the Atlantic trade, Frank Tannenbaum made a single contribution to the development of the discussion in the more restricted sphere with his *Slave and Citizen: The Negro in the Americas*, which first came out in 1947. A large amount of high-quality work in comparative slavery has followed since, and C. Vann Woodward has enlarged upon the thesis of the Dutch scholar Wilhelmina Kloosterboer concerning comparative emancipations.[13]

To C. Vann Woodward must also go at least some of the credit for opening up American history as a whole to comparative consideration, a move in line with historiographical development elsewhere and especially promoted by medieval historians, two of whom, Marc Bloch and Henri Pirenne, made particular efforts to persuade their colleagues to think in such a manner. As far as the essentially non-medieval case of the United States is concerned,

Woodward points out in *The Comparative Approach to American History* that 'The striking paradox of a nation that professes historical parochialism and practises cosmopolitan involvement calls for attention from professional historians.'[14] Somewhat surprisingly, this paradox has been as applicable to the historians of the New Left as to the more conservative 'consensus' school.[15] While at least one of them, Jesse Lemisch, wishes to encourage 'a Left historian who wants to work on 12th century trade patterns',[16] he himself and most of his colleagues specialise in American history, thus still echoing in their own manner the famous words of Stephen Decatur, 'our country, right or wrong', even if giving fresh emphasis to the wrong.

Even as far as foreign policy is concerned, David Donald, putting forward his own argument and quoting others, tells us:

> The Radicals usually do research only in American archives, and they concentrate on showing how United States policy was formed. As a result, Henry Pachter has observed, their monographs frequently tend 'to attribute too much of what happened in the last 80 years to American initiatives. *We* did this, *we* did that – as though diplomacy was not an interaction of many powers.' Dean Ernest May of Harvard points out that this single-archive approach to diplomatic history often leads to another kind of distortion: 'Those historians who concern themselves exclusively with American events tend also to be those who are on the hunt for villains.'[17]

May himself elsewhere points the way towards an exit from such an impasse[18] by declaring that: 'In fact, there may be only one nation in all of history that has had anything like America's post-1945 experience, and that is its contemporary and adversary, the USSR.'[19] If this be so, historians must surely recognise that the pre-1945 experience of the superpowers is also to some extent comparable. So it has certainly appeared to many observers from at least as far back as the end of the eighteenth century onwards. Here we are concerned with investigating the degree of similarity of their historiographies from the point of view of their nationalist framework.

The first obvious obstacle to the implementation of an exercise which is very heavily burdened with difficulties of many kinds is that the Russian Revolution is of much more recent provenance and of much more bloody immediate consequences than the American. The result of a comparative exercise may well be to show that the differences outweigh the similarities, as we proceed to the investigation of Russian historiography, both pre-revolutionary and post-revolutionary.

Russian historians of the nineteenth century shared with their counterparts in the United States and most European countries a nationalist 'Whig' outlook. They saw their primary task as the explanation of the process by which the Russian Empire had come to be formed, and by strong implication gave encouragement to the view that the Russian Empire would continue to exist, and in its own peculiar fashion prosper. The greatest of them, S. M. Solovev and his pupil V. O. Kliuchevsky, were both men of broad and cosmopolitan culture, and yet both gave their major emphasis to the study of the organic growth of the Great Russian state. At the same time neither could be as lyrical in the celebration of their major theme as was Bancroft, since each of them was by far too honest a scholar to conceal from himself the inefficiency and injustice of the tsarist régime. Yet even though Kliuchevsky was still active throughout the first turbulent decade of the twentieth century, he never ceased to hope that the organic growth could continue without any form of revolutionary discontinuity.[20]

The tensions with which the historians of the last days of tsarism had to reconcile themselves are most appropriately embodied for us by Pavel N. Miliukov, who was an active politician as well as an outstanding scholar. Among other aspects of his career which are particularly relevant to our theme is his close association with the United States, where in 1903 at the University of Chicago he gave what was probably the first American series of lectures on Russian civilisation by a Russian.[21] Published as *Russia and Its Crisis*, the series concluded with Miliukov's affirmation that 'Russia wants a political representation, and guaranties of what are called the fundamental rights of individuality'.[22] Nearly twenty years after, having struggled unsuccessfully for the establishment of a liberal democracy, Miliukov remained convinced that his views were correct, agreeing with the leader of the ill-fated Root Mission about 'the meaning of that Revolution which lies at the bottom of the American policy towards Russia, the only policy that is sound and really friendly'. Miliukov quoted with approval Root's observation that 'We must remember that a people in whom all constructive effort had been suppressed for so long, cannot immediately develop a genius for quick action.'[23] Miliukov continued to present his evolutionary view of Russian history which would culminate in the establishment of something like the American system of government.

Before 1917 there had been no shortage of attempts to show that Russia could peacefully evolve in such a direction, even though most of his colleagues were not as Americanophile as Miliukov himself.[24] After the October Revolution, an almost complete rejection of such an optimistic view took place under the aegis of M. N. Pokrovsky, who dominated Soviet historiography throughout most of the 1920s.[25] According to Pokrovsky the whole of pre-revolutionary Russian history was to be seen as a preparation for the October Revolution. Such a terminal point was its only positive feature; the rest was a tale of the most vicious exploitation in feudal, capitalist and imperialist eras alike. All the great national heroes, including Peter the Great, were reduced to ciphers completely controlled by the relentless forces of the class struggle and the development of the exploitation of natural resources. Even Lenin found Pokrovsky's approach too broad and impersonal for easy comprehension and recommended that a chronological appendix be appended to his general history.

Soon after his death in 1932 Pokrovsky's work was denounced as schematic and mechanical, and during the Stalinist era of 'Socialism in One Country', 'Pokrovskyite' became a term of opprobrium. Nationalist history made a triumphant comeback, and such figures as Peter the Great were rehabilitated as outstanding contributors to the early formation of the Socialist Fatherland.[26] This tendency became even more marked during the years of the Second World War, and with the ensuing onset of the cold war 'Soviet patriotism' was still the most desirable feature of historical writing while 'cosmopolitanism' had become the quality most to be deplored. As in the American case, universalist aspirations became the disguise of nationalism. Even the most distinguished historians were suspected or accused of deviations away from the good norm or towards the bad. As in other cultural fields, such as education and literature, a necessary accompaniment of the construction and reconstruction of socialism first in one country, then throughout Eastern Europe, was rigid conformity to narrowly if not always clearly defined regulations of orthodoxy.

With the death of Stalin and the ensuing 'thaw' historians joined in the difficult exercise of establishing different norms for published works. Some went too far in the new direction, notably the majority of the editorial board of the principal journal, *Voprosy istorii* ('Problems of History'). The second-in-command, E. N. Burdzhalov, came under heaviest fire for his over-enthusiastic participation in the campaign of Destalinisation. While it was a hopeful sign that Burdzhalov made a substantial comeback so that his excellent book on the February Revolution of 1917 could be published in 1967, neither he nor his colleagues could yet feel confident that harsh criticism and demotion might not be meted out to them for work unacceptable to the Party. Historians such as Andrei Amalrik have been sent into harsh Siberian exile, admittedly for works that are closer to political pamphleteering than to academic scholarship; Amalrik is now in the West. Others have been demoted for alleged misinterpretation of the Russian Revolution.[27]

At the same time even militantly anti-Soviet Western historians could now admit that work of real value to them has been published in the Soviet Union with official approval in recent years, for example the monographs on the nineteenth century by P. A. Zaionchkovsky.[28] Moreover in recent years we can see historians moving towards an acceptance of the comparative approach for pre-revolutionary, if not revolutionary and post-revolutionary history. The partial rehabilitation of M. N. Pokrovsky could be seen as a step in the same direction. But the base of the Soviet 'Whig' view is still that of the Fatherland.

Before we turn to consider the question of the extent to which such trends mark a convergence of American and Soviet historiography, we must summarily investigate the consideration of Soviet history by Americans and vice versa, although in an even more summary manner than our survey so far. Among the friends of Pavel N. Miliukov at the University of Chicago at the beginning of the twentieth century was Samuel Harper, who was among the first American university professors to concern themselves with the study of Russia. Predictably enough, like the outstanding British historian of Russia of the period, Sir Bernard Pares, Harper was a great supporter of Russian liberalism. Accompanying Elihu Root on his mission to the Provisional Government in 1917, Harper was encouraged to conclude that the cause in which he believed was now triumphant, even though there were a few dampers to his enthusiasm such as the enforced resignation from the Foreign Ministry of Miliukov and the growing threat of Bolshevism. Harper encouraged Root to think that democracy of the American type would in the end be victorious, although this view was modified later when he came to publish his memoirs under the title '*The Russia I Believe In*'.[29] Harper helped set the essential tone for American writing on Russian history that has persisted down to more recent times, the basis for which is that the Soviet Union will one day be freed from Communist oppression and assume a form of government similar to that of the United States. It has received encouragement from many émigrés sharing the outlook of Miliukov. In such a perspective the pivotal point of Soviet history, the October Revolution of 1917, is looked upon as a sad and unfortunate incident which might have been avoided and was not profound enough in its influence to be inevitable. Christopher Lasch believes that such 'optimism' persisted down into the thirties and forties, writing:

The depression and the New Deal, by making the issue of economic inequality a matter of general concern, gave weight to the argument that the Bolshevik revolution was primarily an experiment in social justice; the rise of the Nazis made the Bolsheviks seem innocuous by comparison; and the war brought the United States into outright alliance with communism. Thus the full significance of the revolution, already made explicit under Stalin, went largely unnoticed in this country until the late 1940s. But even then it was difficult for Americans to believe that the revolution was not only a bad thing for liberalism but that, equally important, it was here to stay. On the contrary, Americans persuaded themselves that the communist dictatorship would topple of its own weight (providing the West stood firm). So autocratic a form of government, they thought, was inherently unstable. Even Mr. George F. Kennan, who otherwise did so much to make Americans aware of the nature of the Soviet system, insisted that the only hope of the West lay in an eventual liberalizing of the system. Thus it may be questioned whether Americans ever resigned themselves to coexistence with evil.

Lasch concludes by saying that 'To live in a world half of which is dominated by one's enemies is not something that comes easily to Americans brought up in the benevolent assumptions of the eighteenth century Enlightenment.[30]

Turning to the men of the thirties and the forties, let us single out for special attention perhaps the most influential of them as Lasch suggests, Mr. George F. Kennan, who has produced both academic work and political advice of generally accepted high quality, while enjoying a successful career as diplomat and university professor. Kennan was one of the principal advocates in the years following the Second World War of the 'containment' of communism, although he insists that he did not want such a policy to be military in its emphasis but rather political and economic. Recognising that the Soviet government had essential interests to protect, he also argued that

If it were not for the peculiar personality and behavior of the Soviet regime itself – its ideological preconceptions against the West, its cruelties at home, the traditionally Russian sense of suspicion and insecurity vis-à-vis the outside world by which it was inspired, and above all its cultivation for domestic–political purposes of the myth of a hostile external environment – the problem of the protection of Soviet power within Russia might never have been what it was.[31]

Kennan believes that the employment of historical perspective encourages understanding of the peculiar personality and behaviour of the Soviet régime itself. He goes back beyond his father's exposure of the harshness of the tsarist government's usage of the Siberian exile system to the reign of Nicholas I to find an administration closely similar to that of the 1970s.[32] While historical continuity is certainly an observable fact in Soviet as well as American and every other kind of history, it could well be going too far to equate the government of a pre-industrial, predominantly peasant society by a monarch with the support of a religious ideology and a land-owning nobility, with that of the heavy industrialised, at least half-urban society by an individual or group with the support of Marxist–Leninist ideology and a privileged, but not in any major sense, property-owning political party. It is doubtful that American historians would feel that the United States could best be understood by an examination of the presidencies from Jackson to Buchanan, granted that some still useful insights were provided by Alexis de Tocqueville and other foreign visitors in a manner broadly comparable to that of de Custine in tsarist Russia. And would Soviet historians be likely to use such analogies as Kennan in a similar fashion? That is among the questions to which we must now turn.

N. N. Bolkhovitinov informs us that 'American studies in the Soviet Union are a comparatively young branch of historical science . . . one may justifiably speak of American studies as an independent field in the Soviet Union only in the 1950s and 1960s'[33] In these two decades, from starting-points such as the writings of Marx, Engels and Lenin, A. V. Efimov's *Towards the History of Capitalism in the USA*, which was first published in 1934, and a whole series of dissertations, monographs and general works have been completed. (The Old Left in the USA (the internal émigrés) help them through their publications rather as external Russian émigrés render assistance to American historians of the USSR.) Special attention has been paid to the questions of the Negro and imperialism among others. While little use has so far been made by them of archival materials, Soviet historians may be said to have provided some interesting insights and to have made some contribution to one of American historiography's least developed areas, its conceptual framework.[34] At the same time, obviously enough, they present a view of American development which is as adversely critical in its own way as is that of Soviet development from the American point of view. Heavy emphasis is given to the belief that the USA needs a revolution of the Russian type, even though this is not explicitly stated.[35] Thus we may conclude that Soviet historians continue to visit their own preconceptions on American history at least as much as do American historians on Soviet history.

Now let us move on to methodology. At the end of an article on contemporary American historiography, N. N. Bolkhovitinov writes:

> Attested and well-founded factual data and conclusions, however paradoxical they seem at first glance, must receive a correct scholarly explanation and recognition. On the other hand, sensational and insufficiently founded conclusions must be decisively rejected.[36]

To him the principal means of discerning the incorrectness of the theoretical positions is through their incompatibility with the tenets of Marxism–Leninism. Thus while showing some respect for the empirical approach, Bolkhovitinov takes up a clear, fundamental methodological position.

From the other side A. P. Mendel believes that he has detected some movement on the part of Soviet historians away from such constrictions, writing:

> Present achievements are providing realistic grounds for the hope and expectation that the first Russian Marxists could derive only from Marxist historical mythology. With tangible scientific and economic success winning allegiance for the regime from those who matter politically, the authorities may feel secure enough to lessen their dependence on Marxist eschatology. Consequently, if this is correct, the historian can begin to withdraw from service on the 'historical front' and to return, at least partly, to his traditional pursuit of historical truth.[37]

Elsewhere Mendel develops his own ideas concerning the 'traditional pursuit of historical truth', arguing that it can make a significant contribution to the raising of the quality of life in the post-industrial age. He argues that:

> It is long past time we junked the curriculum of economic man and got back to the 'liberal arts', the free arts, the arts of free men. . . . The essential concern of our schools should be to provide for our children the sensitivities and proclivities that will enable them to live lives of creative leisure, to find deep gratification – as their parents cannot – in great art, thought, literature and music, in 'listening to the essence of things', feeling themselves in accord with the natural world (not regarding it as an enemy to be conquered and dissected), in living the kind of life that gave meaning and richness to the earlier aristocracies.[38]

In other words, history should concentrate on improving the flavour of life rather than contributing in any useful manner to its scientific explanation. While not agreeing in general with Mendel, many of his colleagues would shy away from 'scientific explanation'.[39]

The argument could be put forward that if Mendel is correct in his view that 'scientific socialism' is in retreat even in the Soviet Union, this is a clear indication that the Soviet Union has lost its revolutionary dynamic to an extent that it can no longer be looked upon as a progressive society.[40] Certainly, as already mentioned above, few if any of the New Left group of American historians appear to look upon the Soviet Union as capable of providing any guidance as to the direction that the United States should take. Among their persistent themes has been the call for a return to the ideals of 1776. For their part many Soviet dissidents appear to have moved away from earlier infatuation with the ideals of contemporary American society to concentrate on a reasoned exposé of the evils of Stalinism, while looking for a solution to Soviet problems in a return to 'pure' Leninism or even in a re-examination of the beliefs of pre-revolutionary Slavophiles or Westerners. In other words, the American dream has turned as sour for many Soviet dissidents as has the Soviet dream for American liberals.

This tendency itself marks a kind of convergence, but a negative kind in that both dissatisfied groups are essentially looking back, hoping for the restoration of a world lost rather than a world to be won. But a more positive kind of historiographical convergence is possible and may already be in process. This needs to be seen within the framework of convergence theory in general. A. G. Meyer has written that there are basically three theories of convergence, firstly:

. . . one that posits the development of both Soviet and American societies within the framework of democratic socialism, a model similar to the Swedish system. The basic assumption here is that a pluralistic society will be able to govern itself only with the help of a democratic, participatory, pluralistic political system based on a civic culture of mutual toleration. A second theory of convergence regards the same social pluralism as the basis for a political order modeled rather on the modern corporation or perhaps on the company town – an order stressing hierarchy, coordination, structured communications, rational elite recruitment, and the like. Hence this is convergence on a bureaucratized polity. Finally, we have an apocalyptic theory of convergence in a new fascist-like totalitarianism engendered by the psychological cost of modernization and the resulting crisis style of political rule. The model here would be the Third Reich. Some would add a fourth theory forecasting the end of both the Soviet Union and the United States in their

present forms in a revolution, followed by the thorough restruc-
turing of both polities according to anarcho-syndicalist or socialist
ideals. I have not considered this last possibility because it is not,
strictly speaking, a theory of convergence, and it is in my view the
least likely of all the possible alternatives.

In any application of these theories of convergence Meyer warns of
the dangers of teleology, ethnocentrism and determinism – precon-
ceived direction, national self-preoccupation and absence of free
will. He also points to various counter-theories or at least limitations
– 'residual differences' and national culture. He asserts that:

> Given the primitive state of social science, a choice between these
> various theories and counter-theories can be made only on ideo-
> logical, moral, or political grounds. To become convinced that
> convergence is or is not likely, the scholar must make a political
> choice between essential and incidental elements of the social
> system. That choice is subjective.[41]

Is historiography in an equally primitive state?[42] Do historians
also realise that their choice is subjective when they talk of historical
trends? What, in particular, is their attitude to the question of convergence? At least one practitioner of the craft, J. H. Plumb, appears
to have little doubt that

> Ancient patterns of living are crumbling before the demands of in-
> dustrial society . . . life in the suburbs of London, Lagos, Jakarta,
> Rio de Janeiro and Vladivostok will soon have more in common
> than they have in difference.[43]

In his book *The Death of the Past*, as we have noted above, Plumb
welcomes the demise of national history, to him false history, and the
dawn of universal, true history.

Possibly nationalistic history has declined in the West since, after a
period of readjustment, a wider framework than that of one nation is
being accepted by practitioners of the craft.[44] If so, the enormous
problems of data collection and processing will have to be carried out
in a manner more defined, even more scientific, than in the phrase
'the traditional pursuit of historical truth', to quote A. P. Mendel
again. As far as America and Soviet historiography is concerned, the
same process might already be under way. By indicating the past development of what Meyer calls 'residual differences' and national
culture in the cases of the USA and the USSR, historians are not only

breaking down the national framework and moving towards 'the death of the past', towards universal history, but also contributing to the discussion of convergence theory by their social science colleagues. Genuine universal history may take some time to come, but any move towards it helps to avert the worst kind of convergence discussed by Meyer, the fascist totalitarian. And in this particular case, the comparative history of the USA and the USSR might contribute in some small degree to a truer, less nationalistic application of the ideals of both American and Russian Revolutions: individual freedom and social justice. But in early 1978 the future looks less rosy than black; a totalitarianism more crippling than that conceivable when the word was first coined about thirty years ago looms all too large on the horizon of many different analysts with widely varied world views. The major reason for this is the world's continued division into great camps where domestic virtues and alien vices are proclaimed in as strident a manner as the available communications media will allow. The Western world loudly proclaims 'democracy' and respect for 'human rights' as its major positive characteristics, underplaying or even completely ignoring its own limited implementation (and more than occasional violation) of such concepts. It visits upon its rivals, especially on the Soviet Union, a thorough-going antipathy and continuous militant opposition towards popular political participation and freedom, saying little or nothing about the advancement of such worthy causes where it may be found on the part of its opponents. The truth of the matter, which is elusive, does not necessarily lie in the middle; it is certainly not to be found in the Manichaean world view which has been too evident in all camps during the cold war. Amid much talk of the arrival of *1984* some years before its time, we should perhaps recall that in George Orwell's novel, an essential policy of the totalitarian state is the continued artificial stimulation of rivalry between Oceania, Eurasia and Eastasia.[45]

A contemporary Western variation of this theme, expressed in a manner ranging from a politician's caricature to a scholarly interpretation, is the equation of the Soviet Union with Nazi Germany under the 'totalitarian' heading. Yet an increasing number of scholars have put forward arguments along the same lines as V. R. Berghann, who believes that 'to subsume Communism and Fascism under one and the same term is a heuristic blind alley'.[46] To varying degrees, many would concur with the reservation of D. Schoenbaum:

Can we assume a meaningful identity with a conspiratorial group of highly intellectual, professional revolutionaries and a heterogeneous collection of provincial cranks; between an underdeveloped country with a vast rural population in the throes of industrialisation and a well developed industrial society in the midst of a worldwide economic crisis?[47]

Certainly, as set out in chapter 3 above, there is a considerable basis for the fairly close comparison between the imperial predecessors of the Soviet Union and Nazi Germany. Moreover, we have seen in chapter 5 above that Lenin and his associates looked chiefly to Germany for a development of the revolutionary drive initiated in Russia. Yet the Bolsheviks clearly recognised the more fully fledged nature of the German proletariat and the more mature level of Germany's modernisation. In the 1930s, such differences were if anything more pronounced. And so, while the basis for comparison remains in such features as the degree of state control and bureaucratic procedure, the case for an identification of the Soviet Union and Nazi Germany is more difficult to place on a firm foundation.[48]

On the other hand, there are few analysts in both Western and Third Worlds who would want to defend the Soviet Union of today as the fulfilment of the Bolshevik aspirations of October 1917. Left-wing Western opponents of the USSR attack it for its conservatism while errant Eurocommunist friends are prepared to compromise with the once reviled social democrats. Explaining such behaviour, one of the latter declares:

> We are fully aware of the fact that our conception of the relation between democracy and socialism does not correspond with that elaborated by Lenin. But this conception has been developed, not by abandoning Lenin's method, but by taking stock of profoundly different historical conditions which Lenin himself could never have predicted.[49]

The first group argues for the overthrow of the Soviet government, the second still hopes for its reform. For their part, Soviet apologists denounce Trotskyism and other 'infantile' left-wing deviations, while chiding Communists in France, Italy and elsewhere for their unnecessary and possibly dangerous revisionism. And some Third World ideologues have been able to see in October a model for their own pattern of development, one of them writing:

> If Uganda is serious about developing as an African country, then we must adopt socialism. . . . When African countries became independent all their institutions were colonial creations, thus the cultural values of the country were not African and the economic systems were capitalistic. . . . The 1917 revolution came at the time

when USSR was in a similar state to that of the African states at the time of independence. The Russians demonstrated an alternative to a liberal capitalist society. Liberal democracy was no longer to be copied by everyone. . . .[50]

But such a path has not been followed by Uganda, and even where African socialism has made some progress, it has not attempted to repeat the route taken by the Soviet Union. As for the Chinese, while still revering Lenin and even Stalin, they attack the USSR bitterly for its 'social imperialism'. Meanwhile, in the USSR itself, there is no shortage of dissidents asserting that the ideals of October have not been realised, or even in some cases wanting to reject the whole tradition that stems from 1917.

But in conclusion let us revert to the principal argument of this book, which has been for the insertion of the Russian Revolution in its appropriate global, historical context. At least as much as its great predecessors, it had universal aspirations and therefore belongs not to any one locale but to the whole world. Like them, it aroused in human beings the desire to struggle for the overthrow of an old, unjust society and the institution of a new society that would be just. Wise statesmen perceived this powerful force, sharing the view of Richelieu, who saw, in the early seventeenth century, that 'for him who knows how to use it there is no lever in the world like that of a rising cause, for a rising cause embodies the growing dissatisfaction of men with a long-established evil which they have learned to detest, but which they have not yet learned to overthrow.'[51] If the Russian Revolution failed to live up to the expectations of most of its supporters, this feature too puts it in the same general category as the English, American and French Revolutions. In the world today there is again 'a rising cause', an overwhelming necessity for a new revolution incorporating the best of the spirit of 1649, 1776, 1789 and 1917, as well as addressing itself primarily to the 'long-established evil' with which we are all too familiar. This is not a call to the barricades, for any major domestic disturbance is likely to upset the delicate international balance; the argument is rather for a revision of our historical consciousness which will help to avert conflict and promote progress. If that sounds like Utopia, 'the world has now become too dangerous for anything less.'[52]

Notes and References

Part One   Russia and Modern Revolutions

1. At the First World Congress on Soviet and East European Studies, Banff 1974, a panel on this subject did not meet because none of the panellists was able to put in an appearance.

2. See chapter 1, notes 1 and 48.

3. J.V.Polišenský, *War and Society in Europe, 1618–1648* (Cambridge, 1978) p. 11.

4. See chapter 2, notes 1–3. Among the Western specialists who do believe in the inclusion of Russia in discussion about the international impact of the French Revolution is Max Okenfuss 'who is personally convinced that both before and after 1789 more Russians knew about and sympathized with European political writings and French revolutionary movements than is generally realized'. See *Kritika*, vol. 10 (1973–4) 46.

5. See chapter 3, note 1.

1. The General Crisis of the Seventeenth Century

1. Trevor Aston (ed.), *Crisis in Europe, 1550–1660* (London, 1965) p.3. And see note 48 below.

2. John Milton, *A Brief History of Moscovia* (London, 1682) from *The Works of John Milton*, vol. 10 (New York, 1932) 327–8.

3. The precedent was Paulus Jovius, or Paolo Giovio (1483–1552), historian and geographer.

4. J.Q.Cook, 'The Image of Russia in Western European Thought in the Seventeenth Century', from *Dissertation Abstracts*, 20 (Ann Arbor, 1959) 2247. For a general description and illustration of this process, see Anthony Cross (ed.), *Russia under Western Eyes, 1517–1825* (London, 1971).

5. Ph. Cluver, *Introductionis in universam geographiam* . . . . (Lugduni Batavorum, 1629) p.47.

6. Pierre Chaunu, 'Réflexions sur le tournant des années 1630–1650', from *Cahiers d'histoire moderne et contemporaine*, 12 (1967).

7. Ibid., p.262.

8. For a penetrating analysis of the significance of this infiltration, see

M. Mancall, *Russia and China: Their Diplomatic Relations to 1728* (Cambridge, Mass., 1971).

9. Ph. Briet, *Parallela geographiae veteris et novae*, I (Paris, 1648) 161.

10. S.R.Gardiner (ed.), *Letters Relating to the Mission of Sir Thomas Roe to Gustavus Adolphus, 1629–1630* (London, 1875) p.2.

11. See, for example, D.Eeckaute, 'Le commerce russe au milieu du XVIIe siècle d'après la correspondance du chargé d'affaires suédois Rodès', *Revue historique*, 233 (1965) 323–38; L.V.Cherepnin, 'Russian 17th-Century Baltic Trade in Soviet Historiography', *Slavonic Review*, 43 (1964–5) 1–22; M.Grokh, 'K voprosu ob ekonomicheskikh otnosheniiakh stran vostochnoi i zapadnoi Evropy v period trinadtsatiletnoi voiny', *Srednie veka*, 24 (Moscow, 1963) 225–39.

12. R.O.Crummey, *The Old Believers and the World of Antichrist; The Vyg Community and the Russian State, 1694–1855* (Madison, Wisc. and London, 1970) p.10.

13. P.Pascal, *Avvakum et les débuts du raskol* (Paris, 1938) pp.xx–xxv; C.B.H.Cant, 'The Archpriest Avvakum and His Scottish Contemporaries', *Slavonic and East European Review*, 44 (1965–6) 381–402.

14. See, for example, L.R.Lewitter, 'Poland, the Ukraine and Russia in the 17th Century', *Slavonic and East European Review*, 27 (1948–9) 157–71 and 414–29; N.A.Baklanova, 'Kul'tura i byt vo vtoroi polovine XVIIv', in B.A.Rybakov *et al.* (eds), *Istoriia SSSR*, 3 (Moscow, 1967) 160–9; S.F.Platonov, *Moscow and the West* (translated and edited by Joseph L.Wieczynski with an introduction by Serge A.Zenkovsky) (Hattiesburg, W. Va., 1972) pp.97–141.

15. Henry Brereton, *Newes of the Present Miseries of Russia . . . .* (London, 1614) p.37.

16. A.V.Borodin, *Inozemtsy – ratnye liudi na sluzhbe v moskovskom gosudarstve* (Petrograd, 1916) p.7.

17. A.F.Steuart, *Scottish Influences in Russian History* (Glasgow, 1913) p.32.

18. Borodin, *Inozemtsy*, pp.8–9.

19. A.V.Chernov, *Vooruzhennye sily russkogo gosudarstva v XV–XVIIvv, s obrazovaniia tsentralizovannogo gosudarstva do reform pri Petre I* (Moscow, 1954) pp.152–5. The manual was *Uchenie i khitrost' ratnogo stroeniia pekhotnykh liudei*, a translation of *Kriegskunst zu Fuss . . .* by Johann Jacobi von Wallhausen (Oppenheim, 1615).

20. For the most scholarly yet broad treatment of this subject, see Richarrd Hellie, *Enserfment and Military Change in Muscovy* (Chicago and London, 1971). See also the valuable article by Thomas Esper, 'Military Self-Sufficiency and Weapons Technology in Muscovite Russia', *Slavic Review*, 28 (1969). On pp.204–5 Esper writes:
'The decision to reorganize and restructure the Russian army along modern lines was made in the early 1630s, although no significant changes occurred until the second half of the century. . . . By the early 1660s . . . seventy-nine per cent of the army (about 77,000 men) was composed of what were called "foreign" units – cavalry, dragoons, hussars, infantry. This was the core of the new army, trained and to some extent officered by foreign mercenaries.'

21. See, for example, B.F.Porshnev, 'Les rapports politiques de l'Europe occidentale et de l'Europe orientale à l'époque de la guerre de trente ans', in *XIe Congrès international des sciences historiques, rapports IV, histoire moderne* (Goteborg–Stockholm–Uppsala, 1960) 136–63. Some of Porshnev's views are more fully presented in his books *Frantsiia, Angliiskaia revolitsiia i evropeiskaia politika v seredine XVIIv* (Moskva, 1970) and *Trinadtsatiletniaia voina i vstuplenie v nee Shvetsii i Moskovskogo gosudarstva* (Moscow, 1976). A commentary on his views, based mostly on the first of those books, now follows.

22. This is the principal theme of Porshnev's *Trinadtsatiletniaia voina*. And see note 18 above.

23. Porshnev, *Frantsiia* pp.70–4.

24. Ibid., p.337.

25. E.N.Williams, *The Ancien Regime in Europe: Government and Society in the Major States, 1648–1789* (London, 1970) p.17.

26. See Michael Roberts, 'The Military Revolution, 1560–1660', in *Essays in Swedish History* (London, 1967); Hellie, *Enserfment*, pp.254–8.

27. See, for example, S.H.Baron, 'The Weber Thesis and the failure of capitalist development in "early modern" Russia', *Jahrbücher für Geschichte Osteuropas* 18 (1970) 321–36. At the same time, it is as well to keep in mind the argument of N.Steensgard that the part played by the state in the economy has been a generally neglected subject for research on seventeenth-century Europe. See his 'The Economic and Political Crisis of the Seventeenth Century' in *XIIIe Congrès international des sciences historiques* (Moscow, 1970).

28. On the Russian social system in this context, see in particular John Keep, 'The Muscovite Élite and the Approach to Pluralism', in *Slavonic and East European Review* 48 (1970). For suggested parallels with Spain and France, see respectively A.N.Chistozvonov, 'Nekotorye aspekty problemy genezisa absoliutizma', in *Voprosy istorii* 5 (1968); S.M.Troitskii, 'Le système de John Law et ses continuateurs russes', in F.Braudel *et al.* (eds) *La Russie et l'Europe, XVIe–XXe siècles* (Paris–Moscow. 1970) p.32.

29. See, for example, P.N.Miliukov, *Gosudarstvennoe khoziastvo Rossii v pervoi chetverti XVIII stoletiia i reforma Petra Velikogo* (St Petersburg, 1905).pp.53–4.

30. Karl Pommerening, 'Donoseniia koroleve Khristine i pis'ma k korolevskomu sekretariu shevdskogo rezidenta v Moskve Karla Pommereninga' in *Chteniia v obshchestve istorii i drevnostei rossisskikh pri Moskovskom universitete*, kn. I (1898) pp.417–21; S.V.Bakhrushin, 'Moskovskii miatezh 1648g', in *Nauchnye trudy*, 2 (Moscow, 1954) 50–2.

31. For a good general survey, see M.N.Tikhomirov, *Sobornoe ulozhenie 1649g* (Moscow, 1961) pp.5–26.

32. Quoted by Bakhrushin, in *Nauchnye trudy*, 2, 53.

33. Ibid., 59.

34. Ibid., 59.

35. Samuel Collins, *The Present State of Russia* (London, 1671) pp.104–5.

36. Bakhrushin, *Nauchnye trudy*, 2, 78.

37. Tikhomirov, *Sobornoe ulozhenie*, pp.9–15.

38. Bakhrushin, *Nauchnye trudy*, 2, 80–1.

39. Ibid., 81–91.

40. Tikhomirov, *Sobornoe ulozhenie*, pp. 22–61. For accounts in English, see J.L.H.Keep, 'The Decline of the Zemsky Sobor', *Slavonic and East European Review*, 36 (1957–8); Hellie, *Enserfment, passim*, particularly pp. 134–40. And see above, pp. 11–12.

41. M.P.Alekseev, 'Angliia i anglichane v pamiatnikakh pis'mennosti XVI–XVIIvv', *Uchennye zapiski Leningradskogo Gosudarstvennogo Universiteta, seriia istoricheskikh nauk*, vyp. 15 (1948) pp. 84–109; Z.I.Roginskii, *Poezdka gontsa Gerasima Semenovicha Dokhturova v Angliiu 1645116446gg: Iz istorii anglo-russkikh otnoshenii v period angliiskoi revoliutsii XVII veka* (Iaroslavl, 1960); J.J.Lubimenko, 'Anglo-Russian Relations during the English Revolution' in *Transactions of the Royal Historical Society*, 4th ser., 11 (London, 1928).

42. K.I.Iakubov, *Rossiia i Shvetsiia v pervoi polovine XVII veka* (Moscow, 1898) p. 470. For events in Turkey, see A.N.Kurat, 'The Ottoman Empire under Mehmed IV', *The New Cambridge Modern History*, vol 5 (Cambridge, 1964) pp. 504–5.

43. Steuart, *Scottish Influences*, pp. 35–6.

44. Z.I.Roginskii, 'Missiia lorda Kolpepera v Moskvu (Iz istorii anglorusskikh otnoshenii v period angliiskoi revoliutsii XVIIv)', L.G.Beskrovnyi *et al.* (eds) *Mezhdunarodnye sviazi Rossii v XVII–XVIIIvv, (ekonomika, politika, kul'tura)* (Moscow, 1966) pp. 906–102; L.Loewenson, 'Did Russia intervene after the execution of Charles I?' in *Bulletin of the Institute of Historical Research*, 18 (1940) 13–20.

45. *A Collection of the State Papers of John Thurloe Esq.*, III (London, 1742) p.50; A.S.Kan, 'Svedeniia russkikh ob angliiskoi revoliutsii', *Izvestiia akademii nauk SSSR, seriia istorii i filosofii*, vol. 6 (1949) 464–5.

46. The phrase is from Samuel Hartlib and quoted by Christopher Hill in his article 'The English Revolution and the Brotherhood of Man', reprinted in *Puritanism and Revolution* (London, 1968) p. 127.

47. See S.D.Skazkin, 'Osnovnye problemy tak nazyvaemogo "vtorogo izdaniia krepostnichestva" i srednei i vostochnei Evropy' in *Voprosy istorii*, No. 2 (1958). For a useful collection of documents, see R.E.F.Smith, *The Enserfment of the Russian Peasantry* (Cambridge, 1968).

48. Among the relevant articles which have appeared in *Past and Present* since the publication of Trevor Aston (ed.) *Crisis in Europe* are: H.Kamen, 'The economic and social consequences of the Thirty Years War', 39 (1968); J.V.Polišenský, 'The Thirty Years War and the Crises and Revolutions of Seventeenth-Century Europe', 39 (1968); J.H.Elliott, 'Revolution and Continuity in Early Modern Europe', 42 (1969); and M.O.Gately, A.L.Moore and J.E.Wills, 'Seventeenth-Century peasant "Furies"; Some Problems of Contemporary History', 51 (1971). The last of these articles is a critique of Roland Mousnier's *Peasant Uprisings in Seventeenth-Century France, Russia and China*, trans. Brian Pearce (London, 1972).

49. For an interesting discussion of this point, see T.K.Rabb, *The Struggle for Stability in Early Modern Europe*, (New York, 1975).

50. C. Hill, *The Century of Revolution, 1603–1714* (London, 1969) p. 165.

51. Paul Avrich, *Russian Rebels, 1600–1800* (London, 1972) p.115; G.A.Sanin and I.S.Sharkova in L.V.Cherepnin *et al.* (eds), *Krest'ianskie voiny v Rossii XVII–XVIII vekov: problemy, poiski, resheniia* (Moscow, 1974) pp. 369, 377–9; B.G.Kurts, *Russko-kitaiskie snosheniia v XVI, XVII i XVIII stoletiiakh* (Khar'kov, 1929) p.136.

2. The Democratic Revolution of the Eighteenth Century

1. J.Godechot, R.R.Palmer, 'Le problème de l'Atlantique du XVIIIème au XXème siècle', *Relazioni del X Congresso Internazionale di Scienze Storiche* vol. 5 (Firenze, 1955) pp.175–239, particularly pp.219–33.

2. For Godechot's later views, see his *France and the Atlantic Revolution of the Eighteenth Century, 1770–1779* (New York and London, 1965).

3. R.R.Palmer, *The Age of the Democratic Revolution: A Political History of Europe and America, 1760–1800: The Struggle* (Princeton and London, 1964) p. 140. For Palmer's later assessment of his own work, see his contribution to L. Perry Curtis (ed.), *The Historian's Workshop* (New York, 1970).

4. Russian title – *Trudy vol'nogo ekonomicheskogo obshchestva k pooshchreniiu v Rossii zemledeiia i domostroitel'stva,* I (St Petersburg, 1765) i, iii, vi, ix–x.

5. E.V.Tarle, 'Byla li ekaterininskaia Rossiia ekonomicheskoi otstaloi stranoiu?', *Sovremennyi mir* v (St Petersburg, 1910).

6. Tarle, *Sovremennyi mir*, v, 7.

7. A.Burja, *Observations d'un voyageur sur la Russie, la Finlande, la Livonie, la Curlande et la Prusse* (Berlin, 1785) p. 214.

8. Burja, *Observations*, p.49; Tarle, *Sovremennyi mir* v, 8.

9. See, for example, B.B.Kafengauz, *Ocherki vnutrennego rynka Rossii pervoi poloviny XVIII veka* (Moskva, 1958); M.Ia.Volkov, 'Otmena vnutrennykh tamozhen', *Istoriia SSSR*, No.2 (1957).

10. See, for example, L.G.Beskrovnyi *et al.* (eds), *Istoriia SSSR*, vol.3 (Moscow, 1967) p.440.

11. F. Crouzet, 'Angleterre et France au XVIIIe siècle: Essai d'analyse comparée de deux croissances économiques', *Annales: économies, sociétés, civilisations*, No.2 (1966) 271.

12. N. G. LeClerc, *Histoire physique, morale, et politique de la Russie ancienne et moderne* 6 vols (Paris, 1783–94) quoted by Tarle, *Sovremennyi mir* v, 11.

13. Tarle, *Sovremennyi mir* v, 13–5, points out that in 1785, a comparatively good year for France, she exported to Russia goods to the value of 5,485,675 livres while importing from Russia goods worth 6,412,339 livres. He goes on to give more comparative figures on p.17. J.L.Van Regemorter, 'Commerce et politique: Préparation et négociation du traité franco-russe de 1787', in *Cahiers du monde russe et soviétique* No. 3 (1963) draws somewhat different conclusions from Tarle on the balance of trade between France and Russia.

14. Tarle, *Sovremennyi mir* v, 17–8; P.W.Bamford, *Forests and French*

Sea Power, 1660–1789 (Toronto, 1956) p. 211.

15. R.G.Albion, *Forests and Sea Power: The Timber Problem of the Royal Navy, 1562–1682* Harvard Economic Studies, xxix (Cambridge, Mass., 1926) p.x.

16. *Hansard's Parliamentary History of England* xvii (London, 1813) 1142.

17. John Marshall, *A digest of all the accounts . . . of the United Kingdom of Great Britain and Ireland, etc.* (London, 1833) pp.71–5. E.B.Schumpeter, *English overseas trade statistics, 1697–1808* (Oxford, 1960) p. 18, gives a slightly different picture. For the Scottish connection in particular, see David S. Macmillan, 'The Scottish–Russian Trade: Its Development, Fluctuations and Difficulties, 1750–1796', in *Canadian–American Slavic Studies* vol.4 (1970).

18. Beskrovnyi *et al.* (eds), *Istoriia SSSR* 3, 422. See also Preceptor K.-G. Hildebrand, 'Foreign markets for Swedish iron in the 18th century' in *Scandinavian Economic History Review* 6 (1958) 9–10.

19. *Hansard,* xvii, 1137. For the importance of Russian exports wider afield, see Alfred W.Crosby, Jr, *America, Russia, Hemp and Napoleon: American Trade with Russia and the Baltic 1783–1812* (Columbus, Ohio, 1965).

20. See, for example, V.I.Shunkov *et al.* (eds), *Perekhod ot feodalizma k kapitalizmu v Rossii* (Moskva, 1969); Samuel H.Baron, 'The Transition from Feudalism to Capitalism in Russia: A major Soviet historical controversy', *American Historical Review* 77 (1972).

21. H.F.Von Storch, *Historisch-statistisches Gemälde des russischen Reichs am Ende des Achzehnten Jahrhunderts* 6 vols (Riga, Leipzig, 1797–1802) quoted by Tarle, *Sovremennyi mir* v, 9.

22. Tarle, *Sovremennyi mir* v, 22–7. Tarle maintains, for example, that while a French factory at the end of the eighteenth century would be considered large if it employed 100–200 workers and a rare exception if 300–400 and more, the corresponding figures for a Russian factory would be higher.

23. Roger Portal, 'The Industrialization of Russia', *The Cambridge Economic History of Europe*, 6 (Cambridge, 1966) 802.

24. *Trudy vol'nogo ekonomicheskogo obshchestva*, vi (1770) 59–68.

25. Iu.P.Klokman, *Sotsial'no-ekonomicheskaia istoriia russkogo goroda: vtoraia polovina XVIII veka* (Moscow, 1967) pp. 316–7, puts the percentage of Russian town-dwellers at the end of the eighteenth century at 4.1 per cent of the poll-taxpaying population, but he also says that other Soviet historians, using unpublished figures, have suggested a figure of 7.5 per cent and even 8.3 per cent. These variations largely result from the fact that government statistics referred to official town dwellers, while many people living in towns seasonally or permanently were officially registered as rural inhabitants. On pp. 321–2 of his book, Klokman maintains that towns throughout Europe shared the political powerlessness of Russian towns, at least up to the French Revolution. Russia's population as a whole, according to V.M.Kabuzan, rose from 22,236,000 in 1762 to 37,414,000 in 1795. See his *Narodonaselenie Rossii v XVIII-pervoi polovine XIXv (po materialam revizii)* (Moscow, 1963) pp. 164–5.

26. C.B.A.Behrens, *The Ancien Régime* (London, 1967) pp. 34, 38, 176. Behrens makes some interesting comparisons between the French and Russian peasants.

27. See, for example, the remarks made on the French economy by F. Crouzet, *Annales*, No.2 (1966) 273–5.

28. V. N. Bochkarev, *Voprosy politiki v russkom parlamente XVIIIogo veka: Opyt izucheniia politicheskoi ideologii XVIIIogo veka po materialam zakonodatel'noi komissii 1767–1768* (Tver, 1923) p.28.

29. Isabel de Madariaga, *Britain, Russia, and the Armed Neutrality of 1780* (London, 1962); N.N.Bolkhovitinov, *Stanovlenie russko-amerikanskikh otnoshenii, 1775–1815* (Moscow, 1966) pp.50–90.

30. See, for example, A.Lobanov-Rostovsky, *Russia and Europe, 1789–1825* (Durham, North Carolina, 1947); K.E.Dzhedzhula, *Rossiia i Velikaia Frantsuzskaia Burzhuaznaia Revoliutsiia kontsa XVIII veka* (Kiev, 1972) pp.330–430.

31. P.P.Epifanov, '"Uchennaia druzhina" i prosvetitel'stvo XVIII veka', *Voprosy istorii* No.3 (1963) 53.

32. From a lecture by Professor C.R.Boxer at the 1967 Anglo-American Conference of Historians in London. I am grateful to Professor Boxer for confirming and enlarging upon this information by letter. For other cultural contacts between the two extremities of Europe in the early eighteenth century, see C.R.Boxer, 'An enlightened Portuguese: Antonio Ribeiro Sanches', *History Today* (April, 1970).

33. L.G.Beskrovnyi, B.B.Kafengauz (eds), *Khrestomatiia po istorii SSSR: XVIIIv* (Moscow, 1963) pp. 585–6; P.N.Miliukov, *Ocherki po istorii russkoi kul'tury*, vol.3 (Paris, 1937) p.396.

34. The number of books published in Great Britain in the eighteenth century is incalculable.

35. Marc Raeff, *Origins of the Russian Intelligentsia: The Eighteenth-Century Nobility* (New York, 1966): M.M.Shtrange, *Demokraticheskaia intelligentsiia Rossii v XVIII veke* (Moscow, 1965).

36. D.S.Von Mohrenschildt, *Russia in the Intellectual Life of Eighteenth-Century France* (New York, 1936); E.Haumant, *La culture française en Russie* (Paris, 1910).

37. See, for example, Göte Carlid and Johann Nordström (eds), *Torbern Bergman's Foreign Correspondence* vol.1 (Uppsala, 1965) pp. 284, 320, 322, 323; N.N.Bolkhovitinov, 'Beginnings of the Establishment of Scientific and Cultural Relations between America and Russia', *Soviet Studies in History* 5 (1966) 48–59; L.W.Labaree et al. (eds), *The Papers of Benjamin Franklin* (New Haven, 1959 –) vol.10 p.299; vol. 12, p.194. This last reference indicates direct contact between Franklin and his Russian contemporary, Lomonosov.

38. K. A. Papmehl, *Freedom of Expression in Russia: The History of the Idea and Its Practical Application* (The Hague, 1971); A.M.Skabichevskii, *Ocherki istorii russkoi tsenzury, 1700–1863g* (St Petersburg, 1892) pp.33–40.

39. Gunning to Suffolk, *State Papers* 91, vol.95, p.146; vol.96, p.43; vol.97, pp.38, 42.

40. A.T.Bolotov, *Zapiski*, from Beskrovnyi and Kafengauz, *Khrestomatiia*, pp. 412–3.

41. See, for example, the contributions of A.L.Shapiro and A.P.Pronshtein to *Soviet Studies in History* vols. 5 and 6 respectively; and J.T.Alexander, *Emperor of the Cossacks: Pugachev and the Frontier Jacquerie* (Lawrence, Kansas, 1973). Roger Portal talks of 'Pugachev: une révolution manquée', *Ètudes d'histoire moderne et contemporaine*, I (Paris, 1947).

42. A.N.Filippov, 'Moskva i Pugachev v iiule i avguste 1774 goda', *Trudy obshchestva izucheniia Kazakhstana* 6 (Orenburg, 1925) 16–7.

43. Ibid., 22–4.

44. S.A.Golubtsov, 'Moskovskaia provintsial'naia vlast i dvorianstvo v ozhidanii Pugacheva', *Staraia Moskva*, no. 1 (Moscow, 1929) 8.

45. All of this paragraph from ibid., 9–10.

46. D.I.Malinin, 'Otgoloski Pugachevshchiny v Meshchovskom uezde: (po sekretnym delam Meshchovskoi voevodskoi kantseliarii)', *Izvestiia kaluzhskoi uchenoi arkhivnoi komissii*, XXI (Kaluga, 1911) 9–29.

47. All these quotations from D.I.Malinin, *Otgoloski Pugachevshchiny v Kaluzhskom krae* (Kaluga, 1930) pp. 4–6.

48. A.T.Bolotov, in Beskrovnyi and Kafengauz, *Khrestomatiia*, p.413.

49. All of this paragraph from M.D.Kurmacheva, 'Otkliki krest'ianskoi voiny 1773–1775 gg v tsentral'nykh guberniiakh Rossii', *Voprosy agrarnoi istorii tsentra i severo-zapada RSFSR: materialy mezhvuzskoi nauchnoi konferentsii* (Smolensk, 1972) pp.24–5.

50. Ibid., pp. 13–7.

51. Golubtsov, *Staraia Moskva* no. 1, pp. 14, 26–8, 31.

52. Ibid., pp. 38–41; Filippov, *Trudy* VI, 10–11.

53. V. V. Mavrodin, 'Osnovnye problemy krest'ianskoi voiny v Rossii 1773–1775 godov', *Voprosy istorii* no. 8, (1964) 62. See also Shapiro and Pronshtein, note 41 above.

54. Alexander, *Emperor of the Cossacks*, pp. 206–11. See also Leo Yaresh, 'The "Peasant Wars" in Soviet Historiography' *Slavic Review* vol. 16 (1957); and, for a different interpretation of the Cossack theme, Philip Longworth, 'The Last Great Cossack Rising', *Journal of European Studies* vol. 3 (1970).

55. Kurmacheva, *Voprosy* p. 111.

56. R. R. Palmer in a letter to the author, 20 April 1970.

57. M. D. Kurmacheva, 'Ob uchastii krepostnoi intelligentsii v Krest'ianskoi Voine 1773–1775 gg', in L. V. Cherepnin *et al.* (eds), *Krest'ianskie voiny v Rossii XVII–XVIII vekov: Problemy, poiski, resheniia* (Moskva, 1974) pp. 307, 310.

58. R. V. Ovchinnikov (ed.), 'Sledstvie i sud nad E. I. Pugachevym', *Vopros istorii* 4 (1966) 123.

59. Beskrovnyi and Kafengauz, *Khrestomatiia* p. 394

60. J. T. Alexander, 'Recent Soviet Historiography on the Pugachev Revolt: A Review Article', *Canadian–American Slavic Studies* vol. 4 (1970); John T. Alexander, 'Western Views of the Pugachov Rebellion', *Slavonic and East European Review* vol. 48 (1970); O. E. Kornilovich, 'Obshchestvennoe mnenie Zapadnoi Evropy o Pugachevskom bunte', *Annaly* vol. 3 (St

Petersburg, 1923); A. I. Andrushchenko, 'Pugachevskoe vosstanie i Kiuchuk–Kainardzhiiskii mir', *Voprosy voennoi istorii Rossii XVIII i pervaia polovina XIX vekov* (Moscow, 1969).

61. *Sbornik imperatorskogo russkogo istoricheskogo obshchestva* XXXVI, 26–9.

62. V. N. Bochkarev, 'Russkoe obshchestvo ekaterininskoi epokhi i frantsuzskaia revoliutsiia', *Otechestvnennaia voina i russkoe obshchestvo* I (Moscow, 1911) 59.

63. An important source here is K. E. Dzhedzhula, *Rossiia* (full title in note 30). In many ways an imperfect work, it nevertheless contains much useful information and some stimulating hypotheses. See the review by Max Okenfuss in *Kritika* vol. 10 (1973–4).

64. É. Dumont, 'Dnevnik', *Golos minuvshego* 2 (1913) 153.

65. Count Ségur, Memories and Recollections III (London, 1827) 420.

66. *Sbornik IRIO* XXIII, 481, 495, 593.

67. *Russkii arkhiv* 1 (1878) 294.

68. *Arkhiv Vorontsova* XII (Moscow, 1877) 117.

69. See Dzhedzhula, *Rossiia* p. 151, for early reaction in the provinces.

70. *Sbornik IRIO* XVI, 431–2.

71. Dzhedzhula, *Rossiia* pp. 158–9.

72. S. N. Glinka, *Zapiski* (St Petersburg, 1895) p. 29.

73. A. Rambaud, *Recueil des Instructions données aux ambassadeurs et ministres de France depuis les traités de Westphalie jusqu' à la revolution française: Russie* II (Paris, 1890) 518–9.

74. *Arkhiv Vorontsova* IX (Moskva, 1876) 267.

75. E. L. Trifil'ev, *Ocherki iz istorii krepostnogo prava v Rossii: Tsarstvovanie Imperatora Pavla Pervogo* (Khar'kov, 1904) pp. 278ff; E. I. Koreneva, *Krest'ianskoe dvizhenie v Rossii v 1796–1798gg: Avtoreferat dissertatsii na soiskanie uchenoi stepeni kandidata istoricheskikh nauk* (Moscow, 1954) pp. 1, 9–10; M. De-Pule, 'Krest'ianskoe dvizhenie pri Imperatore Pavle Petroviche', *Russkii Arkhiv* (1869) 530, 548.

76. De-Pule, *Russkii Arkhiv* (1869) 536–7.

77. A. A. Bibikov, *Zapiski o zhizni i Sluzhbe A. I. Bibikova* (Moscow, 1865) p. 260.

78. Dzhedzhula, *Rossiia* pp. 171–2.

79. T. G. Snytko, 'Novye materialy po istorii obshchestvennogo dvizheniia kontsa XVIIIv', *Voprosy istorii* no. 9 (1952) 113–6. The evidence that Snytko presents does not appear to justify fully his assertion that the Smolensk group can be called a Jacobin circle.

80. A. Karasev, 'Kazn brat'ev Gruzinovykh: 27-ogo oktiabria 1800g', *Russkaia starina* VII (1873) 573; O. Gvinchidze, *Brat'ia Gruzinovy* (Tbilisi, 1965) p.6.

81. All the above from Dzhedzhula, *Rossiia* pp. 192, 204–20. Of course, Radishchev and Novikov, to some extent Chelishchev and Krechetov too, incurred Catherine's wrath for other reasons as well as for alleged sympathy with the French Revolution.

82. G. R. Derzhavin, *Zapiski* (Moscow, 1860) p. 381. See also the case of Kotzebue in *The most remarkable year in the life of Augustus von Kotzebue*

written by himself and translated by the Rev. Benjamin Beresford, 3 vols (London, 1802). And see for further examples, some of them debatable, Dzhedzhula, *Rossiia* pp. 220–34 and M. M. Shtrange, *Russkoe obshchestvo i frantsuzskaia revoliutsiia 1789–1794gg* (Moscow, 1956) pp. 159–61.

83. E. N. Burdzhalov, *Tsarizm v bor'be s frantsuzskoi burzhuaznoi revoliutsiei* (Moscow, 1940) p. 13.

84. Gvinchidze, *Brat'ia Gruzinovy* p. 34.

85. M. V. Klochkov, *Ocherki pravitel'stvennoi deiatel'nosti vremeni Pavla I* (Petrograd, 1916) pp. 134–5.

86. Gvinchidze, *Brat'ia Gruzinovy* p. 34.

87. C. F. Masson, *Mémoires secrets sur la Russie* II (Paris, 1800) p.39.

88. V. V. Sipovskii, 'Iz proshlogo russkoi tsenzury', *Russkaia starina* XCVIII (1889) 164.

89. A. McConnell, *A Russian Philosophe: Alexander Radishchev, 1749–1802* (The Hague, 1964) p. 130.

90. Dzhedzhula, *Rossiia* pp. 234–54; Shtrange, *Russkoe obshchestvo* pp. 176–7.

91. A. A. Fursenko, 'The American and French Revolutions of the Eighteenth Century: An attempt at a Comparative Characterization', *Soviet Studies in History* vol. 13 (1974) argues that the French Revolution has a much greater significance than does the American. Albert Soboul, 'La revolution française dans l'histoire du monde contemporain', *Studien über die Revolution* (Berlin, 1969) also insists on the pre-eminence of the French Revolution over the American.

92. Edmund Burke, *Works* vol. 3 (London, 1901) 367.

93. Marquis de Condorcet, *Outlines of an Historical View of the Progress of the Human Mind* (London, 1795) p. 265.

3. The Peaceful Modernisation of the Nineteenth Century

1. There is a vast literature on this subject taking such an 'optimistic' view. See, for example, G. Katkov *et al., Russia Enters the Twentieth Century, 1894–1917* (London, 1971); T. G. Stavrou (ed.), *Russia under the Last Tsar* (Minneapolis, Minn., 1969); Paul R. Gregory, 'Russian Industrialisation and Economic Growth: Results and Perspectives of Western Research', *Jahrbücher für Geschichte Osteuropas* vol. 25 (1977).

2. See note 27 below.

3. This passage comes from near the beginning of *The Communist Manifesto*.

4. Two books which examine this theme, albeit in a different manner, are W. Laqueur, *Russia and Germany* (London, 1965) and H. Schreiber, *Teuton and Slav* (London, 1961). In some respects, our approach follows that of Perry Anderson, *Lineages of the Absolutist State* (London, 1974) and of Barrington Moore Jr, *Social Origins of Dictatorship and Democracy: Lord and Peasant in the Making of the Modern World* (Hardmondsworth, 1969).

5. See, for example, J. L. H. Keep, 'Russia 1613–45' in J. P. Cooper (ed.), *The New Cambridge Modern History*, vol. 4 (Cambridge, 1971) and chapter 1 above.

6. See, for example, L. R. Lewitter, 'Poland, the Ukraine and Russia in the 17th Century', *Slavonic and East European Review* vol. 27 (1948–9). And see chapter 1 above.

7. Hans Rosenberg, 'The Rise of the Junkers in Brandenburg–Prussia 1410–1653', *American Historical Review* XLIX (1943–4) 1–22, 228–42; F. L. Carsten, *The Origins of Prussia* (London, 1954) pp. 176–7.

8. Carsten, *Origins* pp. 179ff.

9. Ibid., p. 181.

10. See E. J. Feuchtwanger, *Prussia: Myth and Reality* (London, 1970) pp. 38ff.

11. Ibid., p. 47. For Russia, see S. M. Troitskii, 'Finansovaia politika russkogo absoliutizma vo vtoroi polovine XVII–XVIII–vv', in Druzhinin, *Absoliutizm* p. 295.

12. Feuchtwanger, *Prussia* p. 49.

13. For informed views on this subject, see H. Schreiber, *Teuton and Slav*, p. 256ff; Marc Raeff, 'The Enlightenment in Russia and Russian Thought in the Enlightenment' in J. G. Garrard (ed.), *The Eighteenth Century in Russia* (Oxford, 1973).

14. See N. M. Druzhinin, 'Prosveshchennyi absoliutizm v Rossii' in Druzhinin, *Absoliutizm*; I. A. Fedosov, 'Prosveshchennyi absoliutizm v Rossii, *Voprosy istorii* No. 9 (1970); and the World Profiles on Frederick II and Catherine II edited respectively by Peter Paret and Marc Raeff.

15. See, for example, W. H. Bruford, *Germany in the Eighteenth Century: The Social Background of the Literary Revival* (Cambridge, 1965); H. Rogger, *National Consciousness in Eighteenth-Century Russia* (Cambridge, Mass., 1960).

16. Quoted by D. B. Horn, *British Public Opinion and the Partition of Poland* (Edinburgh, 1945) pp. 18–9. Compare Goethe's observation that: 'It was Frederick the Great and the Seven Years War that first gave German literature a subject with a real greatness and living interest': Bruford, *Germany* p. 296; and Kliuchevskii's assertion that 'Russians under Catherine felt themselves to be not only people, but almost the first people of Europe: V. O. Kliuchevskii, *Sochineniia* vol. 5 (Moskva, 1958) 370.

17. See, for example, G. A. Craig, 'Engagement and Neutrality in Germany: The Case of Georg Forster, 1754–94', *Journal of Modern History* 41 (1969); M. A. Bond, 'The Political Conversion of Friedrich von Gentz', *European Studies Review* 3 (1973) 1–12; and, for an interesting attempt to go beyond the familiar arguments about French influences during this period, see R. M. Berdahl, 'New Thoughts on German Nationalism', *American Historical Review* 77 (1972) 65–80. The East German historians, with their socioeconomic approach, have been able to bring out well the positive developments in Germany during the Napoleonic period. See Andreas Dorpalen, 'The German Struggle against Napoleon', *Journal of Modern History* 41 (1969) 488. For Russia, see chapter 2 above.

18. J. G. Blum, 'The Rise of Serfdom in Eastern Europe', *American Historical Review* 62 (1956–7).

19. E. D. Domar, 'The causes of slavery or serfdom: A hypothesis', *Journal of Economic History* 30 (1970).

20. See chapter 2 above and H. J. Habbakuk and M. Postan (eds), *The Cambridge Economic History of Europe* vol. 6 (Cambridge, 1966), especially the remarks by D. S. Landes on pp. 363–5 and R. Portal on p. 602. For some interesting qualifications of the notion of German backwardness see K. Borchardt, *The Fontana Economic History of Europe* IV (London, 1972) ch. 4; T. Kemp, *Industrialization in Nineteenth-Century Europe* (London, 1969) pp. 81–2.

21. The passage comes from near the end of *The Communist Manifesto*.

22. See, for example, Otto Pflanze, *Bismarck and the Development of Germany: The Period of Unification, 1815–71* (Princeton, 1963): H. Böhme, *The Foundation of the German Empire* (London, 1971) pp. 40ff.

23. See, for example, W. M. Pintner, *Russian Economic Policy under Nicholas I* (Ithaca, New York, 1967) pp. 5–7, 22–5.

24. Ibid., pp. 250–5.

25. Marx and Engels, quoted by N. M. Druzhinin in A. P. Bazhova *et al.* (eds), *Istoriia SSSR,* (Moskva, 1967) 260.

26. For a good introduction to the abolition, see T. Emmons (ed.), *Emancipation of the Russian Serfs* (New York, 1970).

27. See, for example, V. I. Lenin, *Collected Works* 4th Ed., vol. 13 (Moscow and London, 1962) p. 239.

28. For one aspect of the Kaiser's (and the Tsar's) influence, see R. A. Kann, 'Dynastic Relations and European Power Politics, 1848–1918', *Journal of Modern History* 45 (1973).

29. For a discussion and qualification of an important work on this subject, see O. Pflanze, 'Another Crisis among German Historians?: Helmut Böhme's *Deutschlands Weg zur Grossmacht*', *Journal of Modern History* 40 (1958) 118–29.

30. A. Gerschenkron, *Europe in the Russian Mirror: Four Lectures in Economic History* (Cambridge, 1970) p. 102.

31. On this question, see the informative and perspicacious discussion in the *Times Literary Supplement* (1 Feb., 1974) pp. 93ff.

32. See A. Rosenburg, *Imperial Germany: The Birth of the German Republic, 1871–1918* (London, reprint 1970) pp. 44ff.

33. Hans-Ulrich Wehler, 'Bismarck's Imperialism, 1862–1890', *Past and Present* no. 48 (1966) 119–55.

34. K. D. Barkin, *The Controversy over German Industrialization* (Chicago, 1972) pp. 40–2.

35. Wehler, *Past and Present* nos 48, 134, 146, 153. Compare the first two chapters of V. R. Berghahn, *Germany and the Approach of War* (London, 1973) and the interesting review of this book by J. Steinberg, who stresses the strength of the German Empire rather than its 'insoluble' problems, in *Historical Journal* XVI (1973) 203.

36. T. H. Von Laue, 'A Secret Memorandum of Sergei Witte on the Industrialization of Imperial Russia', *Journal of Modern History* 26 (1954).

37. See, for example, J. P. McKay, *Pioneers for Profit: Foreign Entrepreneurship and Russian Industrialization, 1885–1913* (Chicago, 1970), who argues on p. 387 that: 'The Russian experience suggests that strategies of development based on market economies can use large-scale private foreign

investment to help meet the challenge of industrial revolution.' For a contrary view, see B. V. Anan'ich, *Rossiia i mezhdunarodnyi kapital, 1897–1914: Ocherki istorii finansovykh otnoshenii* (Leningrad, 1970) p. 299; 'Even the most perfect financial system could not save the already doomed political regime of the last Russian tsar.'

38. Pleve, quoted in *The Memoirs of Count Witte* (New York and London, 1921) p. 250.

39. See chapter 4 below and H. D. Mehlinger, J. M. Thompson, *Count Witte and the Tsarist Government in the 1905 Revolution* (Bloomington, Indiana, 1972) pp. 32–3. Omitted here for reasons of space have been the late nineteenth-century crises of tsarism as analysed by P. A. Zaionchkovskii and other Soviet historians.

40. G. A. Hosking, *The Russian Constitutional Experiment: Government and Duma, 1907–1914* (Cambridge, 1973) p. 113. Nicholas and the extreme right tended to cut themselves off from the Duma as Wilhelm and his entourage did from the Reichstag.

41. O. Hoetzsch, *The Evolution of Russia* (London, 1966) p. 176. For contrasting views of the success of Stolypin's peasant policy, see W. E. Mosse, 'Stolypin's Villages', *Slavonic and East European Review* 43 (1965) and G. B. Tokmakoff, 'Stolypin's agrarian reform; An appraisal', *Russian Review* 30 (1971). Lenin believed that the Stolypin reform followed the Prussian path. See *Collected Works* vol. 13, pp. 243–4.

42. A. Gerschenkron, 'Problems and patterns of Russian economic development', in C. E. Black (ed.), *The Transformation of Russian Society* (Cambridge, Mass., 1960) p. 61.

43. L. D. Trotsky, *The History of the Russian Revolution* (London, 1965) pp. 27–8.

44. Marx and Engels, *The Communist Manifesto*, preface to the Russian edition. For a general scholarly study, see R. P. Koniushaia, *Karl Marks i revoliutsionaia Rossiia* (Moscow, 1975).

45. For Durnovo's memorandum, see F. A. Golder (ed.), *Documents of Russian History, 1914–1917* (New York, 1927) pp. 3–23.

46. Quoted by Michael D. Biddiss, 'From Illusion to Destruction: The Germanic bid for world power, 1897–1945', review article, *British Journal of International Studies* 2 (1976) 183.

47. This was clear enough at the time to Miliukov and others. See Trotsky, *History* p. 845.

48. *Sbornik IRIO* xxxiii, 293–4.

49. Quoted by J. C. Miller in *Triumph of Freedom, 1775–1783* (Boston, 1948) p. 586.

50. Quoted by Paul Dukes, *The Emergence of the Super-Powers: A Short Comparative History of the USA and the USSR* (London and New York, 1970) p. 49. Some of the following argument is taken from that work.

51. R. W. Emerson, *Works* (Edinburgh, 1906) p. 949.

52. From *Correspondence Respecting Central Asia* HMSO C. 704 (London, 1873) pp. 72–5.

53. These quotations from L. A. Rand, 'America views Russian serf emancipation', *Mid-America* 50 (1968) 43–4, 47–8.

54. See Douglass C. North, *Growth and Welfare in the American Past: A new economic history* (Englewood Cliffs, New Jersey, 1966) especially chs 10 and 11.

55. Quoted by Dukes, *The Emergence* pp. 80–1.

56. For an interesting Soviet view of the Progressive movement, see I. A. Beliavskaia, *Burzhuaznyi reformizm v SSHA* (Moskva, 1968).

57. John Higham, quoted by Marilyn Blatt Young, 'American Expansion, 1870–1900: The Far East', in Barton J. Bernstein (ed.), *Towards a New Past: Dissenting Essays in American History* (New York, 1969) p. 185.

58. Woodrow Wilson, quoted by Lloyd C. Gardner, 'American Foreign Policy, 1900–1921: A Second Look at the Realist Critique of American Diplomacy', in Bernstein, *Towards a New Past* p. 212.

59. O. H. Palmer, Secretary, *Statement of the Origin, Organisation and Progress of the Russian–American Telegraph Western Union Extension, Collins' Overland Line . . . .* (Rochester, New York, 1866) p. 33.

60. Glyn Barratt, 'The Enemy that never was: The New Zealand "Russian Scare" of 1870–1885', *New Zealand Slavonic Journal* no. 1 (1976).

Part Two   The Russian Revolutions and Their Impact

1. L. Trotsky, *The History of the Russian Revolution* (London, 1965) p. 27.

2. Ibid., p. 31. And see, for example, A. Gerschenkron, *Europe in the Russian Mirror: Four Lectures in Economic History* (Cambridge, 1970) pp. 109–10.

3. See Frantz Fanon, *The Wretched of the Earth* (Harmondsworth, 1971) and Jean-Paul Sartre's prefatory remark on p. 9, that in this book '. . . the Third World finds *itself* and speaks to *itself* through his voice.'

4. Victor Zorza in *The Guardian Weekly*, 1 Jan. 1978. Of course, the Chinese make the distinction between the 'imperialism' of the USA and the 'social imperialism' of the USSR, and also seek to drive a diplomatic wedge between them.

5. See, for example, Zbigniew Brzezinski, *Between Two Ages: America's Role in the Technetronic Era* (New York, 1970) pp. 293–301, and the comments on his outlook by Jonathan Steele in the *Guardian* 29 Dec. 1977.

4. The Three Russian Revolutions

1. Leon Trotsky, *1905* (Harmondsworth, 1973) p. 7.

2. See W. Sablinsky, *The Road to Bloody Sunday* (Princeton, 1976).

3. Quoted by Lionel Kochan, *Russia in Revolution* (London, 1970) p. 93.

4. Trotsky, *1905* pp. 98–9.

5. John Keep, *The Rise of Social Democracy in Russia* (Oxford, 1963) pp. 195–6.

6. Trotsky, *1905* p. 122.

7. E. D. Chermenskii, *Burzhuaziia i tsarizm v pervoi russkoi revoliutsii* (Moscow, 1970) assesses the manner in which the middle-class centre

claimed for itself the achievements of 1905.

8. Trotsky, *1905* p. 141.

9. Ibid., p. 91.

10. Julius Braunthal, *History of the International, 1864–1914* (London, 1966) p. 298.

11. Ibid., pp. 298–9.

12. Lenin and Pavlovich quoted in Ivar Spector, *The First Russian Revolution: Its Impact on Asia* (Englewood Cliffs, New Jersey, 1962) p. 123.

13. See especially *Mother* and *The Life of a Useless Man*.

14. Maureen Perrie, trans., ed. and intro., 'The Russian Peasantry in 1907–1908: A Survey by the Socialist–Revolutionary Party', *History Workshop* no. 4 (1977) 182, 187, 190. See also Maureen Perrie, 'The Social Composition and Structure of the Socialist–Revolutionary Party before 1917', *Soviet Studies* vol. 24 (1972).

15. Leopold Haimson, 'The Problem of Social Stability in Urban Russia, 1905–1917', *Slavic Review* 23 and 24 (1964–5) and later comments by Arthur P. Mendel, T. H. Von Laue, George L. Yaney, Truman B. Cross and Alfred Levin.

16. Norman Stone, *The Eastern Front, 1914–1917* (London, 1975) pp. 20–4.

17. See, for example, Violet Conolly, 'The "nationalities question" in the last phase of tsardom' and Hans Bräker, 'The Muslim revival in Russia' in G. Katkov *et al.* (eds), *Russia enters the Twentieth Century, 1894–1917* (London, 1971).

18. Stone, *The Eastern Front* pp. 12–3.

19. E. N. Burdzhalov, *Vtoraia russkaia revoliutsiia: Vosstanie v Petrograde* (Moskva, 1967) p. 85.

20. See Raymond Pearson, *The Russian Moderates and the Crisis of Tsarism, 1914–1917* (London, 1977) especially ch. 7 – 'The Reluctant Revolutionaries'.

21. Burdzhalov, *Vtoraia: Vosstanie* p. 92.

22. On 'spontaneity' and the debate concerning it in the Soviet Union, see David Longley, 'Some Historiographical Problems of Bolshevik Party History (The Kronstadt Bolsheviks in March 1917)', *Jahrbücher für Geschichte Osteuropas* vol. 22 (1974); and Tsuyoshi Hasegawa, 'The Bolsheviks and the Formation of the Petrograd Soviet in the February Revolution', *Soviet Studies* vol. 29 (1977). For complete opposition to the concept of 'spontaneity', see G. Katkov, *Russia 1917: The February Revolution* (London, 1967).

23. John Keep, *The Russian Revolution: A Study in Mass Mobilization* (London, 1976) p. 52 quotes the Moscow police chief's view that the bread queues in the old capital had the effect of 'tens of thousands of revolutionary proclamations'.

24. Leon Trotsky, *The History of the Russian Revolution* (London, 1965) pp. 223–232.

25. Lenin, *Collected Works* vol. 24, pp. 21–4.

26. Ibid., vol. 23, 253. Lenin is talking here in a lecture on 1905 given on 9 Jan. 1917 to an audience of young 'friends and comrades' in Zurich with a context of Europe and the world rather than Russia alone. He also says: 'We

must not be deceived by the present grave-like stillness in Europe. Europe is pregnant with revolution.'

27. From Miliukov's note of 1 May 1917. See Trotsky, *The History* p. 350, where he describes the note and talks of Miliukov's aim to 'use the war against the revolution'.

28. These two quotations from Branko Lazitch and Milorad M. Drachkovitch, *Lenin and the Comintern* vol. 1 (Stanford, California, 1972) pp. 21, 28–9.

29. *The Times* 29–31 August, 11–15 Sept. 1917.

30. For contrasting interpretations of this process, see Keep, *The Russian Revolution*, and Trotsky, *The History*.

31. Lenin, *Collected Works* vol. 26, 74.

32. For contrasting interpretations of the event, see R. V. Daniels, *Red October: The Bolshevik Revolution of 1917* (London, 1967; New York, 1969) and P. N. Sobolev et al., *History of the October Revolution* (Moscow, 1966). Lenin quotation from *Collected Works* vol. 26, 236.

33. Notably O. H. Radkey, *The Election to the Russian Constituent Assembly of 1917* (Cambridge, Massachusetts, 1950).

34. Arthur Ransome, 'Russia', *The Encyclopaedia Britannica* supplementary vol. III (London and New York, 1926) p. 415. And see Lionel Kochan, 'Kadet Policy in 1917 and the Constituent Assembly', *Slavonic and East European Review* 45 (1967). For an appreciation of Arthur Ransome as analyst of Russian revolutionary affairs, see W. Mandel, 'Arthur Ransome: Eyewitness in Russia, 1919', *Slavic Review* 27 (1968).

35. Ransome, *The Encyclopaedia* vol. III, p. 415.

36. Ibid., p. 415. And see Keep, *The Russian Revolution* parts IV and V.

37. Ransome, The Encyclopaedia vol. III, p. 415.

38. Lenin, *Collected Works* vol. 30, pp. 253–75. And for a scholarly Soviet analysis of the Constituent Assembly, see O. N. Znamenskii, *Vserossiiskoe uchreditel'noe sobranie* (Leningrad, 1976). Gorky quotation from R. E. F. Smith (ed.) *The Russian Peasant 1920 and 1984* (London, 1977) pp. 27.

39. See generally J. Wheeler-Bennett, *Brest-Litovsk: The Forgotten Peace* (London, 1934; New York, 1971).

40. Ransome, *The Encyclopaedia*, vol. III, 415, 417–8.

41. A Competent account may be found in D.Footman, *Civil War in Russia* (London, 1961).

42. Ransome, *The Encyclopaedia* vol. III, p. 419.

43. Quoted in Louis Fischer, *The Soviets in World Affairs* vol. 1 (London, 1930) p. 157.

44. Quoted in John M. Thompson, *Russia, Bolshevism and the Versailles Peace* (Princeton, 1966) p. 84. For a comparable approach to that of Thompson, see A. J. Mayer, *Politics and Diplomacy of Peacemaking: Containment and Counter-revolution at Versailles, 1918–1919* (New York, 1967).

45. James B. Scott, *President Wilson's Foreign Policy* (New York, 1918) pp. 354–63; Thompson, *Russia* p. 335. And see generally N. G. Levin Jr, *Woodrow Wilson and World Politics: America's Response to War and Revolution* (New York and London, 1970), and the many works of

W. A. Williams.

46. Quoted by I. D. Buzinkai, 'The Bolsheviks, the League of Nations, and the Paris Peace Conference, 1919', *Soviet Studies* vol. 19 (1967–8) p. 258.

47. Thompson, *Russia* p. 319.

48. Quoted by O. G. Gankin, 'The Bolsheviks and the Founding of the Third International', *Slavic Review* 1 (1941) 99.

49. Thompson, *Russia* p. 343.

50. Ibid., p. 319.

51. Quoted by Buzinkai, *Soviet Studies* vol. 19, p. 259.

52. Quoted by Carr, *The Bolshevik Revolution* vol. 3, p. 116.

53. Ibid., p. 130. A British delegate Fineberg was present in a 'consultative' capacity.

54. Ibid., p. 132n.

55. Ibid., p. 192. The atmosphere of the Second Comintern Congress is well caught in A. Rosmer, *Lenin's Moscow* (London, 1971).

56. For the '21 Conditions' see Jane Degras (ed.), *The Communist International* 1 (1956) 168–172. For the context, see *The Second Congress of the Communist International: Minutes of the Proceedings* (London, 1977).

57. See Brian Pearce (ed.), *Baku: Congress of the Peoples of the East, September 1920: Stenographic Report* (London, 1977) pp. 34, 36; S. White, 'Communism and the East: The Baku Congress, 1920', *Slavic Review* 33 (1974).

58. See Paul Avrich, *Kronstadt 1921* (Princeton, New Jersey, 1957); R. V. Daniels, 'The Kronstadt Revolt of 1921: A Study in the Dynamics of Revolution', *Slavic Review* 10 (1951); E. Mawdsley, 'The Baltic Fleet and the Kronstadt Mutiny', *Soviet Studies* vol. 24 (1973).

59. Lenin, *Collected Works* vol. 32 pp. 275–82; See also Rosmer, *Lenin's Moscow* pp. 119–22.

60. *The First Congress of the Toilers of the Far East, Moscow–Petrograd 1922* (Petrograd, 1922; reprint London, 1970) pp. 141–8.

5. *The Western World*

1. Ron Grant, 'The Society of Friends of Russian Freedom (1890–1917) – A case study in Internationalism', *The Journal of the Scottish Labour History Society* no. 3 (1970) 12.

2. Ibid., 15–16. See also Barry Hollingsworth, 'The Society of Friends of Russian Freedom: English Liberals and Russian Socialists, 1890–1917', *Oxford Slavonic Papers* New Ser., 3 (1970) 45–64.

3. Grant, *The Journal* no. 3; 17.

4. W. S. Adams, 'British reactions to the 1905 Russian Revolution', *Marxist Quarterly* 2 (1955) 173.

5. I. S. Iazhborovskaia, 'Revoliutsiia 1905–1907 godov i mezhdunarodnoe rabochee dvizhenie', *Istoriia SSSR*, 1 (1975) 29–36. Iazhborovskaia quotes Rosa Luxemburg, *Gesammelte Werke* Bd. 2 (Berlin, 1972) 150. Compare Robert Looker (ed. and intro.), *Rosa Luxemburg: Selected Political Writings* (London, 1972) pp. 117–33.

6. See, for example, Teddy Roosevelt to Upton Sinclair on 15 Mar. 1906, *Letters* vol. 5, pp. 179–80.

7. A. V. Piaskovskii, *Revoliutsiia 1905–1907gg v Rossii* (Moscow, 1966) p. 288.

8. Concerning later opposition to asylum in Great Britain for Nicholas II, George V wrote: 'Those damn politicians, if it had been one of their kind, they would have acted fast enough. But merely because the poor man was royal. . . .' See Robert D. Warth, *The Allies and the Russian Revolution: From the Fall of the Monarchy to the Peace of Brest–Litovsk* (Durham, North Carolina, 1954) p. 36.

9. Lloyd George, *War Memoirs* vol. 3 (London, 1934) pp. 1636–46.

10. E. N. Burdzhalov, *Vtoraia russkaia revoliutsiia: Moskva, front, periferiia* (Moscow, 1971) pp. 416–8.

11. See, for example, A. P. Mendel (ed.) *P. N. Milyukov: Political Memoirs, 1905–1917* (Ann Arbor, Michigan, 1967) pp. 435–9.

12. General Sir Alfred Knox, the British military attaché, made the following comment when Miliukov said that Russia would fight to the last drop of blood: 'I have no doubt that Miliukov would, but can he answer for Russia?' See Warth, *The Allies* p. 32.

13. Burdzhalov, *Vtoraia: Moskva* pp. 428–32.

14. William Gallacher, *Revolt on the Clyde: An Autobiography* (London, 1936) p. 137.

15. See, for example, G. A. Williams, *Proletarian Order: Antonio Gramsci, Factory Councils and the Origins of Italian Communism, 1911–1921* (London, 1978) p. 61.

16. Quoted by Burdzhalov, *Vtoraia: Moskva* p. 435.

17. Stephen White, 'Soviets in Britain: The Leeds Convention of 1917', *International Review of Social History*, vol. 19 (1974) p. 166.

18. Alastair Davidson, *Antonio Gramsci* (London, 1977) p. 83.

19. Burdzhalov, *Vtoraia: Moskva* pp. 438–40.

20. Lloyd George, *War Memoirs* vol. 4 (London, 1934) p. 1933 wrote: 'The coming of the Russian Revolution lit up the skies with a lurid flash of hope for all those who were dissatisfied with the existing order of society. It certainly encouraged all the malcontents in the ranks of labour to foment discord and organise discontent. Fishers in troubled waters, they did not create the unrest, but they took full advantage of it. Their activities sprang into special prominence in 1917, and seriously added to our difficulties.'

21. Burdzhalov, *Vtoraia: Moskva* pp. 440–1.

22. Ibid., pp. 442–3; Gerhard Schulz, *Revolutions and Peace Treaties* (London, 1974) p. 72.

23. John Paton, *Proletarian Pilgrimage* (London, 1935) p. 299.

24. Ken Coates, intro., *British Labour and the Russian Revolution: A Report from the Daily Herald* (Nottingham [no date]) p. 20.

25. For Gallacher's comments on this, see his *Revolt* pp. 164–5.

26. Ralph Miliband, *Parliamentary Socialism: A Study in the Politics of Labour* (London, 1961) pp. 56–7. Anderson quotes from Coates, *British Labour* pp. 12–13, 30. See also S. R. Graubard, *British Labour and the Russian Revolution, 1917–1924* (Cambridge, Massachusetts and London,

1956) pp. 39–41, including an account by Will Thorne of an interview with George V who was worried about the outcome of the Leeds Conference. Thorne assured the King that 'in my humble judgment there will never be a physical violent revolution in this country'. Compare Lloyd George, *War Memoirs* vol. 4 (1938). And see White, *International Review*, vol. 19, who describes the discussions throughout Great Britain concerning the establishment of Soviets or Councils in 1917 and 1918. And, for echoes as far away as Aberdeen, see Lewis Grassic Gibbon and Hugh MacDiarmid, *Scottish Scene: or The Intelligent Man's Guide to Albyn* (London, 1934) pp. 242–3, where Grassic Gibbon talks of 'the founding of the Aberdeen Soviet when the news of the Bolshevik Revolution came through from Russia: and how I and a cub reporter from another paper attended the foundation meeting; and were elected to the Soviet Council . . . .'

27. The passage is to be found towards the end of *The Communist Manifesto*.

28. This analysis of the German Revolution taken from Schulz, *Revolutions*; E. H. Carr, *The Bolshevik Revolution* vol. 3 (Harmondsworth, 1966); A. S. Lindemann, *The 'Red Years': European Socialism versus Bolshevism, 1919–1921* (Berkeley, California, 1974); A. J. Ryder, *The German Revolution of 1918* (Cambridge, 1967); and R. Rürup, 'Problems of the German Revolution 1918–19', *Journal of Contemporary History* 3 (1968)

29. See R. L. Tökes, *Bela Kun and the Hungarian Soviet Republic: The Origins and Role of the Communist Party of Hungary in the Revolutions of 1918–1919* (New York, 1967).

30. See, for example, C. A. Macartney, *The Social Revolution in Austria* (Cambridge, 1926); F. L. Carsten, *Revolution in Central Europe, 1918–1919* (London, 1972) pp. 78–126.

31. Schulz, *Revolutions*; Carr, *The Bolshevik Revolution* vol. 3.

32. Lindemann, *The 'Red Years'* pp. 249–86; R. Wohl, *French Communism in the Making, 1914–1924* (Stanford, California, 1966) especially ch. 5; Williams, *Proletarian Order* ch. 11.

33. See, for example, G. H. Meaker, *The Revolutionary Left in Spain, 1914–1923* (Stanford, California, 1974); A. F. Upton *et al.*, *Communism in Scandinavia and Finland* (New York and London, 1973); *Encyclopaedia Britannica* Supp. Vol. ii (London and New York, 1926) p. 1036.

34. Gallacher, *Revolt* p. 221. For confirmation of Gallacher's assessment of army unrest, see Dave Lamb, *Mutinies, 1917–1920* (London, no date). For the navy, see Public Record Office, Admiralty Digest 1919, listing items such as 'Bolshevik Agents in the Fleet' and 'Distribution of Bolshevik Literature'. See also letter from Tom Hadwin, *History Workshop* no. 4 (1977).

35. Minutes of the War Cabinet, 30 Jan. 1919, quoted in *Glasgow 1919: The Story of the 40 Hours Strike* (Glasgow, [no date]) no pagination. And see R. Desmarais, 'Lloyd George and the development of the British government's strikebreaking organisation', *International Review of Social History* vol. 20 (1975). Desmarais argues that Lloyd George agreed with the advice of Tom Jones that 'Bolshevik propaganda is only dangerous in so far as it can lodge itself in the soil of real grievances', but at the same time was determined to crush unrest wherever it appeared.

36. See, for example, R. Challinor, *The Origins of British Bolshevism* (London, 1977); J. Klugmann, *The History of the Communist Party of Great Britain* vol. 1 (London, 1968); L. J. Macfarlane, *The British Communist Party: Its Origin and Development until 1929* (London, 1966). For evidence of revolutionary feeling in Glasgow, the Rhondda Valley and elsewhere in the summer of 1920, see Whiting Williams *Full up and Fed up: The Worker's Mind in Crowded Britain* (London and New York, 1921). I owe this reference to Raphael Samuel.

37. See, for example, Stephen White, *Britain and the Bolshevik Revolution: A Study in the Politics of Diplomacy, 1920–1924* (London, 1978) chs. 7 and 8, and Conclusion.

38. Marcus Wheeler, 'Soviet Interest in Ireland', *Survey* 21 (1975) 81–5; *The Second Congress of the Communist International* 1 (1977) 143, 317–26.

39. William M. Brown, *Communism and Christianity: Analyzed and Contrasted from the Marxian and Darwinian points of view* (Galion, Ohio, 1927) under frontispiece.

40. See, for example, T. Draper, *American Communism and Soviet Russia: The Formative Period* (New York, 1960) pp. 13–24. For a Soviet analysis, see A. V. Berezkin, *Oktiabr'skaia revoliutsiia i SSHA 1917–1922* (Moscow, 1967) ch. 4.

41. Draper, *American Communism* p. 16.

42. Ole Hanson, *Americanism versus Bolshevism* (New York, 1920) pp. 283–4.

43. Clayton R. Lusk *et al.*, *Revolutionary Radicalism: Its History, Purpose and Tactics* (Albany, New York, 1920) pp. 2294, 2322–3, 2385–6.

44. Compare the celebrated remarks of Mr Dooley, Finlay Peter Dunne's creation: 'We're the greatest crusaders that iver was – f'r a short distance.'

45. See, for example, the *Calgary Daily Herald* 16 June 1919.

46. Lamb, *Mutinies* pp. 20–7, for an account, a reconstruction and an assessment of the Kinmel Mutiny. See also *The Times* 8, 10, 26 Mar. 1919. Possibly, the red flags were used as signals in addition to their revolutionary implications, themselves accentuated by the fact that one of the leaders was William Tarasevich, of Russian descent. He and four others were shot or bayonetted dead.

47. *The Calgary Daily Herald* of that date also carried stories with the headlines 'Human Flesh Sold in Russia to Famine Stricken People' and 'Spartacans Fighting like Wild Beasts' as well as the declaration by Sir Rider Haggard that the Kinmel Mutiny had clearly demonstrated that 'The Empire should be kept for the citizens of the Empire.'

48. *The Calgary Daily Herald* 26 May 1919. Threatened with deportation for their alleged infringement of Orders in Council prohibiting socialist meetings and circulation of socialist literature, 'aliens' – mainly of Russian descent on this occasion – had issued a joint protest earlier in the year. See J. G. Eayrs, *In Defence of Canada* vol. 1 (Toronto, 1964) p. 43. *The Calgary Daily Herald* 27 May 1919 called for the censorship of *The Soviet* being published in Edmonton.

49. Nevertheless, Roy Maclaren, *Canadians in Russia, 1918–1919* (Toronto, 1976) p. 516 argues that labour unrest in Canada in the year 1919 has been

under-emphasised.

50. I. Avakumovic, *The Communist Party of Canada* (Toronto, 1975) pp. 10ff.

51. H. J. and R. E. Simons, *Class and Colour in South Africa, 1850–1950* (Harmondsworth, 1969) pp. 88, 183, 285–6. See W. H. Harrison, *Memoirs of a Socialist in South Africa, 1903–1947* (Cape Town [no date]) pp. 68–72 for a description of the foundation of the Communist Party of South Africa. For biographies of the other two leaders, see R. K. Cope, *Comrade Bill: The Life and Times of W. H. Andrews, Workers' Leader* (Cape Town, 1943) and E. Roux, *S. P. Bunting: A Political Biography* (Cape Town, 1944). Bunting argued in 1922 that the maintenance of the colour bar by the Rand strikers was really a fight for civilised standards. Roux, on p. 27 of his biography, says that Bunting ended up in the 'negrophilist camp'.

52. Alastair B. Davidson, *The Communist Party of Australia: A Short History* (Stanford, California, 1969) p. 6.

53. Davidson, *The Communist Party* chs. 1 and 2. For earlier background, see Robin A. Gollan, *Radicals and Working Class Politics, 1850–1910* (Melbourne, 1960).

54. Manning Clark, *A Short History of Australia* (New York, 1969) p. 215.

55. P. J. O'Farrell, *Harry Holland: Militant Socialist* (Canberra, 1964) p. 108.

56. More respectable newspapers such as the *Lyttelton Times*, the *New Zealand Herald*, and *The Christchurch Press* took a line similar to that of the *Sydney Morning Herald*.

57. O'Farrell, *Harry Holland* p. 111. Holland and his colleagues were denounced by the Marxian Association as 'the Kerenskys and Scheidemanns of New Zealand'. Ibid., p. 110.

58. John A. Lee, *Rhetoric at the Red Dawn* (Auckland and London 1965) p. 7.

59. H. O. Roth, 'The October Revolution and New Zealand Labour', *Political Science* 13 (1961) 45–55.

60. Keith Sinclair, *A History of New Zealand* (Harmondsworth, 1969) p. 244.

61. Sinclair, *A History*.

62. Kikuchi Masanori, *Roshiya Kakumei to Nihonjin* (*The Russian Revolution and the Japanese* (Tokyo, 1973) as summarised and translated by Tsuyoshi Hasegawa, pp. 61–7, 103–6, 247–50, 256–7, 259–65.

63. Chitoshi Yanaga, *Japan since Perry* (New York and London, 1949) pp. 468–82.

64. Robert A. Scalapino, *The Japanese Communist Movement, 1920–1966* (Berkeley and Los Angeles, California, 1967) pp. 14–21. For some worthwhile articles on the development of Japanese socialism, see *Rivista Storica Italiana* Anno LXXXIX (1977).

65. Carr, *The Bolshevik Revolution* vol. 3, pp. 516–7.

66. W. K. Hancock and Jean Van der Poel (eds), *The Smuts Papers* vol. 4 (London, 1966) pp 83–7.

67. G. Pitt-Rivers, *The World Significance of the Russian Revolution*

(Oxford, 1920) p. 44.

68. Frank Anstey, *Red Europe* (Glasgow, 1921) p. 176. For a fictional representation of Anstey, see the character of 'Frank Ashton' in Frank Hardy's novel *Power Without Glory*.

6. The Third World

1. Vilhjalmur Stefansson, *The Northward Course of Empire* (London, 1922); *The Adventure of Wrangel Island* (London, 1926).

2. See, for example, the brief account of the Bellingsgausen–Lazarev Expeditions, 1819–1821, in Dimitri M. Lebedev and Vadim I. Grekov, 'Geographical Exploration by the Russians', a contribution to Herman R. Friis (ed.) *The Pacific Basin: A History of its Geographical Exploration* (New York, 1967) pp. 194–7. I owe the references in notes 1 and 2 to Terence Armstrong.

3. See, for example, *The Second Congress of the Communist International*, 1 (London, 1977) 109–20. See also Dov Bing, *Revolution in China: Sneevlietian Strategy* Auckland University, Unpublished M.A. Thesis, especially ch. 5.

4. Lenin, *Imperialism: The Highest Stage of Capitalism* (Moscow, 1970) pp. 73–4.

5. *Appendix to the Journals of the House of Representatives of New Zealand, 1920* 1, A4, A5.

6. C. E. Russell, *Bolshevism and the United States* (Indianapolis, 1919) p. 4.

7. *Encyclopaedia Britannica* 11th ed. (Cambridge, 1910).

8. H. W. Wilson and J. A. Hammerton (eds), *The Great War: The Standard History of the All-Europe Conflict* vol. 3 (London, 1915) p. 177.

9. PRO, WO 95, 4532.

10. David Mitchell, *1919: Red Mirage* (London, 1970) p. 124.

11. J. F. Cody, *Man of Two Worlds: Sir Maui Pomare* (Wellington, 1953) pp. 112–14.

12. All the above communications from PRO, CO 209:300.

13. Council for World Mission Archives, School of Oriental and African Studies, London, South Seas 1919, Box 59.

14. PRO, CO 209:301.

15. *Appendix*, vol. 1 A4.

16. Cody, *Man of Two Worlds*, pp. 132–3.

17. PRO, CO 83:150, 211, 263, 343, 372, 383.

18. Ibid., 558.

19. K. Dhanesh, *Adolf von Plevitz: The Precursor of Manilal Doctor* (Mauritius, no date) pp. 45–7.

20. PRO, CO 83:151, 101, 102, 129, 230.

21. H. Roth, 'The October Revolution and New Zealand Labour', *Political Science* 13 (1961) 52.

22. For later developments in Fiji, see K. L. Gillion, *The Fiji Indians: Challenge to European Dominance, 1920–1946* (Canberra, 1977).

23. Ian Willis, 'Rabaul's 1929 Strike', *New Guinea* vol. 5 (1970) pp. 13–4. I owe this reference to Hugh Laracy.

24. Pre-revolutionary Russo-African connections from Edward T. Wilson, *Russia and Black Africa before World War II* (New York and London, 1974) pp. xiv–xv, 3, 73, 79–89.

25. PRO, CO 96:597, 600, 601.

26. Latter part of this paragraph from Wilson, *Russia and Black Africa* pp. 110–20.

27. John D. Hargreaves, 'Assimilation in Eighteenth-Century Senegal', *Journal of African History* 6 (1965) 183.

28. A. B. Letnev, 'Politicheskoe probuzhdenie vo frantsuszkoi zapadnoi Afrike posle pervoi mirovoi voiny, 1918–1923gg', in A. B. Davidson *et al.* (eds), *Tropicheskaia Afrika: Problemy istorii* (Moscow, 1973) pp. 16, 17, 19–21, 22, 29, 33–34, 54, 61–8. André Marty, *La révolte de la Mer Moire* (Paris, 1939) refers to Senegalese participation in a revolt only at Itea in Greece on 26–7 June 1919. See pp. 449–50. I am grateful to Marc Michel for his comments on the Senegalese in the War and Intervention. M. Michel is sceptical about Letnev's account.

29. I. Milton Sacks, 'Marxism in Viet Nam', in Frank N. Trager (ed.), *Marxism in Southeast Asia: A Study of Four Countries* (Stanford, California, 1959) pp. 103–11.

30. Jeanne S. Mintz, 'Marxism in Indonesia', in Trager, *Marxism*, pp. 171–80. See generally the works of Ruth T. McVey, including *The Rise of Indonesian Communism* (Ithaca, New York, 1965) and *The Social Roots of Indonesian Communism* (Brussels, 1970).

31. G. Adhikari, *Documents of the History of the Communist Party of India*, vol. 1, 1917–1922 (New Delhi, 1972) pp. 1–2.

32. Goutam Chattopadhyay, in conversation with the author, May 1974.

33. This paragraph from Ivar Spector, *The First Russian Revolution: Its Impact on Asia* (Englewood Cliffs, New Jersey, 1962) pp. 94–8.

34. Ibid., pp. 98–100.

35. Lenin, 'Inflammable Material in World Politics', quoted by Goutam Chattopadhyay, 'Impact of the Russian Revolution on the Indian Freedom Movement – Some Aspects', in Horst Kruger (ed.), *Neue Indienkunde: Festschrift Walter Ruben zum 70 Geburtstag* (Berlin, 1970) p. 177.

36. Quoted in ibid., p. 178.

37. Ibid., p. 178. See also T. G. Fraser, 'Germany and Indian Revolution, 1914–1918', *Journal of Contemporary History* 12 (1977).

38. Chattopadhyay, *Neue Indienkunde*, p. 178. See also Zafar Imam, 'The Rise of Soviet Russia and Socialism in India, 1917–1929' in B. R. Nanda (ed.), *Socialism in India* (Delhi and London, 1972) pp. 42–3. I owe this reference to Rosemary Tyzack.

39 Zafar Imam, *Colonialism in East–West Relations: A Study of Soviet Policy towards India and Anglo-Soviet Relations* (New Delhi, 1969) pp. 54–5, 56–72, 74–7.

40. Adhikari, *Documents* vol. 1, p. 15.

41. Ibid., pp. 15–6; Chattopadhyay, *Neue Indienkunde* p. 180; Imam, *Colonialism*, pp. 59–62.

42. Quoted by Adhikari, *Documents* vol. 1, p. 19. See also A. I. Iunel, 'V. I. Lenin i stanovlenie sovetsko-indiiskikh obshchestvenno-politicheskikh otnoshenii v 1917–1922gg', *Istoriia SSSR* no. 1 (1974).

43. Imam, *Colonialism* pp. 71–4, 117–19; Adhikari, *Documents* vol. 1, pp. 16–20.

44. Ibid., pp. 33–46.

45. Ibid., p. 52.

46. Ibid., p. 52. See also L. F. Rushbrook Williams, *India in 1920: A report prepared for presentation to Parliament* . . . (Calcutta, 1921) p. 1: 'It is impossible to understand on the one hand the relations between India and Afghanistan, and on the other hand the relations between India and the Frontier Tribes, without some knowledge of the stormy background of Bolshevik activity upon which both in greater or less degree largely depended.'

47. Adhikari, *Documents*, vol. 1, 50–2.

48. E. H. Carr, *The Bolshevik Revolution, 1917–1923* vol. 3 (Harmondsworth, 1966) pp. 239–42, 290–2, 463–4.

49. Sir Cecil Kaye, *Communism in India* ed. by Subodh Roy, p. 132; Imam, *Colonialism* pp. 74–7.

50. And in books such as Edmund Candler, *Bolshevism: The Dream and the Facts* (Bombay, 1920). See, for example, p. 79: 'The adoption of Bolshevism in principle would mean that the Brahmin would have to do the work of the chamar, clerks would be employed as scavengers, and bankers and merchants would be seen cleaning the common sewers.'

51. Quoted by Chattopadhyay, *Neue Indienkunde* p. 181.

52. Quoted in ibid., pp. 183–4.

53. See P. G. Robb, *The Government of India and Reform: Policies towards Politics and the Constitution, 1916–1921* (Oxford, 1976).

54. The section on Turkey from Spector, *The First* pp. 62–6; George S. Harris, *The Origins of Communism in Turkey* (Stanford, California, 1967) ch. 1.

55. The section on Iran from Spector, *The First* pp. 38–50. For the views of an English contemporary, see E. G. Browne, *The Persian Revolution of 1905–1909* (Cambridge, 1910). For Lenin's views, see 'Events in the Balkans and in Persia', October 1908, in *Collected Works* vol. 15, pp. 220–30.

56. Carr, *The Bolshevik Revolution* vol. 3, p. 247.

57. Ibid., pp. 246–51, 266–7, 294–304, 468–72; Harris, *The Origins* chs. 4–6.

58. Carr, *The Bolshevik Revolution* vol. 3, pp. 246, 292–4, 464–8. See also Sepehr Zabih, *The Communist Movement in Iran* (Berkeley and Los Angeles, 1966) pp. 43, 45; and Nasrullah Saifpour Fatemi, *Diplomatic History of Persia, 1917–1923* (New York, 1952). The section on Turkey and Iran has been modified somewhat, following expert comment generously given by William Olson.

59. Hans Kohn, *A History of Nationalism in the East* (London, 1919), especially ch. 7; Walter Laqueur, *Communism and Nationalism in the Middle East* (London, 1956), especially ch. 2. And for a scholarly survey of the Bolshevik threat to the British sphere of influence in general, see Stephen White, *Britain and the Bolshevik Revolution: A Study in the Politics of Diplomacy,*

1920–1924 (London, 1978), especially chs. 4–6.

60. Lucien Bianco, *Origins of the Chinese Revolution, 1915–1949* (Stanford, California, and London, 1971) pp. 4–12. For a distinctive, anti-socialist approach to the subject, see Donald W. Treadgold, *The West in Russia and China: Religious and Secular Thought in Modern Times* vol. 2 (Cambridge, 1973).

61. This paragraph from Spector, *The First* pp. 77–87.

62. Ibid., p. 85.

63. Joseph W. Esherick, *Reform and Revolution in China: The 1911 Revolution in Hunan and Hubei* (Berkeley, California, and London, 1976) p. 258.

64. This paragraph from Carr, *The Bolshevik Revolution* vol. 3, pp. 489–98; A. S. Whiting, *Soviet Policies in China, 1917–1924* (New York, 1954) especially p. 30.

65. Carr, *The Bolshevik Revolution* vol. 3, pp. 528–30.

66. Treadgold, *The West* vol. 2, p. 136.

67. Bianco, *Origins* 39–43, 54. And for the part played by about 2000 émigrés, see C. Brandt, 'The French returned élite in the Chinese Communist Party' in E. F. Szczepanik (ed.) *Economic and Social Problems of the Far East* (Hong Kong, 1962). I owe this reference to Delia Davin.

68. Carr, *The Bolshevik Revolution* vol. 3, pp. 524–8, 533–4.

69. Ibid., pp. 488–9, 505–14, 522–4. See also *The First Congress of the Toilers of the Far East* (Petrograd, 1922; reprint London, 1970) pp. 95–121 and *passim*. And see Owen Lattimore, intro., Gerard M. Friters, *Outer Mongolia and its International Position* (London, 1951).

70. K. M. Panikkar, *Asia and Western Dominance* (London, 1959) p. 152.

71. Brian Pearce (ed.), *Baku Congress of the Peoples of the East* (London, 1977) p. 85.

72. Angelica Balabanova, *My Life as a Rebel* (London, 1938) pp. 318–19.

73. Robert J. Alexander, *Communism in Latin America* (New Brunswick, New Jersey, 1957) p. 34.

74. Ibid., pp. 319–22.

75. This general survey taken from ibid., *passim*. See R. E. Poppin, *International Communism in Latin America: A History of the Movement, 1917–1963* (New York, 1964). I am grateful to David Waddell for his perusal of the section on Latin America.

76. A. I. Sizonenko, 'Sovetskaia Rossiia i Latinskaia Amerika v 1917–1924gg', *Voprosy istorii* 6 (1973).

Part Three   Revolutions in Retrospect and Prospect

1. Daniel Field, 'The Reforms of the 1860s', *Windows on the Russian Past: Essays on Soviet Historiography Since Stalin* (Columbus, Ohio, 1977) pp. 92, 95.

7. *Sixty Years After*

1. David Layzer, quoted by G. J. Whitrow, *The Nature of Time* (Har-

mondsworth, 1972) p. 132.

2. P. N. Miliukov, *Istoriia vtoroi russkoi revoliutsii* (Sofia, 1921) pp. 11–22, quoted by Arthur E. Adams, *The Russian Revolution and Bolshevik Victory: Why and How?* (Boston, Massachusetts, 1960) p. 1.

3. J. H. Plumb, *The Death of the Past* (Harmondsworth 1973) p. 115.

4. George Bancroft, *History of the United States of America from the Discovery of the Continent* the author's last revision vol. 4 (New York, 1886) p. 4. Although not giving specific approval to this passage and while making subtle reservations which cannot be entered into here, Edmund S. Morgan nevertheless suggests that 'the Whig interpretation of the American Revolution may not be as dead as some historians would have us believe, that George Bancroft may not have been so far from the mark as we have often assumed'. See his *The Challenge of the American Revolution* (New York, 1976) p. 57.

5. M. M. Klein, 'The American Revolution in the Twentieth Century', *The Historian* vol. 34 (1972) p. 229; Richard B. Morris, *The American Revolution Reconsidered* (New York and London, 1967) p. 85.

6. See, for example, G. A. Billias, 'The First Un-Americans: The Loyalists in American Historiography' in A. T. Vaughan and G. A. Billias (eds), *Perspectives on Early American History: Essays in Honor of R. B. Morris* (New York, 1973).

7. See, for example, Jesse Lemisch, 'The American Revolution Seen from the Bottom Up', in Barton J. Bernstein (ed.), *Towards a New Past: Dissenting Essays in American History* (New York, 1969); and for a convenient review essay, see R. C. Simmons, 'Class Ideology and Revolutionary War', *History* vol. 62 (1977).

8. Richard Hofstadter, *The Progressive Historians: Turner, Beard, Parrington* (New York, 1968) pp. 29, 39, 66.

9. George L. Beer, *African Questions at the Paris Peace Conference* (New York, 1923) p. 4.

10. H. E. Bolton, 'The Epic of Greater America', *American Historical Review* 38 (1932–3) 473–4. Bolton went on to modify his assertion significantly: 'Before closing I wish to repeat with emphasis that I do not propose such a synthesis as a substitute for, but as a setting in which to place, any one of our national histories.' And see *Wider Horizons of American History* (New York and London, 1939).

11. *American Historical Review*, 39 (1933–4) 227–8, Hofstadter, *The Progressive Historians* pp. 72, 102–3, 135, 333.

12. See chapter 2 above. And see A. J. Mayer, *Politics and Diplomacy of Peacemaking: Containment and Counterrevolution at Versailles, 1918–1919* (New York, 1967) p. viii: 'My conception of the age of the Russian Revolution owes much to Robert Palmer's treatment of an earlier age.'

13. W. Kloosterboer, *Involuntary Servitude since the Abolition of Slavery: A Survey of Compulsory Labour throughout the World* (Leiden, 1960); C. Vann Woodward, 'Emancipations and Reconstructions: A Comparative Study', *XIII mezhdunarodnyi kongress istoricheskikh nauk: Doklady kongressa* tom 1 (Moscow, 1973).

14. C. Vann Woodward (ed.), *The Comparative Approach to American*

History (New York, 1968) p. 3.

15. Aileen S. Kraditor attacks the 'conflict' concept as well as that of the 'consensus', since both lead to the posing of 'yes-type' questions for which the answers are predetermined. See her 'American Radical Historians and their Heritage', *Past and Present* no. 56 (1972) 137.

16. Jesse Lemisch in debate with Staughton Lynd at the New University Conference in Spring 1968, appendix to Staughton Lynd's pamphlet, *Intellectuals, the University and the Movement* (Boston [no date]).

17. David Donald, 'Radical Historians on the Move', *New York Times* Book Review section, 19 July 1970.

18. For further discussion of such an exit see, for example, Louis Hartz, 'American Historiography and Comparative Analysis', *Comparative Studies in Society and History* vol. 5 (1962–3); Walter Hugins, 'American History in Comparative Perspective', *Journal of American Studies* 11 (1977); and P. P. McCormick, 'The Comparative Method; Its Application to American History', *Mid-America* no. 61 (1974).

19. Ernest R. May, 'The Cold War', in Woodward, *The Comparative*, p. 342. For pre-1914 American-Russian comparisons, see chapter 3 above.

20. V. E. Illeretskii *et al.* (eds), *Istoriografiia istorii SSSR* (Moskva, 1961) pp. 305–16. For the early formation of the Russian school, see J. L. Black, 'The State School Interpretation of Russian History: A Re-Appraisal of its Genetic Origins', *Jahrbücher für Geschichte Osteuropas* Band 21 (1973). See also J. L. Black *Nicholas Karamzin and Russian Society in the Nineteenth Century* (Toronto, 1975) pp. 164–89.

21. S. Harper, *The Russia I Believe In* (Chicago, 1945) p. 9 points out that Miliukov was preceded by the Czech statesman Masaryk in 1902.

22. P. N. Miliukov, *Russia and Its Crisis* new ed. (New York, 1962) p. 408.

23. P. N. Miliukov, *Russia Today and Tomorrow* (London, 1922) p. 294.

24. See, for example, A. E. Presniakov, 'Tri stoletiia' vol. 1, 1–3, and other contributions to V. V. Kallash (ed.), *Tri veka* (Moscow, 1912–13), a six-volume celebration of the tercentenary of the Romanov dynasty.

25. See H. Asher, 'The Rise, Fall and Resurrection of M. N. Pokrovsky', *The Russian Review* 31 (1972); J. D. White, 'Historiography of the Russian Revolution in the Twenties', *Critique* vol. 1 (1973); S. H. Baron, 'Plekhanov, Trotsky and the Development of Soviet Historiography', *Soviet Studies* vol. 26 (1974).

26. Perhaps the outstanding example of a patriotic historian was E. V. Tarle. See A. K. Erickson, 'E. V. Tarle: The Career of a Historian under the Soviet Regime', *Slavic Review* 19 (1960).

27. H. J. Ellison, 'Soviet Historians and the Russian Revolution', in L. H. Legters (ed.) *Russia: Essays in History and Literature* (Leiden, 1972); George M. Enteen, 'A Recent Trend on the Historical Front', *Survey* vol. 20 (1974); John Keep, 'The Current Scene in Soviet Historiography', *Survey*, vol. 20 (1974); D. A. Longley, 'Some Historiographical Problems of Bolsheviks Party History (The Kronstadt Bolsheviks in March 1917)', *Jahrbücher für Geschichte Osteuropas* vol. 22 (1974).

28. One of these has been translated into English by D. Jones –

P. A. Zaionchkovskii, *The Russian Autocracy under Alexander III* (Gulf Breeze, Florida, 1976).

29. Samuel Harper, *The Russia I Believe In* (Chicago, 1945) p. 108 writes that 'we Americans were guilty of wishful thinking.' For examples of such thinking, especially by Harper, see C. Lasch, *The American Liberals and the Russian Revolution* (New York, 1962) pp. 28, 45, 73, 105–7, 159.

30. Ibid., pp. xv–xvi.

31. G. F. Kennan, *Soviet Foreign Policy, 1917–1941* (Princeton, New York and London, 1960) p. 115.

32. G. F. Kennan, *The Marquis de Custine and his Russia in 1839* (Princeton, 1971). For Kennan's later views see 'Mr X – 30 Years On: An Interview with George Urban', *Encounter* (September 1976) and 'The Russian Question', *Encounter* (March 1978). He now defends détente.

33. N. N. Bolkhovitinov, 'The Study of United States History in the Soviet Union', *American Historical Review* 74 (1968–9) 1221. Pre-revolutionary Russian writing on the United States was not for the most part at an academic level. For an example of the work of perhaps the most notable figure, see M. Kovalevsky, 'American Impressions' *Russian Review* 10 (1951).

34. See, as a small translated example, N. N. Bolkhovitinov's own article, 'The role of the "frontier" in the history of the USA (a critical analysis of the views of F. J. Turner)', *Soviet Studies in History* vol. 2 (963–4).

35. See, for example, A. A. Fursenko, 'The American and French Revolutions of the eighteenth century: An attempt at a comparative consideration', *Soviet Studies in History* vol. 13 (1974).

36. N. N. Bolkhovitinov, 'Sovremennaia amerikanskaia istoriografiia: novye techeniia i problemy', *Novaia i noveishaia istoriia* no. 6 (1969) 129.

37. A. P. Mendel, 'Current Soviet Theory of History: New Trends or Old?', *American Historical Review* 72 (1966–7) 72–3.

38. A. P. Mendel, 'On the Eve of Freedom', *Ingenor 4* (Michigan University College of Engineering, 1968) 24.

39. During a tour of the United States in 1970, the writer found very few historians sympathetic to the concept of 'scientific explanation'.

40. James P. Scanlan, 'From Historical Materialism to Historical Interactionism: A Philosophical Examination of Some Recent Developments', in Samuel H. Baron and Nancy W. Heer (eds), *Windows on the Russian Past: Essays on Soviet Historiography since Stalin* (Columbus, Ohio, 1977) p. 20.

41. A. G. Meyer, 'Theories of Convergence' in C. Johnson (ed.), *Change in Communist Systems* (Stanford, 1973) pp. 336–7.

42. For stimulating discussion on this point, see D. A. Hollinger, 'T. S. Kuhn's Theory of Science and Its Implications for History', *American Historical Review* 78 (1973); C. Vann Woodward, 'The Future of the Past', *American Historical Review* 75 (1970).

43. J. H. Plumb, in his Introduction to The History of Human Society Series, for example, in J. H. Parry, *The Spanish Seaborne Empire* (London and New York, 1966) p. 17.

44. So argues P. M. Kennedy, 'The Decline of Nationalistic History in the West, 1900–1970', *Journal of Contemporary History* 8 (1973).

45. For an interesting discussion of how Orwell chose his title, see 'Note on the sources of George Orwell's *1984*' in R. E. F. Smith (ed.), *The Russian Peasant 1920 and 1984* (London, 1977) pp. 9–10. One of the possibilities referred to by Smith is Jack London's *The Iron Heel*. Another is A. V. Chayanov's *The Journey of my Brother Alexei to the Land of Peasant Utopia*, first published in Moscow in 1920, in which the following passage describing one future development occurs: 'After six months of bloodshed, peace was restored by the joint efforts of America and the Scandinavian Union, but at the price of dividing the world into five closed economic systems – German, Anglo–French, American–Australian, Japan–China and Russian. Each of these isolated systems was allocated pieces of territory in all climatic zones, sufficient to ensure their economic existence, and thereafter, while preserving a community of culture, they developed altogether different political and economic ways of life'. See Smith, *The Russian Peasant* p. 86.

46. In a book review, *Journal of European Studies* 3 (1973) 309. See also the remarks of Ronald G. Suny in another book review, in *Sbornik* of the Study Group on the Russian Revolution (Leeds, 1975) p. 24: 'The concept "totalitarianism" has in recent years been subject to acute criticism, its underlying values and biasses exposed, and its essential fuzziness revealed . . . .'

47. D. Schoenbaum, *Hitler's Social Revolution: Class and Status in Nazi Germany 1933–1939* (London, 1967) p. xiv.

48. For a fuller assertion of this argument, see Paul Dukes and John W. Hiden, 'Towards an Historical Comparison of Nazi Germany and Soviet Russia in the 1930s', *New Zealand Slavonic Journal* no. 2 (1978).

49. Giorgio Napolitano interviewed by Eric Hobsbawm, *The Italian Road to Socialism* (London, 1977) p. 99.

50. Ahmed Mohiddin, 'Socialism the Answer to Africa', *Uganda Argus* 5 Sept. 1969, quoted in James Mulira, *The Role of Soviet Bloc Countries in the Political, Economic and Social Developments of Uganda, 1945–1970* unpublished Ph.D. Dissertation in History (Princeton, 1974).

51. S. R. Gardiner, *The Thirty Years War, 1618–1648* (London, 1903) p. 199.

52. J. R. Platt the physicist, quoted by Arthur Koestler in a book review in the *Observer* 25 Sept. 1977.

Bibliographical Note

There is a vast literature on the Russian Revolution and on modern Russian history. Yet, as far as I know, there is no other work in English which attempts to consider these subjects in the manner undertaken here. For that reason, a bibliography of a general nature cannot be provided. True, books such as Stanley W. Page, *Lenin and World Revolution* (New York, 1959) and Arnold Toynbee, *The Impact of the Russian Revolution: The Influence of Bolshevism on the World outside Russia* (London, 1967) suggest an approach similar to Part 2, but both are essays of a somewhat broader nature and less close in focus. The third volume of E. H. Carr's *The Bolshevik Revolution* (London, 1953) subtitled 'Soviet Russia and the World' is a much more scholarly treatment than that given in Part 2, yet it says little about the Southern Hemisphere or about the course of the Russian Revolution itself. Crane Brinton, *The Anatomy of Revolution* (London, 1953) is a stimulating comparison of the great revolutions of modern times. W. H. Chamberlin, *The Russian Revolution. 1917–1921*, 2 vols. (New York, 1935) and several later editions is generally agreed still to be the best of its kind. Chapter 38, 'The Drive for World Revolution' is an introduction to the themes tackled in chapters 5 and 6 of the present work. As far as studies of a more specific nature are concerned, they are introduced with full title as well as place and date of publication on their first appearance in each chapter.

Index